The Best
Stage Scenes
of 1992

Jocelyn A. Beard has edited

The Best Men's Stage Monologues of 1992
The Best Women's Stage Monologues of 1992
The Best Men's Stage Monologues of 1991
The Best Women's Stage Monologues of 1991
The Best Men's Stage Monologues of 1990
The Best Women's Stage Monologues of 1990
One Hundred Men's Stage Monologues from the 1980's
One Hundred Women's Stage Monologues from the 1980's

and has co-edited

The Best Stage Scenes for Men from the 1980's
The Best Stage Scenes for Women from the 1980's

i

MONOLOGUES
The Best Men's Stage Monologues of 1992
The Best Men's Stage Monologues of 1991
The Best Men's Stage Monologues of 1990
The Best Women's Stage Monologues of 1992
The Best Women's Stage Monologues of 1991
The Best Women's Stage Monologues of 1990
Street Talk: Character Monologues for Actors
One Hundred Men's Stage Monologues from the 1980's
One Hundred Women's Stage Monologues from the 1980's
The Great Monologues from the Humana Festival
The Great Monologues from the EST Marathon
Monologues from Contemporary Literature: Volume I
Monologues from Classic Plays
Uptown: Character Monologues for Actors

YOUNG ACTORS
Great Scenes for Young Actors from the Stage
Great Monologues for Young Actors
New Plays from A.C.T.'s Young Conservatory
Scenes and Monologues for Very Young Actors

ADVANCED ACTORS
The Best Stage Scenes for Women from the 1980's
The Best Stage Scenes for Men from the 1980's
The Best Stage Scenes of 1992
The Actor's Chekhov

PLAYS FOR ACTORS
Women Playwrights The Best Plays of 1992
Seventeen Short Plays by Romulus Linney

If you require pre-publication information about upcoming Smith and Kraus monologues collections, scene collections, play anthologies, advanced acting books, and books for young actors, you may receive our semi-annual catalogue, free of charge, by sending your name and address to Smith and Kraus Catalogue, P.O. Box 10, Newbury, VT 05051.

The Best Stage Scenes of 1992

Edited by
Jocelyn A. Beard

SK
A Smith and Kraus Book

A Smith and Kraus Book
Published by Smith and Kraus, Inc.

Cover and Text Design by Julia Hill
Manufactured in the United States of America

First Edition: February 1993
10 9 8 7 6 5 4 3 2 1

Publisher' Cataloging in Publication
(Prepared by Quality Books Inc.)

The Best stage scenes of 1992 / edited by Jocelyn A. Beard. - 1st ed.
    p. cm.
    Includes bibliographical references.
    ISBN 1-880399-18-0

1. Acting. 2. Monologues. I. Beard, Jocelyn A. II. Title:
Best stage scenes of nineteen ninety-two.

PN2080.B4 1993b   792'.028
                         QBI92-2796

Smith and Kraus, Inc.
Main Street, P.O. Box 10, Newbury, Vermont 05051
(802) 866 5423

iv

Acknowledgments

Grateful thanks

to the playwrights and their agents.

Jocelyn A. Beard

would also like to thank

Kevin Kitowski

for his love and support.

Table of Contents

Foreword *Jocelyn A. Beard*
Introduction *Richard Elliott*

SECTION 1 MEN AND WOMEN

Foreword

As our society changes, so do our interpersonal relationships. While Western Civilization hurries to meet it's rendezvous with the next millennium, people - lovers, friends, families, enemies and strangers - are left with the task of translating these momentous social changes into meaningful dialogue.

The creation of meaningful, believable dialogue is perhaps the greatest challenge facing the playwright. How many times have you read, watched or acted in a play in which the words left you flat? "People don't talk like that!" you mutter to yourself while regretting the loss of opportunity - for every time two or more characters convene on a stage, there is a tremendous opportunity for communication.

Happily, the scenes in this collection have been selected for the quality and innovation of their dialogues, giving you, the actor, the opportunity to join with your fellows in meaningful communication.

1992 has given us superlative theatre, with plays ranging from the warm and wonderful *Dancing in Lughnasa* to the biting satire of Alan Aykbourn's *Man of the Moment*. In 1992, veteran wordsmiths the likes of Craig Lucas and Timberlake Wertenbaker have made a gift to us of their masterfully crafted scenes which show humanity in all of its manifestations.

You will find scenes for many combinations of actors in this collection, freeing you to explore as much of the art of communication as possible. With memorable characters such as the irrepressible Enrico Caruso, Gertrude, Queen of Denmark and Lionel Barrymore, the playwrights of 1992 did well to mine the core of both popular culture and history, creating scenes with depth and power.

Enjoy, and break a leg!

Jocelyn A. Beard
Patterson, New York
Autumn, 1992

ix

Introduction

One HUGE aspect of my job as artistic director is conducting auditions. I see literally hundreds, if not more each year in preparing for our productions. One common aspect I find in most actors who are called back for productions is their level of training. Invariably, the best actors come with the best training. Usually they are currently studying or have years of training under their belts. Most all of the truly gifted performers maintain on-going voice lessons or dance or some other discipline which keeps the body and voice tuned.

Practicing your craft is essential. Not only is it terribly important that you show the best you have in the short time you are allotted at an audition, but it is equally as critical that you maintain your level of expertise in approaching an entire role. This new collection, The Best Stage Scenes of 1992 provides a wonderfully diverse selection of contemporary pieces for all ages, types and levels of experience.

Students of acting should begin their course of study with absolute basics: a free, open unrestricted voice and body and a highly creative and rept emotional readiness that will allow you to draw upon experiences from your own life that can meld with the characters you will play. This type of relaxation and readiness can be achieved through improvisation, movement, song, and interaction with other actors who are equally willing to share their work with one another. When you are ready to begin scene work, select a scene that best demonstrates what you can give to the part. Be careful not to tackle something that is beyond your realm of experience. One of the first signs of an untrained actor is an inappropriate piece. Often during auditions, many decent actors will do themselves in by presenting peices for which they are definitely not suited.

However, do not underestimate yourselves! Choose scenes and monologues that stretch your abilities. This is especially true for actors of color. Many artistic directors are welcoming non-traditional casting choices with open arms. If you can present the character with truth and understanding, race and sometimes even gender is no issue.

This collection should give you a wide variety from which to choose for your scene work. If you find a scene you like, try to get the entire script. You really need to know where the character is coming from and where he/she is going. This book will introduce you to many new plays that may soom be available at your local bookstore.

Keep working and persevering! The more you stick to a course of study and training, the better your chances are of succeeding as a scrious performer.

Richard Elliott
Artistic Director CitiArts Theatre
Concord, California

The Best
Stage Scenes
of 1992

Section I

Scenes for
Men and Women

AFTER THE DANCING IN JERICHO
by P.J. Barry

The Characters: Jim, 53 an actor, and Kate, 53, a housewife

The Setting: A museum in New York, 1984

The Scene: Jim and Kate grew up together and then drifted apart. Decades later they rediscover their friendship and begin meeting regularly in NYC. Here, they explore an art museum.

(Kate and Jim enter. In no time Katie gets Jimmy into the spirit of the number.)
KATE: I've never been in this museum. Isn't that incredible? An hour and a half by train. I've never taken advantage of the Big Apple. I might as well have been living in Jericho all my life. *(Pause)* I like that picture. It's sad... but I like it.
JIM: It's called *Nighthawks*.
KATE: I can read.
JIM: I can't... without glasses.
KATE: Are you wearing contacts?
JIM: Yes.
KATE: So am I.
JIM: Do you like them?
KATE: Not very much.
JIM: Why do you wear them?
KATE: Vanity. You?
JIM: The business.
KATE: Is that the truth?
JIM: The business and vanity.
(She Laughs.)
JIM: And big news. I just had to get bi-focals.
KATE: Me, too. *(Kate and Jimmy are working well now. They dance off. They both laugh.)*
KATE: Listen, you. We have to meet more often. Here it is June and we've only met twice since-
JIM: Hey, I've been out of town.
KATE: No excuses. Now that you're back we must meet... at least twice a month.
JIM: Now wait-
KATE: Once a month? Promise? Promise?
JIM: I promise.

1

KATE: Oh, good.
JIM: Won't your husband have something to say about that?
KATE: Oh, he won't care. *(Takes his arm, and they move on to another picture.)* Do you think you'll ever marry again?
JIM: Never.
KATE: Are you sure?
JIM: Positive. And you?
KATE: Me? Oh, Howard and I... well, at our age I can't see us getting a divorce.
JIM: Have you thought about it?
KATE: Some. Maybe we will. Who knows.
JIM: Are you still a Catholic?
KATE: Yes. I mean born a Catholic, always a Catholic. Do I go to church anymore? No. Do you?
JIM: No.
KATE: And you a La Salle boy.
JIM: Dreary high school, dreary place.
KATE: Oh. One thing. Something I said when we first met... last February. I said Howard would be waiting for me at the station. Untrue. I parked the car there. I acted as if he still loves me so much he couldn't wait to see me. Oh, he loves me... but...
JIM: Relax. I lied, too. I said I was going to rehearsal that show in upstate New York. Didn't exist. My unemployment had run out.... I was, once again, working at a travel agency. Hadn't done that in five years.
KATE: But your commercials...
JIM: Short cycles; it wasn't all that much money.
KATE: I'm sorry.
JIM: It's okay now. The last three months... it's really picked up. Four commercials, that role in the TV movie. Geezuz, not four commercials, two... two. Why do I exaggerate? Who am I trying to impress?
KATE: Me.
JIM: Yes.
KATE: You're brave.
JIM: *(Examining a painting.)* No. I don't know what else to do at my age. I just keep going. Survive.
KATE: But you're still doing what you want to do.
JIM: Yeah... but I've never had the financial security, Kate. I'm still struggling... like a damn kid.
KATE: Well, I admire you.
JIM: *(In regard to the painting)* What the hell is that?
KATE: *(Shrugs, Then)* Every so often a bell goes off. I really did want to be a dancer... an entertainer... out there! But Dad said no and Mom said no, and I was obedient. We listened to

our parents, didn't we.

JIM: A face! It's a face.

KATE: But I've been brave, too. With both the boys gone now I applied for a couple of teaching jobs in the fall.

JIM: That's terrific. Congratulations.

KATE: I'm very proud of myself. I went through the motions. Thanks to you. *(Jim looks puzzled.)*

KATE: The last time we talked on the phone, I told you I was thinking about it and you said do it and I did it.

JIM: I did?

KATE: Yes. You got me out of my rut.

JIM: Good.

KATE: You're my lifesaver.

JIM: Sure. I'm thinking about making some changes, too. That friend in Chicago. I still have that job offer.

KATE: Are you really considering it? A big move like that?

JIM: Maybe it's that time.

KATE: What about show business?

JIM: Fuck show business.

KATE: But you just auditioned for that Broadway show.

JIM: I didn't get it.

KATE: Oh.

JIM: They offered me understudy. I'm too old for that crap.

KATE: *(Pause)* Something else will turn up... something special!... I just know it. Oh, I hope you don't go off to Chicago... Don't! Please.

JIM: I'm just... kicking it around, that's all. No immediate, earth-shattering decisions.

KATE: Besides, you just promised to meet me twice- once a month and I'm holding you to that.

JIM: You're persistent today.

KATE: *(Laughs)* We're just getting to know each other again, you. I mean you're my roots... kind of. And I'm yours...

JIM: Kind of.

KATE: Yes! Oh look. That picture. *(Tilts her head)* It looks like Johnny.

JIM: You think so? *(Tilts his head)* I don't think so.

KATE: Like he looks now. When did you see him last?

JIM: Ahhh... when we both came home from Korea, God, a thousand years ago.

KATE: Well, last time I visited my mother... Easter... I ran into him in Jericho on Main Street... By the Old Stone Bank - That's still there. He was slightly drunk.

JIM: I went through that.

KATE: But you stopped drinking Jim, and saved your life. His life has been so sad. Last fall he was in that horrible

3

accident on Phoenix Bridge. His wife and daughter were killed. He was driving; he didn't get a scratch.

JIM: Geezuz. That was Maria.

KATE: No. Marie.

JIM: I thought he married Maria?

KATE: Yes, he married Maria first... but she died in childbirth.

JIM: I didn't know that. Did I know that?

KATE: And their son, Johnny Junior, was killed in Vietnam.

JIM: Geezuz.

KATE: But before that he married her twin sister Marie- you used to date her and they had a daughter and she and the daughter were killed in that car crash last fall.

JIM: Geezuz.

KATE: I stood there listening to him by the Old Stone Bank for almost an hour. He said he didn't know why God had cursed him like the Kennedys. He has had such terrible tragedy in his life, I mean he has, Jim. They say that he set his father's house on fire in a drunken rage.

JIM: He set his father's house on fire?

KATE: You didn't know? Well, it was never proved, he got off scot free. His father, his brother, his sister-in-law- you remember Ethel- all perished. They found him outside with a broken arm, the only one who escaped. Supposedly he was still drunk. Why are you laughing?

JIM: It's unbelievable.

KATE: It is, but it happened, it's not funny, I felt so sorry for him. He asked me to go for a drink. I told him he should go to AA; he said he appreciated my concern.

JIM: Unbelievable.

KATE: And I told him I'd seen you. I said you were in AA.

JIM: What did he say?

KATE: He said you were the best friend he ever had... and I was the only girl he ever really loved... and he should've married me.

JIM: Aren't you lucky it was Marie and Maria, and not you.

KATE: Aren't you terrible. You are. *(Pause)* He does look like that picture now. And Jim, he's still so handsome... in a dissipated kind of way. Maybe he should've stayed in the Marines. The discipline seemed-

JIM: I got it. You're planning to divorce Howard, marry Johnny and save him from himself.

KATE: You're rotten.

JIM: What a crusade.

KATE: You are.

JIM: Don't do it.

4

KATE: Better. I divorce Howard, marry you and save you from yourself.

JIM: Too late. I already did that.

KATE: Then it's settled. Johnny needs me, you don't.

JIM: Like old times.

KATE: Not quite. I'm not crazy. Not yet.

JIM: Good. Common sense wins. You saved yourself.

KATE: Oh, you.

JIM: *(Laughs)* Listen. What time do you have to be back tonight?

KATE: I said I'd be home around nine, Why?

JIM: I have an idea. After we have dinner, let's go to The Red Windows.

KATE: What's The Red Windows?

JIM: It's a disco in the Village. But on Tuesdays they have Swing Night. A big dance floor.

KATE: Are you serious?

JIM: Yeah. Let's go there after we have dinner.

KATE: I said I'd be home around nine.

JIM: Call him.

KATE: No, I won't call him. I'll just be late.

JIM: Is that fair?

KATE: I can be late, can't I? Serve him right.

JIM: *(Lightly)* Are you neglected?

KATE: Yes. No, not really- Yes! I won't get the seven-thirty train back, I'll get the eleven o'clock train. Tonight I live dangerously.

JIM: Dancing.

KATE: Dancing! *(Laughs, half hugs him)* Oh, I feel so wicked.

JIM: You are. Not calling your husband.

KATE: He probably won't even notice.

(They exit.)

5

ASCENSION DAY
by *Michael Henry Brown*

The Characters: Nat Turner (African-American, 30) a slave
on the verge of rebellion and Cherry (African-American,
20's), his wife.

The Setting: Virginia, 1831

The Scene: Following his first escape, Nat returns to the
plantation for he believes he is destined to lead his people to
freedom. Here, he and his wife share a quiet moment of love.

*(Night. Nat and Cherry in woods by a tree. Cherry is sitting
with her back against the tree. Nat is standing a few feet away
from her.)*
CHERRY: It be my fault.
NAT: Shush, Gal.
CHERRY: Me ... no youngins ... you be free ... wese a
terrible burden to ya.
NAT: Dem two li'l smilin' faces I seen tonight didn't look like
no burden to me.
CHERRY: I conjured you back here. 'Llowed it to happen ...
didn't put a reign on my feelins ... what I wuz thinkin' ... what
I wuz missin' ... Started to yearn ... started to see you in my
dreams ... started to talk to ya ... Yeah, Nat, I conjured you
back here. I'm jest not strong as I thought.
NAT: You plenty strong, dat's why I marry you.
CHERRY: Massa Reese say me an' Briley should make strong
chil'ren. *(Pause)*
NAT: You mine. *(Pause)* Briley evah touch you, I kill him...
He know dat.
CHERRY: But Massa Reese don't. *(Pause)* When you goin'
back to Massa Travis?
NAT: Pretty soon here... Ol' Brantley went into town
tonight... dat mean he come back drunk... All us catch hell...
CHERRY: I 'member fo' me an' de chil'ren were sol' ...
(Pause) Well ... coulda been worse ...
NAT: Don't see how.
CHERRY: Coulda sent us to 'Bama ... 'sippi...
NAT: Still could... 'Til weez free we gots to live with dat...
Deys got to be a way ...
CHERRY: What can you do?
NAT: Don't rightly know.
CHERRY: De prophet ain't got all de answers? (They both

6

laugh.)
NAT: Ise studyin' on it.
CHERRY: I knowes it.
NAT: How you know dat?
CHERRY: 'Cause evah since you put de babies to sleep ...
you been lookin' at dat sky ... 'steada me. (Nat goes to her.)
Been a month.
NAT: Coulda been a lifetime.
CHERRY: Lotta men come a courtin' while you wuz gone.
NAT: Who?
CHERRY: Don't much matter now.
NAT: I decide dat ... Who been afta you? ... Hark? I be seein'
how he look at you ...
CHERRY: Prophets gits jealous.
NAT: Don't knows 'bout prophets, but Nat kicks ass ... Now
who it be? (Pause)
CHERRY: Redic.
NAT: Redic?
CHERRY: Dat right. He say Mama, now dat Papa gone I
jump de broom wit you. (They laugh.) All dese years an'
you still not sho Ise yours.
NAT: Oh ... Ise sho ... an' youse sho ... jest wanna make sho
everybody else is.
(She pulls him down on top of her.)
CHERRY: Dem stars up dere mo' interesti' den me?
NAT: Jest got some figurin'.
CHERRY: Why don't you figure what dis here baby gonna
be.
NAT: You oughts know dat fo' me ...
CHERRY: Youse de prophet.
NAT: Is dat why I came back ... 'cause Ise a prophet?
CHERRY: You back cause in 'bout six month you got a new
baby.
NAT: You sho' you wit chile?
CHERRY: As sho as you got de prettiest brown skin in
Southhampton county. (Nat kisses her.) Welcome to earth
Nat Turner...
NAT: It be late ... gotta ...
CHERRY: Heaven an' Massa Travis can have you tomorrow ..
but tonight youse mine. (She wraps her legs around Nat. Nat
begins kissing her neck.) Wonder what yo' flock say dey see
you like dis. (Nat laughs. They begin pulling off their
clothes. Nat puts his head on her stomach.) What it gonna be?
NAT: Free.

(They begin to make love.)

7

BLUE STARS
by *Stuart Spencer*

The Characters: Horace and Emma, a dysfunctional couple
(30 - 50)

The Setting: A suburban home, the 1950's

The Scene: In the following scene, Horace and Emma engage
in a breakfast conversation that illustrates the grim and lonely
nature of their lives.

(*Morning. A white kitchen. An old style refrigerator, black
wall phone, coffee percolator. A small breakfast table.
Horace sits sipping coffee, eating a piece of toast and reading
the paper. He is dressed in a suit and tie. A small briefcase
on the floor next to him. Emma enters, looks tentatively,
anxiously into the room.*)
EMMA: You're already up.
HORACE: Hm?
EMMA: You're already up and dressed.
HORACE: I couldn't sleep.
EMMA: Nightmares?
HORACE: No, I just couldn't sleep.
EMMA: (*Moves into the kitchen*) I had nightmares.
HORACE: Did you? I'm sorry.
EMMA: Terrible nightmares. I couldn't wake up. (*Beat*)
You made the coffee.
HORACE: Yes.
EMMA: (*Pours some*) I would have made it.
HORACE: I didn't know when you'd be up.
EMMA: (*Sips*) It's fine.
HORACE: I thought it was pretty good.
EMMA: It is. It's very good. Did you want breakfast?
HORACE: Toast is fine.
EMMA: It won't hold you.
HORACE: It doesn't need to hold me. I can go out for
something at the office.
EMMA: I'll be glad to make you something.
HORACE: You don't need to, really.
EMMA: Pancakes, maybe. With blueberries. We still have a
lot of blueberries from the bunch I picked up at the cottage.
They'd be wonderful in some pancakes. They'll only go bad,

8

sitting in the refrigerator. Would you like some? Some blueberry pancakes?

HORACE: What's the matter with you? Why don't you just sit down and have your coffee. *(Pause)*

EMMA: Have you been outside today?

HORACE: Outside?

EMMA: To get the paper, I mean. Did you go out in front?

HORACE: Yes.

EMMA: Did you see anything out in the front of the house? Anything unusual.

HORACE: Like what, for instance.

EMMA: You'll laugh at me.

HORACE: *(Slight Pause)* No I won't.

EMMA: An airplane.

HORACE: Did I see an airplane out in front of the house?

EMMA: Yes.

HORACE: On the front lawn?

EMMA: Not on the lawn - on the street. At the curb. Pulled up to the curb, like an automobile, only it's a plane. A little plane, with a little stubby nose. Cute, almost. Just big enough for one person or maybe two if you squeeze. The pilot and a passenger. And the pilot is there, dressed like a ... well, like a pilot. A leather jacket with the fleece lining and a scarf and a cap. He's standing next to his plane. Young man. Nice looking.

HORACE: *(Slight Pause)* No, I didn't see that when I got the paper.

EMMA: He wanted me to go with him. He wanted me to get into his airplane.

HORACE: And did you?

EMMA: No, I wouldn't.

HORACE: You refused?

EMMA: Yes, I told him I didn't like to fly. I told him I was afraid of going up in an airplane.

HORACE: So you didn't go.

EMMA: No. Heavens, no.

HORACE: Then why was it a nightmare?

EMMA: It just was. If felt like a nightmare.

HORACE: But you didn't go in the airplane. You didn't want to go and in fact you did not. If you had gone in the airplane against your will, if he had tricked you, or forced you somehow. And then if you had actually taken off and you were flying around up there and something terrible happened, like you crashed, or he threw you out of the plane. That might have been a nightmare. What you had was a dream, that's all. People have them all the time. Some people

9

enjoy them.

EMMA: It was very real.

HORACE: Of course it was real. The stranger they are, the more real they seem. Don't you know that?

EMMA: I guess not.

HORACE: Have your coffee.

EMMA: *(Takes her coffee to the window.)* I suppose it was the prospect of something bad. The potential for it. The potential for something really dreadful happening.

HORACE: It's always the way in dreams.

EMMA: But this one in particular.

HORACE: You might have gone up into the wild blue yonder with an attractive young man in his airplane. You might have done something very exciting that you have never done before and in all likelihood will never do again. Call me a cockeyed optimist, but I do not see that as particularly dreadful.

EMMA: That never occurred to me.

HORACE: Of course it didn't. Now will you please relax?

EMMA: *(Pours more coffee)* The coffee's really very nice.

HORACE: Thank you.

EMMA: I didn't know you could make such good coffee.

HORACE: There are a lot of things I can do by myself.

EMMA: Would you like some more?

HORACE: I'll get some in a minute. I'm not quite ready. *(She unplugs the percolator and puts it on the table.)* It'll get cold sitting there.

EMMA: Not for a while.

HORACE: I'd prefer it back where it belongs, please, and plugged in. I prefer my coffee hot. *(She puts the percolator back on the counter and plugs it in.)*

EMMA: Do you think we'll go back to the cottage this weekend?

HORACE: Do you want to?

EMMA: Oh yes, very much.

HORACE: Then we may go.

EMMA: I hope we do.

HORACE: You're free to go alone, you know. You don't have to have me with you.

EMMA: You mean, me go up and leave you here?

HORACE: That's exactly what I mean.

EMMA: *(Astonished)* Are you serious?

HORACE: If you want to, why not?

EMMA: Me, go up to the cottage by myself?

HORACE: Yes.

EMMA: What would make you think such a thing?

HORACE: Never mind. It doesn't matter.

10

EMMA: It would never have occurred to me. I can't picture it.
HORACE: I only said it in passing.
EMMA: *(Slight Pause)* Do you think we'll go then?
HORACE: We may and we may not. We'll have to see.
EMMA: I'd like to pick more blueberries.
HORACE: I thought you said we had plenty of blueberries?
EMMA: We do.
HORACE: They were going to go bad, you said.
EMMA: They will.
HORACE: And you want to pick more.
EMMA: I like to pick them, that's all. I like going out with the basket and picking. I could do it for hours. All afternoon, nothing to do but pick berries.
HORACE: All by yourself.
EMMA: Yes.
HORACE: Out by yourself all afternoon, picking berries. But when I say, why not go up to the cottage by yourself, you say you can't picture it.
EMMA: It's different.
HORACE: Different how? What's different about it?
EMMA: The one way you're there, and the other way you're not.
HORACE: Either way, I'm not there.
EMMA: One way you're back at the cottage waiting for me when I'm done picking berries. The other way you're not there at all.
HORACE: I'm not there, but I'm here.
EMMA: Well, that's true.
HORACE: I'm somewhere. I still exist. It's not as if I have ceased to exist.
EMMA: It's not the same, that's all. I don't want to go up to the cottage without you. If you don't go, I'm not going.
HORACE: You make it awfully difficult, do you know that? You make things very, very difficult.
EMMA: If you want to go to the cottage, we'll go. If you don't want to go, we won't. And that's that. *(He gets up.)* Where are you going?
HORACE: To work.
EMMA: Already?
HORACE: I like to allow ample time.
EMMA: But it's early.
HORACE: It's not early. You got up late, remember?
EMMA: *(Beat)* When will you be home?
HORACE: I don't know.
EMMA: Call me, will you?

11

HORACE: If I have time.

EMMA: I want to know about dinner, is all.

HORACE: What about dinner?

EMMA: I want to know when we're going to have dinner.

HORACE: I'll call you when I know something.

EMMA: I think that's reasonable, isn't it.

HORACE: I said I'd call you.

EMMA: I have to plan a little bit, don't I?

HORACE: I said I'd call. Don't worry about it. *(Pause)* Will you quit looking at me like that? I'll call you. Don't worry.

EMMA: I'm sorry.

HORACE: I'll call you.

EMMA: All right.

HORACE: Kiss? *(They kiss.)*

EMMA: Don't work too hard. *(He exits. She goes to the window, waits a minute, waves.)* Good bye!

BREAKING LEGS
by Tom Dulack

The Characters: Lou Graziano (55) a restauranteur, and Angie (28) his outspoken daughter.

The Setting: A restaurant in a New England university town, the present

The Scene: During off-hours, Lou and Angie go over restaurant business. Their conversation turns more personal, however, when Lou brings up Angie's single status.

(The back room of an Italian restaurant in New England. It's a private room used for parties; there's a semi-circular booth stage right; a service bar with a couple of stools upstage left; and in front of that a table, checkered tablecloth, candles in a Chianti bottle, three chairs. Plastic flowers and ferns, fountains and garden sculpture comprise the interior decorating scheme.

Upstage is a door leading to the main dining room, and stage left, at the side of the bar, is another door leading to the kitchen. Stage right, behind the booth, a large window overlooks an alley adjacent to a parking lot.

In the restaurant. Lou and Angie, a flamboyant rather tough young woman in a mini-skirt and high heels.)

LOU: So what happened?
ANGIE: *(Opening mail)* Nothing happened. What is this, 469 dollars from Semprini Plumbing?
LOU: They fixed the toilets in the women's john. So what did he do?
ANGIE: Nothing! Forget it! I thought Semprini owed you a favor.
LOU: He did.
ANGIE: 469 dollars? This is a favor? What's he got to do, stick a coat hanger down there, for the love of God.
LOU: Hey, what do I know? His work is guaranteed.
ANGIE: It better be guaranteed!
LOU: Lay off Charlie, he's a nice guy.
ANGIE: Nice, nice.

LOU: You know, it's none of my business, Angel, but you date a guy for fifteen months, what are we supposed to think?

ANGIE: Why do you have to think anything?

LOU: What, I'm not human? Your daughter dates some guy for a year and a half, I'm not supposed to *think*?

ANGIE: He's a creep.

LOU: It took you a year and a half to figure out he's a creep?

ANGIE: I was giving him the benefit of the doubt. *(Opening an envelope and reading)* Mosconi's got a good price on Calamar'.

LOU: We can't buy no fish products from Mosconi. I told you before. My father would turn over in his grave.

ANGIE: Giulani gave us some fish we had complaints last week.

LOU: He had an accident with his refrigerator.

ANGIE: It's not the first time either.

LOU: You know, your grandmother liked this guy.

ANGIE: I don't want to talk about it.

LOU: All I'm saying is she's gonna take this hard. She was counting on you to give her some great-grandchildren before she dies.

ANGIE: She's already got about forty of them. How many does she need?

LOU: You can never have too many. And what about me?

ANGIE: What about you?

LOU: I ain't getting any younger. A man wants to see his daughter settle down, raise a family. I want to play with your kids, take 'em fishing, take 'em to the race track, teach 'em how to shoot craps.

ANGIE: You know our payroll's too big. Why do we need Francine Saturday afternoons? We don't do dick Saturday afternoons.

LOU: Look, Angel, this is none of my business, and I don't want to interfere in your private life. But you know, I mean, you gotta start thinking about your future. Naturally you want to be selective, and a girl like you can afford to bide your time. Still, you're getting to the age - I mean, don't get me wrong, Angel, everybody thinks your 22, 23, 26 ... Still! -

ANGIE: Dad, Marvin is history, okay? Ancient history!

LOU: Yeah, well, I knew it would never work. From the beginning, I told your mother, "Don't get your hopes up. This creep just ain't got what it takes."

ANGIE: I'm going to put Francine in the kitchen Saturday afternoons. What time's Terence coming?

LOU: I told him to come early. Mike's gotta go someplace tonight.

14

ANGIE: I can't wait to see him again. He was such a great teacher.

LOU: He said they did one of his plays in Europe.

ANGIE: Oh yeah?

LOU: Now he wants to do it in New York. He's looking for investors.

ANGIE: So what do you guys know about producing plays?

LOU: What's there to know? How hard can it be?

ANGIE: Everybody I ever heard of invested in a play they lost their shirt.

LOU: You lose your shirt at the track, shooting craps, what's the difference? It'll be nice, it'll be a laugh. Opening night, pulling up to the door in a stretch limousine. Red carpet on the sidewalks, Connie Chung, Channel 5 News. Some bimbo on my arm. You're gonna lose your shirt, you might as well go in style.

ANGIE: Never mind the bimbo on your arm.

LOU: You don't have to repeat that to your mother. I was only kidding.

ANGIE: Well, when Terry comes, just remember who you're dealing with. Don't embarrass me.

LOU: "Embarrass you!" What's that supposed to mean? Since when do I embarrass you?

ANGIE: He's a college professor, that's all I'm saying.

LOU: What are you, telling me something I don't know? I don't know he's a college professor now?

ANGIE: All I'm saying is he's not some scumbag looking to put the bite on you, like Dino or Vinnie. You can't be jerking him around.

LOU: Nobody's gonna jerk him around! Whatsa matter with you?

ANGIE: Just remember who you're dealing with, that's all I'm saying. Did you eat yet?

LOU: Nah, I'll wait for Mike and Tino. Whata we got tonight?

ANGIE: I don't know, I'll go see.

LOU: And ask Billy who won the fifth at Hialeah. Patsy had a horse running down there. *(Angie goes out.)* And call your Aunt Mary! How many times I have to tell you?

ANGIE: *(Offstage)* Okay, okay!

15

THE DAYS OF WINE AND ROSES
by J.P. Miller

The Characters: Joe Clay (30-40), an alcoholic and Kirsten Arnesen (20's), a young woman attracted to Joe.

The Setting: a walk along the east bank of the Hudson River, 1960's

The Scene: On their first date, Joe and Kirsten walk by the river and share details of their lives.

(Joe and Kirsten enter up left. River and city sounds in the background. Kirsten is dreamy. Joe is still full of the day's emotions, but several drinks have helped him to look at things -- at least for now -- in a rosier light.)

KIRSTEN: Isn't it beautiful down here? Like another world.
JOE: *(Chuckles)* To you, maybe. To me it looks like the same world where I made an ass of myself last night.
KIRSTEN: You did, didn't you? But that seems like a long time ago somehow. Joe -- I enjoyed our dinner very much.
JOE: On, me, too. It was great. And no matter what happens to me tomorrow when I go to the office, meeting you has made it all worth it.
KIRSTEN: Thank you. But nothing bad's going to happen. I know Rad Leland. He has no moral principles of his own, but he respects people who do.
(They have arrived down left, where there is a short length of rail running left to right. They lean against the rail, facing down. Joe takes a flat pint of amber liquid out of his jacket pocket and offers it to her. She shakes her head. He takes a drink.)
JOE: Are you on the wagon? Or you just don't drink?
KIRSTEN: I just don't drink.
JOE: Not at all?
KIRSTEN: I don't see the point of it.
JOE: It makes you feel good!
KIRSTEN: I already feel good.
JOE: Maybe it's make you feel better! Oh, I'm not pushing booze, but have you ever tried it?
KIRSTEN: Once.
JOE: Well?

KIRSTEN: Senior prom. Spiked punch. I hung around the punch bowl all night, didn't even dance, fell down, had to be carried to my date's father's car, threw up all over his rented tuxedo and my borrowed prom gown, and the car, inside and out, and had a monster hangover for two days. It was wonderful.

JOE: And you never tried again. A real quitter, huh?

KIRSTEN: I guess so. You drink like this often?

JOE: *(Bursts out laughing.)* Can't afford it! Oh, I do like to drink, but not to excess, you know. Not often, anyhow. Oh, I tie one on once in a while. Everybody has his little quirk. What do you like?

KIRSTEN: Books. *(Pulls book partway out of shoulder bag, drops it back.)* And chocolate. *(Takes chocolate bar out of bag, breaks off piece, pops it in her mouth.)*

JOE: Sugar. If you eat that stuff you probably get sugar highs.

KIRSTEN: *(Thinks about it.)* Maybe. I never thought about that.

JOE: See? Stick with me, kid. An encyclopedia of trivia.

KIRSTEN: You're funny. I like being here with you. Look - - you can see the Prince's yacht. Aren't the lights beautiful? You know what Mr. Trayner told me? Two of the girls stayed with the Prince after the party.

JOE: I guess I oughta be pretty proud, huh? I'm sort of responsible for a menage a trois. *(He takes a drink.)*

KIRSTEN: Sometimes I wish I could be like those girls. They don't have to be anywhere except where they are. They're like -- I don't know -- hummingbirds. They just stand in the air wherever the nectar is. The world's just one big honeysuckle vine.

JOE: As opposed to one big skunk cabbage, for some people - -

KIRSTEN: You know what? It's after midnight, and I feel wonderful!

JOE: *(Without conviction)* Me, too. *(He takes a drink.)*

KIRSTEN: *(Dreamily)* It's funny about the river. If you look close it's filthy. I watch the middle where it's clean. You know what I think? I think I watch the water because I expect a sea monster to come up out of there someday and carry me down to the ocean caves...

(Joe stares at her, then shakes his head at such an incongruous thought.)

JOE: Midnight, huh? Show time. My Mom and Pop are a club act. You know, songs, dances, snappy patter - - old time vaudeville. They're working some loud joint in Vegas right

17

this minute. Show biz baby. Three years old, right out there with 'em. *(Does a little soft shoe, singing:)*
  "Me and my shadow..." *(Stops suddenly)*
KIRSTEN: *(Applauds)* More! More!
JOE: I retired at seventeen, joined the Navy. Mom and Pop are still at it.
KIRSTEN: Are they good?
JOE: *(Shrugs)* You know. Oh, they were on TV, couple times.
KIRSTEN: But you didn't like that kind of life.
JOE: I wanted something steady, something with a little class. Like this Trayner account -- class.
KIRSTEN: Joe -- don't hate yourself. We all have to do things we don't like. That's part of your job.
JOE: *(Explodes)* No! It's not! I want to be a public relations man, not a pimp! *(Seething, he tries to control his anger.)* Classy guy, huh? Meets a beautiful girl, a girl who believes in things in spite of the dirty people all around her, a girl who reads books, and dreams nice dreams. And what does this bum do? He gets half-schnockered and tells her what a tough life he leads.
KIRSTEN: Actually, I'm proud that you confided in me.
JOE: The great lover.
KIRSTEN: And you did me a favor, too.
JOE: I did?
KIRSTEN: I love it down here, but I usually have to come alone.
JOE: Alone? You come down here alone? Kirsten, this place is crawling with all kinds of odd balls! You can't come down here by yourself at night!
KIRSTEN: They walk by me real slow sometimes, and stare, but they never do anything. I don't know why.
JOE: Jesus Christ, Kirsten!
KIRSTEN: I dreamed one time they murdered me in those bushes over there, and my dad drove all the way in from the Island and took my body home in his pickup truck. I could see my body stretched out in the bed of the truck on all the little clods and leaves from all the trees and shrubs he'd been delivering. And all the way home he kept talking to my body. The back window of the cab was broken out, and he talked over his shoulder through that broken window, talked a blue streak all the way home. But I was dead and couldn't answer him. The strange thing is, my father never talks. Oh, he used to talk to my mother. They had a very private love affair. Their favorite toast to each other was "Til samen e himlin." In Norwegian that means "Together in heaven."

JOE: Til samen e himlin.

KIRSTEN: *(Corrects his pronunciation.)* Til samen e himlin. You've got to get the lilt.

JOE: Til samen e himlin.

KIRSTEN: Together in heaven. They meant it, too. After Mama died, he was more silent than ever, almost as though he'd gone with her. *(She suddenly makes an effort to throw off her gloom.)* Well, "gather ye rosebuds while ye may, Old Time is still a-flying."

JOE: You get that out of that book?

KIRSTEN: *(Pulls book out of shoulder bag.)* No, that's Herrick. He's in Go-Ja. *(She pronounces it "Gojay".)* This is Le-Na *("Lenay")*. Dad gave me these for my high school graduation. He said if I read all the way through from Ab-Bu to Ya-Zu I'd have the equivalent of a college education.

JOE: Hey, you're about halfway through your sophomore year, here. *(Hands her the book. She drops it in her bag. He lifts his bottle in a toast.)* Here's to your BA degree. And after that?

KIRSTEN: My dream, you mean? You won't laugh? I hope to get a real degree someday, and be an English teacher.

JOE: English teacher. Great. You want it, you'll get it. *(Flourishes bottle)* Here goes the coup de grace. *(Drains bottle)*

KIRSTEN: Well, it's just about time to get back to the real world.

JOE: *(Finally has the glow he's been looking for.)* Time does not exist on the river. *(He caps the bottle and leans over the rail.)* I ought to put a message in this bottle. But what?

KIRSTEN: *(She leans over the rail with him as he holds the bottle out and drops it. We hear a splash. They watch it float away, right to left.)*

"They are not long, the days of wine and roses.
Out of a misty dream
Our path emerges for awhile, then closes
Within a dream."

(They turn away from the rail and walk toward up left. At Center they stop and look at each other. He puts his arm around her, and they continue off left as lights fade to black.)

DEJAVU
by John Osborne

The Characters: Cliff (50+), a man paying a visit to an old friend; and Alison (20's) an angry young woman

The Setting: A home in the Midlands, England, the present

The Scene: In this sequel to "Look Back in Anger" Cliff, now 30 years older confronts J.P.'s daughter with her feelings for her father.

(Cliff is seated. Alison stares out of the window. Pause)
CLIFF: Teddy's quiet ... I think he's given up brooding over market forces. Just concentrating on trying to become a good European. He's been hanging back for too long from playing a full role in unification, haven't you? Starting a new fast-lane lifestyle aren't you, my old ursine cocky? Even feeling a little less guilty over his colonial past. Aren't you? Less guilty? His part in the slave trade, for instance. About a hundred and fifty years before his time but it bothers him. Wouldn't think he had a colonial past to look at him, would you? Well, that's his considered view of it. Isn't it. *(Cliff gropes among the newspapers for a black, hairy object which turns out to be a dreadlock wig. He arranges it on Teddy's head.)* That degree course in African Studies and Caribbean Culture didn't cheer him up either. He will worry about people, especially if he doesn't know them. Don't you Ted? You *worry* ... That wig's a mistake. Do you think he secretly hates whitey?
ALISON: Teddy - can go fuck himself.
CLIFF: He already thinks he's in a no-win situation.
ALISON: You know what? You two are mad. Barking.
CLIFF: Teddy's not mad. Not he that is gone into England.
ALISON: Oh, do *shut* up, Cliff. When he's not here, *you* start to sound like my father.
CLIFF: Perhaps a little mad but no, not malign. Ted never had a role model, you see. Not even a world that never existed to regret.
ALISON: You've both talked this brand of babyish balls ever since I can remember.
CLIFF: You wrong-footed him pretty adroitly just now.
ALISON: Oh? I goaded him, *I* exposed the vicious oink struggling inside every carping old dodo like J.P. Longing for some petty recompense for a lifetime of useless snarling. No

20

wonder he prefers dogs to people. He came into this world bitching and he'll go out the same way. Unloved, unlovable and unloving.

CLIFF: Teddy's quite fond of him.

ALISON: Then Teddy is mad. *And* malign.

CLIFF: Did you never like him ever? As a little girl? At all?

ALISON: No.

CLIFF: Well-- you didn't see much of each other. Your mother saw to that.

ALISON: She wanted to protect me.

CLIFF: Against what?

ALISON: Someone so rabidly hopeless. With such a second, third-rate, oh, mind.

CLIFF: Well, your mother has an obsession with what her sort of friends call "first-class minds." I don't think J.P.'s second class. What British Rail call "Standard" perhaps. J.P., a most happily prejudiced witness, tells me that your mother's old love, Professor Randy, First Class Brain, was devastated when his wife died before Christmas. The reason being that he no longer had the perfect hostess for his dinners in London when he popped up from Oxford for his weekend performances. More seriously, he found at an advancing age, and to his great astonishment, that he could no longer get it up. He's been inconsolable for weeks. Even your mother's attentions with mid-morning smoked salmon and her best Wine Society claret in the evenings haven't brought him comfort.

ALISON: There's nothing wrong in being brainy.

CLIFF: I met a girl once. In Cannes. I was sitting on the terrace, having breakfast and reading *The Times*. She was sitting at the next table, looking quite gorgeous at that time of day. Suddenly, she looked up and said, rather coldly I thought: "What have you got for seventeen down?" Seventeen what? "The crossword. You've got it there." Oh, I thought: There goes that one. "I'm sorry: I don't do *The Times* crossword." Her beautiful lip curled, it really did. "You don't? And how do you exercise your mind?" No joy there, I thought. Exercise my mind? By fucking intellectual girls like you.

ALISON: Why do you try so hard to be unpleasant? There's nothing wrong in being brainy. She admires intellect. So what? So do I.

CLIFF: There's no such thing as decent intellect. Like dumb insolence.

ALISON: She's accustomed to the company of clever men. She comes from a clever family. Her parents. Her brothers.

21

CLIFF: Ah yes, barristers, judges.

ALISON: Yes, all right: diplomats, scholars, historians.

CLIFF: And the cleverness of strangers too. Not an MEP among them. You wouldn't call J.P.'s family clever. More silly to themselves, eh, Ted. You must have your mother's intellect.

ALISON: *(Fierce)* What's he ever given me - forget *done* for me? And *don't* say "What's he ever done for Teddy?" Sometimes I think you're worse than he is. At least he seems to *enjoy* being a bully and a bigot - every now and then.

CLIFF: J.P.? He's just an old dog. Now, I'd say your mother's a bully.

ALISON: She isn't.

CLIFF: She sends you up here to report on him.

ALISON: Is that what he says?

CLIFF: Why else would you come up here so regularly? When you despise him.

ALISON: Oh, and you think young Jimmy comes up to spy as well?

CLIFF: I think your brother's too unconcerned to hitchhike two hundred miles to eavesdrop on his father. He comes up for free meals, twenty-four hour sleeps, a hefty tip and, possibly, even some respite from your mummy. Dad's place is an all-right squat, and, if there's a great gig up the road in the big city, OK.

ALISON: You must think we're hard up.

CLIFF: You forget. I have children of my own.

ALISON: Well, he's sure not doing much about his son being jumped on by the police.

CLIFF: He's talked about nothing else since *I* came up.

ALISON: Oh yes. Jimmy may have to go to prison. And where's his father? Slumped over a filthy old blanket in his posh drawing room we're not allowed in, keening like a peasant over a cheesy old dog.

CLIFF: I think young Jimmy is happier where he is - with the Rev. Ron. Anyway, the dog does love him.

ALISON: Yeah. Like Teddy, I suppose.

CLIFF: I don't think he is quite sure. "Occasionally held but never moved," as they say. I've learned very little during the time I've seen you grow up, but one small thing has become clear to me, that, apart from the fact of realizing that one's parents may be corrupt or even wicked, your children may also be vindictive and even vengeful. Above all, as with your ironing-board pantomime, something stares you in the early-morning face: that those whom you no longer love can still inflict amazing pain.

22

ALISON: On *him*? Who?

CLIFF: Yourself. Your mother, young Jimmy even.

ALISON: He's never loved anyone. Not even himself and God knows that *does* make sense.

CLIFF: Forgive me, Alison. I was there. You weren't. I really do think you feel oppressed as you say you are because you had a man for a father.

ALISON: Oh, very J. Porter. Most glib. I'd get on the first train to Euston in the morning if I were you. Go back to your wife, even your children, go back to the TV studios, go back to Wales, even. Teddy and J.P. will only bring you down to their own silly level.

CLIFF: I don't come back to spy on him.

ALISON: Do you think my mother cares what happens to him? J. Porter Esquire? He doesn't exist. For any of us.

CLIFF: Perhaps he never did. It's the one thing you might have all agreed about.

ALISON: Don't be so bloody precious.

CLIFF: you're right. Maybe it's these bloody church bells. I always told him it was a mistake having a church tower next door to your runner beans. It was bad enough in the old days, when they made him angry. I dare say the Rev. Ron will silence all that with a strong rock beat soon enough. What message do they have for young people today? Decadence, shabby sentiment, yes, what J.P. calls "the crimson twilight". Those were our Sunday evenings. Bloody bells. Unheeded, elitist bells. But then I was brought up a Methodist. Leave him alone, Alison.

ALISON: With pleasure.

CLIFF: He may not have lightened up your life but he hasn't darkened it.

ALISON: And he won't. Don't you think you can drop all this seedy male conspiracy for a bit? What's he going to do for his own son when he's in such trouble? That's what I've come to find out.

CLIFF: Nothing. I imagine.

ALISON: There you are.

CLIFF: Your mother didn't exactly hurtle back from her US lecture tour. Just a few gushy phone calls and a list of pushy lawyers who only appear for the grievously oppressed.

ALISON: This tour is important to her career.

CLIFF: Quite so. That's a consideration J.P. hasn't got. Still, the Rev. Ron's barged to the front like a funeral parlor executive at a pile-up on the motorway.

(Telephone rings offstage. Alison and Cliff both wait to see if it's answered. It stops.)

23

DOWN THE FLATS
by Tony Kavanaugh

The Characters: Mother (54), a hardworking woman, Father (57), the gruff patriarch of a dysfunctional family, Bridy (23), their vivacious daughter and Fran (25), their angry son.

The Setting: A flat in Dublin, the present

The Scene: As the Flynn's gather for their evening meal, ritualistic arguments begin and escalate to familiar violence.

MOTHER: I'll get the dinner ready. You're father'll be in soon. *(Mother goes to the gas cooker and takes the dinner out of the oven which is in a pot and pan. Fran switches on the radio and a "U2" song, "Pride" comes on. He dances as he looks out the window. After a few minutes ...)* Fran, switch that off, will ya, it's given' me a Jaysus headache.
FRAN: Why? What's wrong?
(Enter Father and Bridy. They both are very cheerful. They take off their coats as they enter. Bridy carries a shopping bag. Fran switches off the radio.)
FATHER: Fifty-pence I put down and I won six Quid.
BRIDY: That's great, Da.
MOTHER: Ya won six quid, yeah? Ya can pay me what ya owe me now.
(Fran sits on the couch, reading a magazine. Bridy exits to the bedroom. Silence. Then Mother puts the plates on the table. Father sits at the table.)
FATHER: What in the name of Jaysus are ya doin', Fran?
FRAN: What!?
FATHER: John Ward seen ya bein' chased by the police today. What the fuck are ya up to?
FRAN: I'm not up to anything.
(The mother now has a pot in her hand. She places it on the table. Fran gets up off the couch and sits at the table. Enter Bridy in a new dress.)
BRIDY: Do ya like me new dress, ma?
MOTHER: O'luvy girl ... Turn around and let me have a look at ya. (Bridy does a twirl.) You're gorgeous.
(Bridy looks at the father. He's not minding her but taking the food from the pot and putting it on the plates. Bridy looks at him a moment then sits down. The mother sits. They begin to

24

eat.)

FATHER: Fran you don't start brin' the police around to this house again ... I'm out workin' hard for me livin' ... I don't get money easy the way you do!

MOTHER: For fuck sack pader - - don't start we'll ya not ... I'm sick a' the ar'gen ... Did ya go down the church?

FATHER: I DID!

MOTHER: WELL?

FATHER: WELL WHA ... I said me prayer and tha was tha' ... *(He pauses and eats. Smacks with his mouth full.)* I naver liked the bollicks anyway.

MOTHER: WHA ... May God for gave ya ... callin' the man a bollicks an he dead.

FATHER: Ah lave me alone ... Are you goin' to get a job, Fran, or wha? *(Long Pause)* Did ya hear me or are ya gone deaf?

FRAN: How goin' to gave me a job wha? Sure the last time I went for an interview ... Everytin was o.k. till I ave them me address ... I knew be the fuck face tha I hadn't got a chance ...

FATHER: Look ... ya can't be thinkin like tha ... you'd get a job in the corporation if ya went over ta'mor'a ...

FRAN: I don't want to work in the corpo!

FATHER: Ah ya don't want to work in the corpo wha' ... *(To Mother)* De ya know wha it is Mary ... he just doesn't want to work. He's too busy be'in chased all over this city by the police ... and his not even out a fuckin' month ... DOESN'T want to work ... Doesn't want to work!

FRAN: *(Getting angry)* Well ya wouldn't let me take the job in the JEWELRY SHOP YEARS AGO WOULD YA ...After the headmaster gavein' me a lovely referency, now would ya ... NO ... you want'd me in the MEAT COMPANY ... the bleedin' meat company killin' cows all day ... I could have been a diamond cutter... not a cow killer wha you want'd me to be ... You were a fread I'd do better than ya!

FATHER: Cuttin' diamon ya woulda, been all right ... Thats a fuckin' laught ... Go way ... ya would of had the kip robbed blind in two weeks ... would ya stop.

(Fran jumps up. Mother and Bridy jump up.)

MOTHER: FRAN SIT DOWN!

BRIDY: FRAN STOP, STOP COM'ON.

FRAN: I jest don't believe you ... I don't believe wha your sayin' ... I naver robbed a thing in me life. When I got that job in the jeweller ... I tought ya would ya been proud of me ... but no ... I ended up at the MEAT COMPANY ... THE FUCKIN' MEAT COMPANY... And the place a den of thieves. *(Pause)* And if ya want to know sometin ... Thats

were I did learn me trade ... SO BOLLICKS YOU AND
DON'T TELL ME TA GETA JOB! ... It was'ent the butcher
trade I learned eider ... it was the robben trade!
(The Father jumps to his feet and throws a punch at Fran.
Fran ducks out of the way.)
FATHER: Ya little fuck ya!
MOTHER: For God sack you's not start' in this carry'on
again ... again ... about fuckin' diamonds. I'm sick hearin'
a'bout ya ... I'm sick of ya.
FRAN: Ya know ... Ya ever put a hand on me, I swear you're
me father ... But I'll kill ya!
FATHER: Ya ... ya wouldn't kill notin. *(Pause. They stare at*
each other.)
FRAN: I'm getin out of hear. *(Fran grabs his coat, As he's*
doing this the mother is speaking.)
MOTHER: Fran have your dinner ... For Gods sack don't
mind him?
FATHER: Let him go! *(Father sits at table.)*
MOTHER: Fran ... Fran ... *(Fran exits. Mother looks at door.*
Sits. Pause.) Jaysus pader ya shoulda let him have his
dinner.
FATHER: *(Eating)* Dinner ... Tha fella doesn't deserve anne
dinner!
BRIDY: *(Sitting down)* He pays his way ya know... He's
entitled to it as mush as you are.
FATHER: He pays his way aright ... Then he borr'ees it back
the next day.
BRIDY: Well he pays back, doesn't he.

(They resume eating.)

EVELYN AND THE POLKA KING
by John Olive

The Characters: Henry Czerniak (40's) a polka king and Evelyn Starkweather (18) a young woman in search of her parents.

The Setting: A small apartment in Chicago, the present

The Scene: Henry has recently stopped drinking after a 25 year bender. His new sobriety has one disturbing side-effect: he goes sleepwalking in the middle of the night. After waking up in the middle of Chicago's vast Graceland Cemetary, Henry hurries home to find a young woman camping out on his doorstep. To his amazement, she claims to be his daughter.

HENRY: Please, door, please be open. *(Evelyn enters, opposite)* Please don't be locked.
EVELYN: Hey.
HENRY: *(Whirls)* Huh!?!
EVELYN: The hell're you doin', out in your skivs and your hightops, middle a the night?
HENRY: I wish I knew.
EVELYN: You're Henry C-Z-E-R-N-I-A-K? Right?
HENRY: Czerniak. Who're you?
EVELYN: My name is Evelyn Starkweather. *(Waits for a reaction, gets none, continues)* I'm from Houston. I got your name out of the Chicago phone book. You gonna invite me in? Stinks in this hallway. I need to talk to you.
HENRY: How'd you get past the security door?
EVELYN: Neiman Marcus.
HENRY: Who?!
EVELYN: Credit card. C'mon. Lemme in. I came all the way up here from Texas, to talk to you.
HENRY: *(Hesitates, terrified)* I'm ... kinda busy. *(Beat. Evelyn takes a fierce step toward Henry.)* All right.
(Lights roll. Henry's cramped apartment. We see an old faded poster of Henry, wearing overalls and a hillbilly hat, holding a jug of whiskey, grinning. "Hank Czerniak, The Polka King". Evelyn looks around, taking in the apartment's squalor, clutching her backpack.)
EVELYN: Don't you have air conditioning?

27

HENRY: No. *(Henry pulls on a ratty robe.)* You want something cold to drink?

EVELYN: Yeah. *(Henry exits. Evelyn notices the old poster, covers her face with her hands, moans)* Ohhhhhhh ...

HENRY: *(Offstage)* I got grape juice, milk, fuzzy water --

EVELYN: *(Shouts)* What!?!

HENRY: *(Re-enters, looks at her, concerned)* What?

EVELYN: What did you say!?

HENRY: *(Flustered)* What? I'm --

EVELYN: Did you say fuzzy water!?

HENRY: Oh. Yeah. Club soda.

EVELYN: That's what *I* call it!

HENRY: *(Looks at her warily)* You want some? *(Evelyn nods: Yes. Henry exists. Evelyn sits. Henry comes back in with two glasses of soda water. He gives one to Evelyn. They both drink, thirstily. Then Henry starts pulling on a pair of pants.)*

EVELYN: Who's Wanda?

HENRY: Look, Miss, I'm sorry about that. I don't know how come I called you Wanda. I guess I got you mixed up with someone else.

EVELYN: Who!?

HENRY: Well, maybe you look like somebody I used to know. *(Evelyn jumps up. Henry cowers, the pants falling around his ankles.)* I'll call the cops!

EVELYN: *(Struggling to calm herself)* Who?

HENRY: I don't know.

EVELYN: What's her last name? Does it begin with an S?

HENRY: *(Buttons the pants, takes a chair, sits near Evelyn.)* Look, Miss. I quit drinking three months ago. I'm coming off what amounts to a twenty-five year blackout. A quart a day. Some things come back to me, sometimes they come back at the strangest times. And lotsa things're gone forever. I lost twenty-five years a my life.

EVELYN: Were you a wino?

HENRY: No. But I could see it coming.

EVELYN: You look like a wino.

HENRY: I ... I had a glass of raw vodka in my hand, and I heard a voice: "This is the last drink you'll ever take." I jumped around, I saw my face in the mirror. It was my voice. I been waiting for it to come back and tell me what to do next. *(After a beat)* I don't know why I called you Wanda.

EVELYN: I just ... I just found out ... that ... that I'm ... adopted. My fa -- *(Forces the word out)* My father, he had this old family lawyer, Mr. Butler. Then Mr. Butler got the queasies 'cause a some a the business deals Daddy got into, so

Daddy had to find another lawyer. Anyway, Mr. Butler died. So I got my friend Earl Dean, he's crazy. Earl Dean'll do anything. He busted into the warehouse where they keep Mr. Butler's files, and he found my ... adoption papers. My mother's name, my real mother's name is listed as "W.S." That's how come, when you called me Wanda, I gotta find out who Wanda is. Wanda begins with a W. *(Henry and Evelyn look at each other. Long moment)*

HENRY: *(Finally)* Who'd it say your father is?

EVELYN: You.

HENRY: *(Stands up, knocking his chair over, staring wildly at Evelyn. He's shaking. Suddenly he lets go a series of shouts.)* Aaaggghhh!!! Aaaggghhh! AAAGGGHHH!!! I knew it! I knew something was gonna happen! WHOOOOOOOOOOO!!!

(Pounding on the wall)

OFFSTAGE VOICE: Hey! Quiet!

EVELYN: Who's "W.S."?! Who's "W.S."!?!

HENRY: What?

EVELYN: Who's - -?

HENRY: Oh, God, I don't believe this! *(Takes a step toward Evelyn, reaching out for her. Evelyn slaps his hand away.)*

EVELYN: No! Who's "W.S."!?

HENRY: *(After a beat, trying to focus)* I ... I don't know.

EVELYN: Can't you remember!?

HENRY: I ... I ... I don't know if I can.

EVELYN: *(Turns away)* He doesn't remember. I don't believe this. *(Faces Henry)* I was born March 13, 1973. Are there itineraries for the Vibra-Tones in 1972?

HENRY: Huh?

EVELYN: Records, of where the band went.

HENRY: Oh. No.

EVELYN: Dammit! Didn't you have a booking agent?

HENRY: No. We just went when people called.

EVELYN: *(Very close to being out-of-control)* CAN YOU REMEMBER ANYTHING ABOUT 1972?!

HENRY: *(Backs away)* 1972? *(Hoping it will help)* I was drunk.

EVELYN: I gotta find out about her. I gotta find out everything there is to know about her. I'll die if I don't.

HENRY: *(A long moment. Then he carefully, gingerly, reaches out his hand to touch Evelyn's face. She stiffens, but doesn't resist. This is very emotionally charged; Evelyn is on the verge of losing control. Softly)* Where'd you come from?

EVELYN: I'm ... I'm pretty sure I got here ... the normal way. *(Wipes her eyes, turns away)* Damn. Here. Lemme read you this. *(Digs in her pocket, pulls out a crumpled piece of paper)* When I found out about you, I did some ... Polka research. *(Evelyn reads. Henry circles her, staring at her, at first not even listening.)* "Polka Music's development mirrors that of the Blues. Both idioms arose out of very specific ethnic communities, African and Polish American, respectively. Both idioms flowered in Chicago, that most quintessentially American city. Both idioms reached heights of popularity in the nineteen-sixties. The Blues, however, has transcended it; Polka Music has not flourished. Its constituency, the white urban working class, is shrinking, becoming suburban, being pulled into the bland TV culture of the nineties, losing its identity, dying. *(Henry reacts, finally getting the gist.)* So, too, is Polka Music."

HENRY: Dying? Polka's dying? What the hell is that? *(Snatches the paper)* Who is this guy?

EVELYN: He's a Professor of American Studies at --

HENRY: He's a moron! I don't know where he gets his information. Polka's big, everywhere. Even in Texas. I bet you never heard of Santiago Jimenez.

EVELYN: He's dead.

HENRY: *(Reacts, horrified)* He is?

EVELYN: So here's my big question. *(Beat)* Are you *the* Polka King or just *a* Polka King?

HENRY: *(After a long moment)* You ... wanna hear one a my songs?

EVELYN: *(Hesitates)* Yeah. Okay.

EVIL LITTLE THOUGHTS
by Mark D. Kaufman

The Characters: Bo (20's) a slow-witted yet attractive man, and Laney (30's) an opportunistic woman.

The Setting: An office supply room, the present.

The Scene: Following a round of lovemaking, Laney demonstrates her superior imagination, and Bo confesses a dark secret.

(An office building basement supply room; shelves of papers, pens, and various desk supplies. Some cushions have been thrown over boxes of xerox paper. Laney is pulling on her dress next to a man in his mid to late 20's, Bo Riverton. Bo, who has little to offer besides his looks, is still lying in his underwear on the cushions, spent.)

BO: You know, when you asked me if I minded that you made love to other men, and I said I didn't, I meant it. *(Pause)*

LANEY: I hope so.

BO: You gotta let someone do what's in their heart if you love them enough. Even if it breaks your heart to see them do it. *(Laney looks at Bo, questioning.)* I don't mean you're breaking my heart; it was only an example. *(Laney nods.)* Another example would be the needless punishment of orphan children. Beating them, starving them. Locking them in a wet basement. Telling them that Santa Claus will bring the one toy they've had their hearts set on - seeing the joy in their faces - then on Christmas morning, when there's nothing under the tree, telling them Santa's changed his mind because their parents are dead. *(Pause)* If you love someone enough, you let them do those things. But I know, no matter who else you're with, we'll end up together.

LANEY: I think we will, too.

BO: It's because of my eyes, isn't it? You said I have the nicest eyes you'd ever seen.

LANEY: You do, Bo. Sometimes I want to just pour your eyes into a glass and drink 'em down so they'll be inside me.

BO: I love to hear you say those things. What else?

LANEY: Well, when I look in 'em it's like I can see who you are, and where you've come from.

BO: You mean Oklahoma?

LANEY: No. I mean like your past lives. Like when you were a slave in ancient Rome, and you had to build these huge buildings all made of these great big stones, and you'd strain your muscles till you thought you'd just die. But you didn't because you knew someday somebody'd come to your rescue. *(Impulsively, Bo grabs Laney's hands.)*

BO: What happened?

LANEY: Ouch! My typing fingers! *(Immediately, Bo begins to massage Laney's hands apologetically.)*

BO: So, did I get rescued?

LANEY: Well, one day along came a real rich Roman lady, and it was on her mind to find a handsome young slave who would fulfill all of her various physical needs, because her husband was an old stiff, and he ate in bed. And the lady refused to go to orgies, although she had lots of invitations, being the looker she was, because she liked to know who she was getting "involved" with, and most of the people who show up at those things: you don't know where they've been. If you know what I mean. *(Bo is completely lost.)*

BO: No, I don't.

LANEY: Anyway, she saw you holding up this two-ton hunk of marble, with beads of sweat shining on your chest and arms through this little torn T-shirt thing you were wearing, and she said, "Well, you're just the man I want to buy." And she went over to your master, and pulled a hundred dollars out of her purse, and bought you right on the spot.

BO: And I went home and made her happy?

LANEY: Until her husband found out. She told him you were a new landscape architect, but that wasn't a very good choice since they lived in a third floor apartment. And sooner or later he got suspicious, and one day caught you fooling around with more than just the philodendron.

BO: What did he do?

LANEY: He threw a fit, and he killed you.

BO: No! How?

LANEY: He poisoned you. He put it in her favorite drink. Both of you had some just before the next time you made love, and you died in each other's arms. With these little half-smile/half-grimaces on your faces, because the moment was a mixture of pleasure and pain all at the same time. *(Pause)*

BO: I don't remember any of this.

LANEY: And her spirit floated around for years and years and finally ended up in another woman's body. But when you find her she'll already be dead this time. Your lives are fated for tragedy.

BO: You see all this in my eyes?

LANEY: With a little imagination.

BO: Oh, I always wanted an imagination: I usually can't think of anything.

LANEY: That's what I love about you! You have nothing going on in your head at all. It's impossible for you to be bad to anybody. I bet you've never had a single mean thought in your life.

BO: That's true; I'd never be mean to anybody.

LANEY: You really like me to tell you stories?

BO: Oh, boy, yes.

LANEY: You see, that's why I have to sleep with all these different men. You need fuel from different experiences to tell stories, and if you're only ever with one man, you don't learn about life. And I have this terrible thirst for knowledge...

BO: Well, drink up!

LANEY: That's just the way I want you to look at it.

BO: I told you before - whatever you like is fine with me.

LANEY: You think it'll be like this when we're married? *(Bo looks around.)*

BO: It'll probably be a little bigger... Not so many pencils.

LANEY: My boss has a good marriage. His wife dresses badly, but she's sweet. If we're at all lucky, our marriage will be just like theirs. And I'll look better. *(Bo continues massaging; thinking.)*

BO: Remember when you said I've never had a mean thought in my head, a couple minutes ago? Well, I have a broth... a friend who's going to murder somebody, and I'm helping him out. *(Pause. Laney looks up.)* I hope that doesn't count.

LANEY: You're going to kill someone?

BO: Not me. I'm just helping out.

LANEY: You Bo? I can't believe it. I... I don't know what to say. Well, is the person you're going to help kill evil or bad at least?

BO: I don't know. I'm doing it more because I like the guy who's doing the killing; not so much that I hate the guy who's getting killed.

LANEY: I don't know about this...

BO: It isn't really a mean thought. I'm not doing it to be mean.

LANEY: I understand that. I'm just concerned that it's not a healthy activity for you to participate in.

BO: Oh, I won't get hurt; don't worry.

LANEY: But there is the possibility you'll get caught. What

33

if you end up in jail? What kind of life am I going to have for myself? When I want to have sex with you, we'll have to do it through the bars of your cell with a bunch of criminals watching. *(Pause)* Not that under the right circumstances that couldn't be kind of fun. But it's no way of life.

BO: Laney, I promise nothing's going to happen to me. If I thought it could mess up our lives I wouldn't do it.

LANEY: You mean that?

BO: Cross my heart. *(Bo crosses his heart with his finger.)*

LANEY: Cross mine, too. *(Bo runs his finger over Laney's chest, crossing her heart.)* That feels nice.

BO: Please don't mind me helping out with the murder.

LANEY: Well... okay. I guess it's sort of like you said; if you love someone enough, you have to let them do what's in their heart. Even if it's a heinous crime. It's just another example.

BO: That's just right. I sure do love you.

LANEY: I think you love me more than anyone else does.

BO: You know, Laney, being with you is about the only good times I have.

LANEY: If this was the only good time I had, I'd kill myself.

(Blackout.)

FOUR PLAY
by Gina Barnett

The Characters: Sam (30's) an Everyman, and Vanessa (30's) his sexy and aloof partner.

The Setting: The apartment. Chinese food cartons, paper plates, pizza box, chopsticks, etc., litter the floor.

The Scene: When this couple's sex life grows stale, they discuss alternatives.

(Sam sits on the floor by himself. Vanessa enters, standing by the bedroom door. She's flossing.)

VANESSA: It's not you Sam.

SAM: Who is it then?

VANESSA: Me. It's my problem.

SAM: But I didn't even know!

VANESSA: Because I've been faking.

SAM: How long?

VANESSA: A few months - - -

SAM: MONTHS!! *MONTHS?* How MANY months?

VANESSA: I don't know. Three, four... seven!

SAM: SEVEN? *SEVEN MONTHS?* WHY haven't you said anything?

VANESSA: Don't be angry.

SAM: I'm not angry. I just can't believe... WHY?

VANESSA: I don't know. It's like... I'm there with you and then all of a sudden everything inside just withers, like my insides are just curling up.

SAM: What do you mean curling up?

VANESSA: I don't know how else to describe it. *(Pause)* My mind starts going and then... I just... click off.

SAM: Well, we'll fix it. It's not the end of the world. It'll pass! It came and it'll Go. *(Pause)* Could be MSG.

VANESSA: It's not you Sam.

SAM: I said MSG.

VANESSA: It's not that either. *(Pause)* I'm sorry.

SAM: I'm the one who should be sorry. I had no idea. You never should've kept it to yourself this long. How about a couple of weeks ago with the ski mask? Did that...? *(Vanessa shakes her head, no.)* Hmmm! *(They sit in silence for awhile. He reaches down and picks up a fortune cookie, cracks it open,*

35

eats the cookie, reads the fortune and snickers.)
VANESSA: What?
SAM: *(Reading)* If you can tickle yourself you can laugh anytime you want. *(Pause)* Shall I get you a feather?
VANESSA: Laughing isn't the problem, Sam.
SAM: *(Pause)* Not yet... Well... I'm bushed. *(He starts to go.)*
VANESSA: Sam?
SAM: Hmm?
VANESSA: I don't know.
SAM: What?
VANESSA: It just, I just thought, I mean it just popped into my head.
SAM: What?...
VANESSA: Oh...
SAM: WHAT already?
VANESSA: What about... someone else...?
SAM: What someone else? You want someone else? you don't want me?
VANESSA: No, that's not what I'm saying.
SAM: What are you saying?
VANESSA: What about someone else along *with* you.
SAM: What, two people? You think if there's two people...?
VANESSA: Just think about it for a second before you--
SAM: Listen, what we decide to do to get your little engine over the mountain is between us. Got it? US. Pulling someone else into it is way over the line if you ask m--
VANESSA: Okay. Okay. It just popped into my head, I thought I'd--
SAM: I mean I'm sorry that you're going through this, and I will do anything in my power, but there are some things I just cannot.
VANESSA: Okay! OKAY. Chill out.
SAM: Well, Jeez. This isn't the easiest thing for a guy to hear, you know.
VANESSA: I know. *(Snuggling)* Remember the time with the figs?
SAM: ...Yeah...
VANESSA: And the Big Truck? Remember THE BIG TRUCK!!? *(Sam laughs.)* It's not *you*, Sam.
SAM: Yeah well, men think that way.
VANESSA: Well stop. Cause it isn't. Don't be angry.
SAM: Will you stop saying that? I'm not angry.
VANESSA: I love you?
SAM: ...I love you too.
VANESSA: Don't give up on me Sam.
SAM: *(They embrace.)* Seven months. You sure it's been

that long? *(Pause)* Come on, let's get some sleep. *(They get up.)* Van?

VANESSA: Hmmm?

SAM: Just out of curiosity. Were you thinking of a male person someone else or a female person someone else?

(BLACKOUT)

GERTRUDE, QUEEN OF DENMARK
by Pat Kaufman

The Characters: Gertrude (40's) the Queen of Denmark and mother of Hamlet, and Claudius (50's) her new husband.

The Setting: Elsinore Castle:

The Scene: When Gertrude is visited by a ghost at night, Claudius wakes too late to behold it and a domestic spat ensues.

GERTRUDE: No! No! No!
(Claudius stirs in his sleep, mutters.)
CLAUDIUS: I'll protect you!
(Gertrude continues to struggle with Ghost.)
GERTRUDE: Go away! Go away! Leave me alone!
(Ghostly figure vanishes.)
CLAUDIUS: Leave his darling? Never!
GERTRUDE: Oh Claudius, you slept through it again!
CLAUDIUS: *(Still deep in his sleepy erotica.)* Mmmmm... Wondrous dreams of his royal rose...
GERTRUDE: A most terrible dream! The ghost trying to make me harm you again. Again! Again!
CLAUDIUS: Hush, hush. It's all right now, your loving lion is here.
GERTRUDE: A most horrible apparition!
CLAUDIUS: There, there. It is the moon time of the month.
GERTRUDE: I didn't do anything wrong.
CLAUDIUS: Of course she did not.
GERTRUDE: I was a good wife to Hamlet Senior, while he lived.
CLAUDIUS: There, there. The moon time of the month and her fancy weighs her down.
GERTRUDE: And a good mother to Hamlet Junior!
CLAUDIUS: And a good daughter to your dear dead mother!
GERTRUDE: I never even let you pinch my nipples.
CLAUDIUS: Claudius the King and his beautiful bride were totally honest and completely honorable.
GERTRUDE: But I wish we had waited the full year.
CLAUDIUS: The Queen is already sated with the King's passion for her!?
GERTRUDE: Please don't get excited.

CLAUDIUS: Claudius is not excited.

GERTRUDE: Please do not shout.

CLAUDIUS: The Queen doesn't love the King anymore.

GERTRUDE: I do. You know I do. But those dreams....

CLAUDIUS: Don't touch him.

GERTRUDE: I have to. His beautiful hands....

CLAUDIUS: No.

GERTRUDE: And his beautiful neck.

CLAUDIUS: No.... Well... And his hair?

GERTRUDE: I love his hair best.

CLAUDIUS: Best? She loves his hair best... O, Gertrude! Gertrude! *(He is thoughtful.)* If you love his hair best, what do you like least? His nose? His nose has always been somewhat too long. It offends her! His brother always had the more shapely nose.

GERTRUDE: Claudius, liking your hair best doesn't mean I like the other things about you least.

CLAUDIUS: Why must Claudius' Queen always judge and weigh and...

GERTRUDE: You used to like it.

CLAUDIUS: Judging Claudius lesser than his dead brother the King.

GERTRUDE: YOU are the King now, Claudius.

CLAUDIUS: Everyone always said he was handsomer.

GERTRUDE: YOU are the most glorious, Claudius, in my heart.

CLAUDIUS: In your heart, but not actually?

GERTRUDE: In my heart AND actually. *(She embraces him. Claudius pulls on his cape.)*

GERTRUDE: Where are you going?

CLAUDIUS: In the dark night, in full terror there lurks young Fortinbras' army and his vengeful ambitions....

GERTRUDE: Where are you going, Claudius?!

CLAUDIUS: To see if the guards are awake.

GERTRUDE: Don't leave me.

CLAUDIUS: Uneasy lies the head of state. Claudius never fully understood that before.

GERTRUDE: Wait!

(Claudius exits.)

GULF WAR
by Joyce Carol Oates

The Characters: Stuart (30's) an aggressive young stock broker, and Nicole (20's) his wife; a woman struggling to cope with tragedy.

The Setting: A suburban home, the present.

The Scene: As they prepare to receive guests, this dysfunctional couple manages to converse without communicating.

The Bells' bedroom. Early evening. Nicole and Stuart are dressing for cocktails. Nicole is wearing a stylishly short skirt (in stark white or black) and is fumbling with the many buttons of a long-sleeved silk blouse. Stuart, newly returned from his office, is changing his shirt, and then knots a floral print tie briskly about his neck. He whistles cheerfully. He regards himself in a full-length mirror with critical exactitude. Nicole stands facing us, her back to Stuart. She addresses the audience conspiratorially, urgently. We must get the distinct impression that Nicole is utterly sincere even as we sense her weakness.

NICOLE: Tonight--I will tell him. I must. I've waited so long... *(Nicole glances back at Stuart to make sure she isn't being observed. She takes a glass (gin-and-tonic) out of its hiding place, perhaps in a dresser drawer or behind a vase; sips form it gratefully; winces; returns the glass to its hiding place. Stuart seems unaware.)*
NICOLE: *(With resolution)* Now we're living in this new house, this house without memory... *(A pause)* Sometimes it's easiest to speak what's in your heart... before witnesses.
STUART: *(Calling over, pleasantly.)* When you called the Whitbecks, darling, I hope you explained why we haven't had them over in some time?-- moving into the new house, and all.
NICOLE: *(Confused, but tries to maintain poise.)* The-- Whitbecks? Isn't it the Witkes who are coming for drinks?
STUART: *(Still pleasantly)* The Whitbecks - - it's written in my date book. Didn't you call *them?*
NICOLE: *(Nervously)* I don't think so, Stuart. I thought you did.
STUART: I'm sure you did, Nicole. Our social engagements are your responsibility, sweetie!

NICOLE: But our friends are all yours...

STUART: *(Without irony)* They aren't my friends, they're my business associates. My distinguished elders.

NICOLE: *(As if trying to make a joke, feminine, hoping to charm her husband.)* They all seem to look alike! I can't keep them straight.

STUART: *(Chuckles, kisses Nicole on the forehead, then reverts to a somewhat dogmatic tone. As if reciting a platitude.)* You can measure your success by the ages of your social acquaintances. If they're your elders, you're doing just fine. *(Laughs, shakes head)* If your prime-time Saturday nights are spent with old college friends, or the neighbors--forget it!

NICOLE: *(Slowly)* It's good, we've moved here... no one knows us here. *(Pause)* I don't think we have any neighbors here. "Fox Hollow Hills" is so spread out.

STUART: *(Correcting her)* "Fox Hills Hollow: A Planned Residential Community."

NICOLE: *(Blankly)* It's so... beautiful here. A view from all the windows. *(As if peering out a window)*.

STUART: *(Good-natured, critical)* And one of these days you might even find time to do a little shopping for the house... We need carpeting, more furniture, lamps...

NICOLE: *(Quickly)* I've been to the Mall. And I- it's so big.

STUART: *(Good-natured)* I don't mind the rooms with an actual echo but our friends are going to wonder!

NICOLE: We'll take the Witkes into the family room, there's enough furniture there.

STUART: *(Laughing, exasperated)* The Whitbecks, Nicole. Not the Witkes. The Whitbecks are more crucial right now than the Witkes--we'll do the Witkes another time.

NICOLE: *(To herself)* Not Witkes but Whitbecks. Yes! I see.

STUART: I wish I could believe you, that you do. *(Frowning at her)* You haven't been drinking, Nicole, have you?

NICOLE: *(Guiltily)* How... would I be drinking? *(Hurt, pouting)* Why would I drink... alone! *(Disdain)* That would be like--making love alone!

STUART: You do eat, don't you, during the day? --and take the vitamins the doctor prescribed? *(When Nicole nods, annoyed)* You still haven't gained back that weight.

NICOLE: I have!--some of it. *(Self-conscious beneath his scrutiny)* Stuart, don't look at me!--like that.

STUART: *(Trying to make light of it)* You're a beautiful woman, why shouldn't I look at you? *(Laughs)* How do you think I fell in love with you? *(Pause)* "Love enters through the eyes."

NICOLE: *(Uneasily):* If it is the Whitbecks who are coming...

I think you must have called them Stuart. Not me.

STUART: When?

NICOLE: When did you call them? How would I know, sweetie!

STUART: It's possible, I suppose, that they called us.

NICOLE: And you invited them over?

STUART: Hell, they may have invited themselves over. You know what they're like.

NICOLE: I... mix them up with the others.

STUART: *(Cheerfully)* Pushy, aggressive. Are they ever! *(A whistling noise as of grudging admiration)* But kind, basically. (Stuart slips on a sports coat, peers at himself in the mirror.) Shit! My hair... I should have had it trimmed today... but I worked right through lunch.

NICOLE: I thought you just had it trimmed.

STUART: That was Monday. This is Friday. It must be my God-damn adrenaline, my hair grows.

NICOLE: *(An effort at maintaining some kind of control)* I think you look--perfect. "The handsomest youngest man in the room."

STUART: *(Not to be co-opted)* I don't want to look perfect--perfection doesn't inspire trust. Like this-- *(Adjusts shirt cuffs to make one just perceptibly more visible than the other; moves tie just to left of center, combs hair to make it appear slightly ruffled, boyish. "Trust enters through the eyes." Now assessing Nicole, who has finally buttoned her blouse.)* And you: how many times have I told you. Glamour isn't the style in Fair Haven, not in our set. *(He musses Nicole's hair just a little; goes to a bureau, returns with a necklace of chunky amber beads.)* How's this?

NICOLE: That doesn't go with this outfit.

STUART: It doesn't go, but it gives the right touch. Sort of-- pretty but clunky. Like, maybe, Judy Whitbeck's daughter, say she's got a daughter your age, might wear. *(Stuart lowers the necklace over Nicole's head. She starts a little, involuntarily; has to restrain herself from pushing from him.)*

STUART: What's wrong?

NICOLE: The floor tilted just now.

STUART: The floor? *(Exasperated)* Maybe if we get some wall-to-wall carpeting in here, it won't. *(A pause)* Do you have something you want to tell me, Nicole?

(A Pause. Nicole looks helplessly at Stuart. She does have something to say, but has not the courage to say it at this moment.)

NICOLE: Tell you...? How?

STUART: *(Briskly, turning away)* Then don't.

                (Lights down.)

HYAENA
by Ross MacLean

The Characters: Patient (60-70) a dying man, and Wife (50-60) his wife.

The Setting: A hospital room, the present.

The Scene: When the dying patient is paid a visit by his wife, the two share an awkward conversation.

(At this point, all the Patient's inflections have a trace of question in them: His "Come in, come in" sounds like a person calling into an empty house, to see if anyone is still living there.)

PATIENT: Come in! Come in! We're all waiting to see you.
WIFE: *(Hesitantly.)* It's me?
PATIENT: Oh, it is you. I thought it was... Hi. Sit down. Close to me. I was afraid it was that- I thought you were that man.
WIFE: What man?
PATIENT: That man that comes around. You've seen him before. He's here all the time. Hangs over me in the bed. I've even seen him in here at night sometimes. Tries to take me places. Horrible man. You know who he is.
WIFE: I'm sure. Is he... here now?
PATIENT: Well look around, you tell me. Do you see him? *(She cautiously shakes her head.)* Good.
WIFE: How are you feeling?
PATIENT: Oh, I don't know.
WIFE: You look well. *(Patient gives her a look that says she's full of shit.)* I brought you this. *(She hands him a little snowstorm.)*
PATIENT: What is it?
WIFE: It's a souvenir of Atlantic City.
PATIENT: Something about that place sounds familiar... I don't know why... Did we ever go there?
WIFE: No.
PATIENT: What do I do with it.
WIFE: It's a snowstorm, dear. You-- *(The patient has no idea what the object is or is for. The wife takes the patient's hand, and turns the globe over. The patient gives a weak cry of delight.)*
PATIENT: Ooooooh...!
WIFE: I hoped you'd like it. I was thinking of you. I really

was.

PATIENT: I haven't heard from Jerry. No more. Do you ever see him?

WIFE: Why do you ask?

PATIENT: I called his office. They said he went away for the day.

WIFE: I thought you couldn't use the phone.

PATIENT: The nurse, she dialed me. For me.

WIFE: Did they say where he went?

PATIENT: Yes, to-- now why can't I remember it, I-- Did you see anyone in the hall? A man?

WIFE: No.

PATIENT: What was I just trying to remember-- Snow? You know: You just said it... I'm sorry, I--- can't say what I think-- always. It's a struggle.

WIFE: I'm glad everyone got a chance to see you the other day. I know it was hard on you, but they all really enjoyed themselves.

PATIENT: Yes, well...

WIFE: I love you.

PATIENT: Be close to me. *(She gets nearer, but is edgy about touching him. She fumbles to get some papers out of her purse.)* I wish I had you to hold while we sleep. I need you.

WIFE: Something else I brought.

PATIENT: Did you see Jerry there?

WIFE: Well-- No. Why would I? I didn't really go there.

PATIENT: Then where did you get this?

WIFE: Jerry gave it to me. To give to you.

PATIENT: How is he?

WIFE: Who?

PATIENT: Jerry! He went to Atlantic City! You saw him, he gave me this.

WIFE: He only went for the day. --I understand.

PATIENT: Why hasn't he come by? Did he say? Did he ask about me?

WIFE: Of course he did.

PATIENT: I need to see him. It's important. We have some very important things to talk about.

WIFE: So do we.

PATIENT: Something's wrong here... Are you cold?

WIFE: Are you?

PATIENT: There was a sudden chill in the room, don't you feel it? I wonder if... What's behind that door?

WIFE: Nothing. That's just the closet.

PATIENT: There's something in there... For me... (The wife cautiously goes to check.)

WIFE: There's... nothing. Your robe.

PATIENT: Bring it to me, will you. I'm cold. *(She does this, and sits him up and helps him into it.)* No one takes care of me anymore. I called him and they said he wasn't in, so I thought he was coming here. He said he would come back, I don't know why he's avoiding me. I haven't seen him for seven months.

WIFE: You've only been in the hospital five, dear. Off and on.

PATIENT: And you haven't been here. At all.

WIFE: I just felt like getting away, thought that a little escape would be... Good for me, you know... I've been getting so... depressed.

PATIENT: So go to Atlantic City.

WIFE: No! What makes you say that-- I couldn't do that... with you here...

PATIENT: Could have gone with Jerry. He went.

WIFE: That would hardly be appropriate. Have you seen anyone else?

PATIENT: Just that-- that hyaena. That blood-sucker. You know who he is, you just don't remember. Would you look under the bed?

WIFE: What for?

PATIENT: See what's under there. The uh-- the uh--Takes me, to walk. You know. Freedom gear.

WIFE: Your slippers.

PATIENT: Put them on, will you? Oh, that's nice. That's nice... You're so good to me. Not like--

WIFE: I don't want to talk about it.

PATIENT: We don't have to talk. You don't know how it feels to have you here. I love you. Hold me. *(The wife obliges.)*

PATIENT: Don't let go of me. Never let me go. *(When he finally lets her go.)* I get so much strength from you.

WIFE: We haven't got much time. I was talking to the doctors. They said--

PATIENT: Oh! Are you taking me home?

WIFE: *(Freezes up.)* What.

PATIENT: Isn't that what you came for?

WIFE: You're not well enough.

PATIENT: I won't be any trouble.

WIFE: Later maybe. Next week.

PATIENT: A week?! No, now, I want to go now.

WIFE: You're making me feel bad. Don't. *(Discreetly wipes her eye.)* I know I haven't been here, but it's not because I've forgotten about you. It's just that--- I have the house to take care of, and no one to help-- There is no reason, is there?

PATIENT: Let's not fight now. There isn't time.

WIFE: I'm not fighting. I've been in touch with the doctors over the phone, so I... I know what's happening. He said you were sleeping almost all the time to me, so I haven't--I thought I should let you rest. *(Patient seems to be drifting off to sleep.)* Are you all right?

PATIENT: Yes... Fine... You want to lay down with me?

WIFE: I don't think I could. We'd better do this now; these are the papers form the bank. Your signatures were a little messy on the last ones, so they asked if you would do it over.

PATIENT: What for? Why?

WIFE: They couldn't read it.

PATIENT: What do I do with this?

WIFE: Sign it.

PATIENT: My name you mean?

WIFE: You always make this so difficult, I can't keep coming back and back for this same thing-- Don't do this to me! All the--

PATIENT: Wait till I'm home. One week.

WIFE: Now. Practice once, I'll help you. *(He has little motor control; his hand goes any direction.)*

PATIENT: Oh, look at what's happening, come on you! I can't even-- My own--

WIFE: *(Gently helps him.)* Let me hold you. *(As he signs one paper, then another, through the whole stack.)*

PATIENT: Is this what you want? This is all you came for.

WIFE: (Strong and patiently, throughout.) Easy now. Steady.

PATIENT: Take it all-- off! Dignity is free, you can't take my dignity! Call the-- teacher.

WIFE: There is no teacher.

PATIENT: Teacher says write everything down, a hundred times till tomorrow.

WIFE: That's right. Everything's going to be OK. It's just one less thing to take care of. One less thing... *(She sorts through the signed papers.)* That's the end of it.

PATIENT: You're not going to come see me anymore, are you?

WIFE: You make it so difficult! How much do you expect me to put up with! It's hard on me too, can't you see that?

PATIENT: You don't think of anyone but yourself.

WIFE: You're all I think of, or can think of, you're like nothing but one helpless--! Oh God, I love you. You must know that.

PATIENT: *(Dies a little.)* Take your pa-- *(Says with great difficulty:)* pppages. Papers! I've signed them. Get!

WIFE: This isn't a good day. I'm sorry to have put you through all this. But it will all be over and we can start again tomorrow, all right? *(Patient withholds response.)* I'll come back every day from now on. Every day.

PATIENT: He's waiting. He'll be here any time.

WIFE: Who's waiting?

PATIENT: You know.

WIFE: I'm not letting you threaten me. I'll come back.

PATIENT: When?!

WIFE: You're going to have days ahead. Beautiful days. And I will be here, with you. I will. OK?

PATIENT: *(Private. Alone.)* Thank you.

(There is no embrace of any kind. She leaves. She joins the Friend at the side of the stage; they go off.)

LYNETTE AT 3 AM
by Jane Anderson

The Characters: Lynette (20-30) a woman having trouble getting to sleep, Bobby (20-30) her sleeping husband and Estaban, (Hispanic, 20-30) a ghost.

The Setting: An apartment in Brooklyn, 3 am.

The Scene: On a sleepless night, Lynette encounters the ghost of a young man who has just been shot in the apartment beneath her.

Lynette sits up. She takes the remote from the bedside table and turns on the TV. She mutes the sound and just stares at the picture. (A beat.) Estaban, a young Latino man appears. He's barefoot and dressed in a white t-shirt and white pants. Lynette stares at him.

ESTABAN: Hello. My name is Estaban. I'm from the apartment below. I just died.

LYNETTE: Oh my God.

ESTABAN: I am sorry to disturb you. I have to pass through so I can go... *(points up)* ...to above.

LYNETTE: Was this like a few minutes ago this happened?

ESTABAN: Yes.

LYNETTE: I thought I heard a gun. Was that you?

ESTABAN: Yes.

LYNETTE: You know, I knew there was something. I told Bobby, I said to him there was definitely a shot. So that was you?

ESTABAN: That was me.

LYNETTE: I was gonna call the police. Should I call the police?

ESTABAN: It doesn't matter anymore.

LYNETTE: Who shot you?

ESTABAN: My brother Jorge.

LYNETTE: Oh my God, your brother?

ESTABAN: I was making love to his wife.

LYNETTE: Oh. Well. That wasn't a smart thing to be doing.

ESTABAN: It couldn't be helped. Lola and me, we fell in love when we were fifteen.

LYNETTE: Really? So this has been going on a long time then.

ESTABAN: Yes. Me and Lola, we grew up in the same village

48

in Puerto Rico.

LYNETTE: I hear Puerto Rico is a very nice place to vacation. Is it nice there?

ESTABAN: Like a paradise.

LYNETTE: I've always wanted to see the islands. But Bobby, he's not a traveller.

ESTABAN: No?

LYNETTE: But you and Lola, I want to hear about. So you met on the island, you were soul mates, go on.

ESTABAN: The first time we made love, it was siesta time. We walked down the street, everyone was asleep. Everything was quiet except for the waves flipping over very soft. It was hot, just a little bit windy from the ocean. Very sexy. I took her to the shade of a vanilla bean tree. We lay down on a blanket. She opened her blouse for me and her skin, it smelled sweet just like the tree. After we made love, I cried.

LYNETTE: I do that. I cry after Bobby and me make love. So you cry too?

ESTABAN: Oh yes. It is because when I make love, my heart leaves my body for heaven. And when it is over and my heart has to come back, it is very sad.

LYNETTE: See, my crying thing is a little different. When I make love and my heart leaves my body I'm always expecting to meet Bobby's heart outside his body. But Bobby's heart - well Bobby has a hard time opening up. If you met his family you'd understand. His heart doesn't really leave his body so my heart is out there all alone waiting while Bobby finishes up. Below. And then he falls asleep and I'm still out there, floating and feeling very lonely. And then I cry and wake Bobby up and he gets annoyed. *(A beat)* Which is not to say that I don't get a lot of other things from him.

ESTABAN: Yes?

LYNETTE: So how come Lola didn't marry you?

ESTABAN: Her parents said, "Lola, marry Jorge, he make better money than Estaban." Jorge, he runs a car service to the airport. I been working for him. Olmos Limos.

LYNETTE: I hate to fly. I see my own death when I fly.

ESTABAN: See, when I drive someone to the airport I always say before they get out, "have a safe trip, God bless." Not one of my passengers ever died in a plane crash. It's part of the service.

LYNETTE: That's nice. *(A beat)* So do you know where you're going? Is anyone gonna be meeting you, like do you have grandparents or anyone who're gonna take you over to the other side?

ESTABAN: No, my family, they're all still alive.

LYNETTE: Are you Catholic?

ESTABAN: Yeh, I grew up with that.

LYNETTE: Do you think the Virgin Mary will be there?

ESTABAN: I don't know.

LYNETTE: Did you go through a tunnel and see a white light?

ESTABAN: No, I haven't even left the building yet.

LYNETTE: Are you scared?

ESTABAN: Why should I be scared? It's nature. Everything dies. Chickens and dogs and pussy cats and movie stars and cockroaches and grandmommies and guys like me who drive people to the airport. We all gotta do it. So how can something that everybody has to do be so bad?

LYNETTE: But you think there's something to go to? You think there's something else?

ESTABAN: Sure, why not?

LYNETTE: Bobby says all that stuff is bullshit, that when you die you die.

ESTABAN: Oh man, don't listen to him. How can a guy who can't make good love know anything about the afterlife? Geez, no wonder you're such a scared lady.

LYNETTE: I didn't paint a fair picture. He's a very good person.

ESTABAN: What's your name?

LYNETTE: Lynette.

ESTABAN: Ah, Lynette, Lynetta. Tu eres muy amable y muy hermosa. Espero que tu te pudiera besar y que tunera sus tetas en las manos como si fueron frutas perfectas, desmasiadas bellas a comer.

LYNETTE: What did you just say?

BOBBY: *(Translating in his sleep.)* "You are very kind and very beautiful. I wish that I could kiss you and hold your breasts in my hands as if they were perfect fruits, too beautiful to eat."

LYNETTE: Bobby?

ESTABAN: Pone la mano en mi pecho. *(Lynette looks at Estaban.)*

BOBBY: *(Still asleep)* He says to put your hand on his chest. That's as far as you go, Lynette.

LYNETTE: I didn't do anything, Bobby.

ESTABAN: Eschucha a la musica. *(Music- very soft mixed in with ocean.)* Esto es lo que esta entre los pulsares de corazon despues de todo se va. *(Lynette looks to Bobby. Estaban touches her chin.)* This is what you hear between heart beats after everything else is gone.

(Estaban kisses Lynette. He caresses her face and lays her down on the bed and continues to caress her. Over this, the alarm goes off. Lights come up to indicate morning. Bobby wakes up, punches the alarm, swears to himself. Lynette starts to set up as if dragging herself up from her sleep. Estaban gently pushes her back down. Bobby sits on the edge of the bed, rubbing his face. He gets up, shuffles to the bathroom. Lynette and Estaban continue their embrace over Estaban's music. We hear the toilet flush, the music fades. Estaban starts to get up. Lynette holds him and tries to pull him back to her. He slips through her hands and disappears as Lynette wakes up.

(FADE OUT)

MAKING BOOK
by Janet Reed

The Characters: Ellen Winston (30's) an idealistic text book editor, and Joel Braun (30-40) a text book editor with the moral instincts of a slimeball.

The Setting: An office at Stroniker Publishing House, New York City, 1987.

The Scene: Principles clash in the following discussion between two textbook editors with decidedly different mindsets.

Joel's Office. (The Indian with Wolf picture is replaced with a photo of an Indian dressed as a cowboy.)

ELLEN: You wanted to see me?
JOEL: *(Pointing to the picture.)* See this? This, I like!
ELLEN: I think it's meant to be a joke.--
JOEL: Oh. Ha. Ha. Yes, I think I knew that. Very funny.... Was this your idea?
ELLEN: I, uh, think the art department sent it over. I think, uh, art was trying to make a point.
JOEL: And what point is that?
ELLEN: Maybe it's better if we don't get into that again.
JOEL: Why don't you just put a sign on my back that says "Kick me". "Kick me hard." Everyone laughs. Laughs at the salesman who became vice-president of the social studies textbook division. They laugh hard, because they don't know how lonely it is at the top. ...I didn't ask for this. Not really.... I want a grilled cheese and tomato on toasted Wonder Bread and a Pepsi-Cola. I want a small bag of Cheetos, and I want to sit in front of the t.v. and watch "Fury: The Story of a Horse and the Boy Who Loved Him"... and then maybe a little Ed Sullivan...
ELLEN: Joel, are you okay?
JOEL: (Hums or whistles "Lassie" theme.) Lassie!
ELLEN: Joel! Joel, what happened...
JOEL: I can't. It's too horrible. It's made me ashamed to be a man.
ELLEN: Joel, is there anybody I should call?
JOEL: NO! No one must know. Why did I say it? Why? Why?
ELLEN: Joel, I think you better tell me what happened.

JOEL: You really want me to? Really?... Okay, but face the door... *(She doesn't.)* Face the door, or I won't tell! *(She does. He mumbles this so she can't hear.)* I'm in this heavy duty meeting with Stroniker - - -

ELLEN: I can't hear you.

JOEL: *(Raises Voice)* I'm in this heavy duty meeting with Stroniker and Runningwater - - Can you hear me now? I presented what I thought was the revised edit about the Indians. You know, the berry-corn thing. They loved that the hunt was omitted. Loved how we avoided the knife thing.

ELLEN: That's good...

JOEL: And of course they loved that it wasn't reverential. And then I quoted from the text, your text that reads: "The following Iroquois legend is about..." And Runningwater laughs. He laughs at me. And he gives Stroniker a knowing look. It was just like the time in Mr. Baldini's gym class when I put my jock strap on the outside of my gym shorts.... But I'm not eleven years old, so I say real smooth, real casual, "What is it guys? What's the problem with Iroquois legends?" Runningwater was so smug. "Don't you mean 'creation myths,' Joe?" He calls me Joe. So I say, "Of course. Of course it's a creation myth...." Ellen - - what the hell is a creation myth?

ELLEN: It's Indian stories of how life on earth began.

JOEL: Well, duh, Ellen. I know that now, but how was I to know it then? I thought "myths" were saved for Zeus, Athena, and Joseph Campbell .

ELLEN: I know. These terms can get very confusing, can't they?

JOEL: Yes they can... but Ellen, Ellen... if you know it's creation myths then why did you write "legends"? Why?

ELLEN: Well, I made a mistake. It happens. I didn't mean to. And Megan was out sick, and when she got back, she caught it. I guess somehow you had the old copy, huh?

JOEL: *(Pause)* Did Megan set me up? She put you up to this?

ELLEN: No, oh no - - -

JOEL: But you're on her side. I can tell.

ELLEN: No. I mean, yes. I mean, but not against... We're all working together to - -

JOEL: Create a best seller. Right. Okay.... And... And do you think the beginning of the book is boring? Because *(he turns his back to her)* Stroniker does. Stroniker said it was boring. He said, "Fix it. It's boring. It's been done to death." And Runningwater nodded and said "Boring." And then they ... they smirked... they smirked at me. Again.

ELLEN: ...Boy, they kind of gave you a tough time, didn't they? I'm sorry...

JOEL: You're sorry, sorry? Sorry won't help me. Pity won't help me. A hug would help. But no. But yes. Hug me Ellen. I need a hug.
ELLEN: Joel, I - -
JOEL: Hug me. *(She hugs him reluctantly.)* Thank you. Thank you. They think I'm in over my head. And I am... but they weren't supposed to know it. And so, you have to help me, Ellen. Have to. I need you. Will you?
ELLEN: I'll try.
JOEL: Trying isn't good enough.
ELLEN: Okay, I'll help you.
JOEL: Thank you. Now let's think of a real boffo way to begin the book. You open the book, and you see... what?... Say anything that comes to mind. *(Pause)* Anything. Don't edit yourself. Freely associate. Okay?
ELLEN: Oh. Why don't I write down some ideas and bring them back in later?
JOEL: NO! I want to do it this way!
ELLEN: Okay! Okay.
JOEL: Anything. Say anything. *(Long pause)* Ooh, I have one. Hamburger. Now what do you say ?
ELLEN: Hot dog.
JOEL: Dachshund.
ELLEN: Dachshund... Peanuts.
JOEL: Popcorn.
ELLEN: Circus.
JOEL: Crowds.
ELLEN: People.
JOEL: People... Who need people.
ELLEN: Are the luckiest.
JOEL: *(Sings to himself: "People in the world".)* World!
ELLEN: World.... Diverse.
JOEL: Hodge-podge.
ELLEN: Mish-mosh.
JOEL: Potpourri.
ELLEN: Melting Pot.
JOEL: Potty Bowl.
JOEL and ELLEN: Melting Pot!!!!!! *(They jump up and end up hugging each other.)* Yes! It'll work. Great! This is the way to go!
(Ellen tries to break away, but Joel holds her and speaks very seductively as he says.)
JOEL: That's it! You get in your Asians, Slavs, Ruskies, talk about them coming over here- -Yes! It'll work! I could kiss you! I will kiss you.
ELLEN: Don't.

54

JOEL: *(Kissing her hair, her neck.)* Don't? It's a friendly gesture. No big deal. Two pros working together-- bonding together...

ELLEN: *(Breaks away.)* Bond somewhere else!

JOEL: My place or yours?

ELLEN: Neither!... Now, I'm pretending you didn't say that, okay? Because I know and you know that when I came in here, you were in an extremely vulnerable state. You didn't know what you're doing. You still don't know. Now, I'm going to go to my desk and write down some ideas. Okay?

JOEL: Whatever you say... darling.

(Ellen looks at the audience. Then exits.)

MAN OF THE MOMENT
by *Alan Aykbourn*

The Characters: Vic (40's) an insensitive talk show host, Trudy (30-40,) his long-suffering wife and Sharon (19) their overweight au pair.

The Setting: The pool area of a Mediterranean Villa, the present.

The Scene: Sharon has fallen in love with her abusive employer, Vic. When it becomes obvious that Vic has nothing but contempt for the unhappy teenager, she decides to kill herself.

Sharon appears, walking along the side of the swimming pool towards the deep end. She has on her black wetsuit, rubber helmet and flippers. She carries a weighted diving belt. She is also crying. In fact, she is in a desperate, heart-broken state. She stops at the end of the swimming pool, a tragicomic, fat, black rubber-calf figure. Trudy watches her, astonished. Sharon, unaware she is being watched, looks towards the house and starts to fasten the diving belt about her waist.

TRUDY: *(Cautiously)* Sharon? Sharon... What are you doing there?

SHARON: *(Between sobs)* Mrs. Parks...

TRUDY: What are you doing, Sharon?

SHARON: I'm going to kill myself, Mrs. Parks.

TRUDY: *(Moving to her, alarmed.)* You are going to what?

SHARON: I'm sorry, Mrs. Parks. I love him so much, and he doesn't care about me at all.

TRUDY: Sharon...

SHARON: *(All in one breath)* He just says I'm fat and I've got to get thin and I've tried to get thin but I can't get thin whatever I do because when he says he doesn't love me I just keep eating because I'm so unhappy you see and then when I eat then I just get fatter you see and then he doesn't love me... and I love him so much, Mrs. Parks, and I'm ever so sorry...

TRUDY: Yes... I'm sorry, Sharon... I know how it is, believe me I do...

SHARON: No, you don't - you can't...

TRUDY: Yes, I do. I promise, Sharon, I do...

SHARON: Nobody knows...

(During the next scene, the music from the house stops as the record comes to an end.)

TRUDY: Sharon, it's a passing thing, I promise. It's something we all go through. Most of us. God help us. It'll pass...
SHARON: No, it won't pass. I've loved Vic for years...
TRUDY: Years? What do you mean, years? You've only been with us two months...
SHARON: I seen him on the telly. I used to watch him on the telly and I used to write to him on *Ask Vic* and he used to write back to me, he did, I promise...
TRUDY: Sharon, he gets thousands of letters a week. He doesn't even read them, let alone write back...
SHARON: He did, he wrote to me and it was in his writing. And he used to tell us on the telly if we had problems how to deal with them and not to worry and then when I got this job working for him I just thought it was going to be so wonderful and he's just been horrible to me... I don't know what I've done... What have I done wrong, Mrs. Parks?

(During the next, Vic comes out of the house and listens, unnoticed.)

TRUDY: *(Fiercely)* The only thing you did wrong, Sharon... The one and only thing you ever did wrong was to love him in the first place... Because he is not a man to love, Sharon, I promise you. Not if you can possibly avoid it. I speak as one who has tried for eight years, Sharon, to keep loving him. While that bastard has abused me and ignored me and taken me for granted--while he has been screwing his way round Television Centre and half of ITV--I have looked after his kids and his house and his bloody, bad-tempered old mother in Beckenham... And I have tried to keep loving him... I swear to God I have tried. And if you are honestly clinging on to life in the hope of getting one tiny scrap of care or consideration back from that self-centered, selfish, scum bucket-then all I can say is, you'd better jump in there now, Sharon, and cut your losses.

(Sharon, understandably, is a little bemused by this outburst. She stands indecisively. Vic steps out further on to the patio. Both women see him for the first time.)

VIC: Well, well. You know what they say. You never hear good about yourself, do you?
TRUDY: Tell her, Vic. Talk to the girl, for God's sake.
VIC: Tell her what?

TRUDY: I just caught her trying to drown herself...

VIC: *(Amused)* What?
TRUDY: Vic, talk to her...
VIC: What do you want to drown yourself for, Sharon?
TRUDY: Why do you think...?
VIC: I have no idea. I have no idea why this great big girl should want to drown herself...

(Sharon sobs and finishes fastening her belt.)

TRUDY: Vic...
VIC: Why? Just tell me?
TRUDY: Because of what you've said to her. Done to her.
VIC: What?
TRUDY: Whatever you said-whatever you did. I don't know. I don't want to know...
VIC: I've never laid a finger on her, have I? Sharon, tell her, I've never laid a finger on you... Have I? Eh?
SHARON: *(Unhappily)* No, Mr. Parks...
VIC: There you are. No. She confirms that...
TRUDY: *(Shouting)* You know bloody well what you've done to her, Vic, now do something about it...
VIC: Right, that's it, forget it. I am not being shouted at. Let her jump...
(He turns to move into the house. Sharon prepares to jump into the pool.
TRUDY: *(Yelling)* Vic...
VIC: *(Furiously)* Let the stupid cow drown herself, what do I care? Go on. Jump, jump, jump then...

(Sharon jumps into the pool. Weighted down by her diver's belt, she sinks rapidly under the dark water and vanishes in a trail of bubbles.)

TRUDY: *(Screaming)* SHARON!
VIC: *(Surprised Sharon has done it.)* Bloody hell! *(He moves towards the pool.)*
TRUDY: Vic, get her out. Dive in and get her out, for God's sake...
VIC: I'm not diving in there. Not in these clothes.
TRUDY: Vic, the girl is drowning.
VIC: She's not drowning. She can stay under for hours. She's built like a bathyscope...
TRUDY: Are you going in to get her, or not?
VIC: You dive in.

TRUDY: I can't get her out, she's far too big for me, she's enormous, Vic...

VIC: We could sprinkle rum babas on the surface, that'll bring her up...

TRUDY: You bastard... *(Desperately)* Oh, dear God. *(Running to the gate and yelling.)* Douglas! Douglas! He's gone...

VIC: *(Peering into the pool, meanwhile.)* Sharon I can see you down there, Sharon.

TRUDY: *(Running to the house and calling.)* Kenny! Kenny, come out here please!

VIC: Kenny went down to the shop-we were running out of vino. . .

TRUDY: If she dies, Vic. If that girl dies...

VIC: Nobody would miss her except the national union of bakers...

TRUDY: *(Running at him in fury.)* You... God, I hate you! I really so hate you! *(She attacks him with both her fists.)*

VIC: *(Amused and fending her off easily.)* Hey, hey, hey!

TRUDY: *(Beating at him.)* I'd so love to... hurt you... like you... hurt... other people, sometimes...

(She lands a blow that Vic doesn't care for. He takes her a little more seriously.)

VIC: Oi! Now, Trudy! That's enough. You've had your fun...

THE NOVELIST
by *Howard Fast*

The Characters: Thomas Crighton (45) a retired sea captain, and Jane Austen (40) a novelist.

The Setting: Jane Austen's cottage in Chawton, Hampshire, England, 1817.

The Scene: Captain Thomas Crighton has fallen in love with Jane Austen via her writing. When he retires, he moves to Chawton with the intention of marrying her. Here, the romantic Captain pays his first visit to the reclusive Miss Austen.

JANE: Who are you, sir?

CRIGHTON: Is that the way you do it, interspersed with petit point?

JANE: Who are you and how do you dare come into my room like this?

CRIGHTON: You are Jane Austen?

JANE: Who I am is beside the point. Who are you, sir, and why are you here, and do you always enter a lady's room in this manner? Cassandra!

CRIGHTON: *(Smiling)* Forgive me, please I beg you. I'm Thomas Crighton. Didn't your brother tell you?

JANE: Tell me what?

CRIGHTON: I stood outside. I knocked once, I knocked twice, I knocked three times. And then the door was open so I came in. You know, all your doors are open.

JANE: Which doesn't mean that a gentleman walks through them without so much as by your leave.

(Crighton stands there staring at her.)

JANE: Do you always stare at people like that, Mr. Crighton? You haven't told me who you are or what you're doing here.

CRIGHTON: Forgive me.

JANE: Or what my brother was supposed to have told me.

CRIGHTON: And he never wrote to you about a Tom Crighton?

JANE: *(Thinking about this.)* Yes, of course he did. You were to visit me in a proper manner. By standing outside until someone had come to usher you in.

CRIGHTON: Shall I go outside? Shall I do it again? Will you

ever forgive me?

JANE: *(Smiling)* You're Captain Crighton of the Invincible.

CRIGHTON: Yes ma'am. *(He pauses.)* Won't you ask me in?

JANE: You are in.

CRIGHTON: Won't you ask me to sit down?

JANE: In a moment. Perhaps. *(She sits down at her desk and thumbs through a group of letters in a letter holder on the desk, selects one, opens it and reads aloud.)* "And this will recommend Captain Thomas Crighton to you. He is a good man, rather impetuous, and perhaps overly romantic. He writes poetry, of which I am no judge, but perhaps this will give him some character in your eyes. He is also an excellent Captain, and the frigate he commands has a remarkable record. I must warn you that he is quite mad on the subject of Jane Austen. Treat him courteously, but I would recommend that you keep him at a distance. He is totally unpredictable." *(She lays down the letter and smiles sweetly at Crighton.)*

CRIGHTON: Your brother wrote that?

JANE: Indeed he did. Is it untrue?

CRIGHTON: It's a damned strange recommendation, if I may say so.

JANE: Now you may sit down, Mr. Crighton. *(Pointing to a chair across the room.)* over there.

CRIGHTON: To keep me at a distance? The man is mad. *(He walks over to the chair, stares at Jane a moment more, and then sits down.)*

JANE: Of course, I don't really know that you are Thomas Crighton.

CRIGHTON: Who else could I be?

JANE: That's no question to ask me, sir. I could invent a hundred personalities for you, and a hundred reasons for your visit here. But whoever you are, you have an honest face.

CRIGHTON: Whoever I am, I am Crighton. Captain Thomas Crighton. At least I have been for a very long time. I'm also reasonably sane. I am forty-five years old. I was married when I was twenty-two to a young woman whose name was Fredricka Bartholomew. The Bartholomews lived in Southampton. She died three years later, in childbirth. We lost the child as well. I have been a widower ever since. I come from a reasonably good family, but nothing at all to boast about. I have an uncle who's a baronet, and until six days ago I commanded one of His Majesty's ships. I am reasonably wealthy, having taken over forty prizes in my time; in good health; of sound mind; and as of the moment, retired. My intention is to live in the country somewhere in this vicinity, to continue to write bad poetry, and to raise roses. What have I left out? Oh yes, my mother was a

Sutherland and she had a second cousin by marriage who married a man who was related to the royal family. I have two sisters, one alive and well in London, the other dead. *(He pauses.)*

JANE: Captain Crighton, you amaze me, you absolutely amaze me. Why are you engaging in this biography of your life and your past? It is not necessary. I haven't asked you who are in terms of your family, and I should think it decidedly impolite and improper to do so. There is no necessity to spell out your antecedents or to enumerate your property.

CRIGHTON: But indeed there is.

JANE: Then I think an explanation is forthcoming.

(Crighton is staring at her intently.)

JANE: And I also think, Captain Crighton, that you might look elsewhere than at me. I realize that a life at sea does not develop the amenities, but I assure you it is very unpleasant to be stared at as if one were simply a curiosity.

CRIGHTON: Let me assure you, Miss Austen, that that is the furthest thing from my mind. I also may specify that I am keeping my distance, as your brother advises in his letter. May I add that I am not dangerous.

JANE: And I am not one of those ladies who faint at the slightest notion of something untoward. I am simply and properly amazed at the fact that a man walks into my room uninvited and proceeds to render his family history to someone to whom he has not even had a proper introduction.

CRIGHTON: But was to have been introduced. Your brother's letter is an introduction.

JANE: Only in a manner of speaking. And I, Mr. Crighton, am still waiting for an explanation of your manner and your actions.

CRIGHTON: As far as my actions are concerned, Miss Austen, I thought I had explained them properly and sufficiently. I knocked at the door and there was no answer. I entered. Here I am.

JANE: Indeed.

CRIGHTON: As far as my manner is concerned, I admit that it lacks polish, but it is not entirely devoid of reason.

JANE: Go on, sir.

CRIGHTON: Our families are not acquainted. I mean, I am acquainted with your brother, but I felt that was insufficient. Therefore I enumerated my possibilities.

JANE: But why, Captain Crighton?

CRIGHTON: Well, this is not easy for me to say, but I'll have a go at it. Because, madam, my intention, my very honorable, decent intention is to marry you.

JANE: What!

CRIGHTON: I'm sorry to put it so bluntly, but I have heard that you esteem honesty as part of a man's character.
JANE: *(Rising, an action which brings Crighton to his feet.)* You, sir are absolutely amazing. And, if I may become just a trifle angry, somewhat buffoonish. I am not a young girl. I am forty-one years old. And without boasting, I may say that I have had a number of proposals of marriage in the past, but never before from someone I did not know. Mr. Crighton, I have no desire to continue this conversation.
CRIGHTON: I am being dismissed?
JANE: Precisely.
CRIGHTON: *(Almost boyishly)* Well there you are. I brought it on myself. I can't complain. I came in like a bull into a china shop, with all the delicacy with which I would storm a French vessel. I can understand your position.
JANE: *(Coldly)* Thank you.
(Hat in hand, Crighton walks toward the door. As he puts his hand on the door, Jane's voice stops him.)
JANE: Mr. Crighton.
CRIGHTON: *(Turning toward her.)* Ma'am?
JANE: Before you leave, speaking simply as a professional writer who has a normal curiosity as to the eccentricities of male behavior, may I ask when you decided that you would ask me to marry you?
CRIGHTON: *(Looking at her, frowning thoughtfully.)* I think it was in 1811 that I received a copy of *Sense and Sensibility*. I remember that the copy was delivered to me just before we sailed, and between Southampton and Malta I read it twice. After the second reading I had more or less made up my mind. But may I say that it was not until some two or three weeks later, when I had a chance to talk with your brother, the Admiral, that I discovered that you were unmarried. It would have been deuced awkward to have come to that decision concerning a married woman, don't you think?
JANE: Are you asking me that?
CRIGHTON: In a manner of speaking.
JANE: Then my answer would be yes. You are absolutely astonishing, Captain Crighton. You stand there and blandly tell me that after reading a book that I wrote, without ever having met me or seen me or knowing me in any way whatsoever, you decide to marry me.
CRIGHTON: Yes, that's the fact.
JANE: But why?
CRIGHTON: Well now, you ask for an explanation. I don't know that there is one. Except that I fell in love with you.
JANE: You fell in love with me?

CRIGHTON: Yes, ma'am, if you will forgive me saying so.

JANE: You know, you are absolutely mad.

CRIGHTON: If you wish.

JANE: And I trust that you will now abandon the idea and say no more about it.

CRIGHTON: No.

JANE: Captain Crighton, you are leaving. I don't think that I will ask you to return. Therefore it appears to me that you have no alternative but to abandon this incredible notion of yours.

CRIGHTON: If you will forgive me, Miss Austen, I don't see it as incredible, and I cannot for the life of me imagine why you should so see it. I read a book that was written by a woman. I fell in love with her. I waited until my circumstances were appropriate, having read in the interval everything else she published and having become more convinced than ever of the correctness of my position, and then I proceeded here and asked for her hand in marriage. I don't find that incredible. I don't even find it extraordinary. Indeed, when I dwell upon it I don't see that I had any alternative.

JANE: Do you know, sir, you leave me speechless.

CRIGHTON: I can't imagine that I do. In fact, I can't imagine that anyone would leave you speechless.

JANE: You are a most extraordinary man.

CRIGHTON: Are you still angry with me?

JANE: Of course I am.

CRIGHTON: But you have no reason to be. I speak gently; my manner is fairly disarming; I make no threats; I make no overtures. I do not descend upon you; I keep an adequate distance between us. Why on earth should you be angry with me?

JANE: I think sir, that you have been too long too far from civilization. If you do not understand why I am angry with you, there is absolutely nothing I can say to make it clear to you.

CRIGHTON: I am not totally a nincompoop, Miss Austen. Let's say that I've been precipitous and outspoken, but I have not been insulting.

JANE: I didn't say you insulted me.

CRIGHTON: Then why the anger?

JANE: Would it please you if I said annoyance instead of anger?

CRIGHTON: Annoyance. Yes, that does ease my mind. Since I am being dismissed, I'll take the liberty of adding to your annoyance. Your brother showed me a picture of you. It does you no justice. You are far more beautiful. You are as well spoken and as witty as I had ever dreamed you would be.

JANE: Thank you, Captain. You have added to my annoyance, Now you will do me the courtesy of leaving.

CRIGHTON: But before I do, madam, one question. You will permit me one question?

JANE: As blunt and as unseemly as your other questions?

CRIGHTON: No, madam, the questions were yours. I made only statements.

JANE: Go ahead, sir.

CRIGHTON: Why, madam, have you never married?

JANE: Your question does not surprise me, Captain Crighton. It is in keeping with everything else you have said today. I could answer that it was no business of yours, but I prefer to say that I have never met a man whom I wanted to marry. Is that sufficient?

CRIGHTON: No, madam.

JANE: And why not?

CRIGHTON: Because we have met today.

JANE: *(Shakes her head impatiently.)* This is incredible. You are absolutely impossible. Now you can only oblige me by leaving.

CRIGHTON: Yes, madam. And when may I call again?

(Jane stares at him without answering. Crighton smiles and exits, closing the door behind him. Jane stands there for a moment, then walks to the door, opens it, and calls out through the doorway.)

JANE: Captain Crighton.

CRIGHTON: *(Offstage)* Yes, Miss Austen?

JANE: Tomorrow at tea time.

CRIGHTON: Yes, Miss Austen.

THE ONLIEST ONE WHO CAN'T GO NOWHERE
by J.E. Franklin

The Characters: Benjamin Henderson (African-American, 70) a grumpy patriarch, Katherine Henderson (African-American, 40) his wife and Benjamin Jr. (African-American, 15) their quick-witted son.

The Setting: A home in a small African-American community in the south.

The Scene: Young Addie Henderson has been invited to the prom. Fearing that her father won't allow her to go, she begs her mother to intercede on her behalf. Here, Ben Sr. is greeted by Katherine and Ben Jr. and the touchy subject of the school dance is broached.

BENNY JR.: Hi, Daddy.
KATHERINE: Hey'dere.
BENNY JR.: Daddy, you seen the front yard?
BENJAMIN: Did you do that back yard?
BENNY JR.: I'm gonna do it... I'm just resting up. *(A beat)*
BENJAMIN: What is this Addie Pearl is wanting now?
KATHERINE: She didn't tell you?
BENJAMIN: I know she done put you up to telling me. *(A beat)*
KATHERINE: She wanna go to that prom-thing.
BENJAMIN: Wanna go to what?
KATHERINE: A prom, Benjamin.
BENJAMIN: What the hell is it?
KATHERINE: *(Impatient)* That school thing you wouldn't let Joyce go to.
BENJAMIN: A dance!? You know I ain't letting Addie Pearl leave out-a here going to no dance in the night-time with no boy!
KATHERINE: Benjamin, she got her heart set on it...
BENJAMIN: Well, she can just unset it!
KATHERINE: All right, Benjamin, I'm through with it! *(A beat)*
BENNY JR.: I think I hear that back-yard calling me.
(Benny Jr. tips out. A beat is felt.)
KATHERINE: Benjamin, you driving all these children away from home.
BENJAMIN: Let 'em go... they don't care nothing about me,

66

nohow.

KATHERINE: That's bunk! All these children love you.

BENJAMIN: That's what you say.

KATHERINE: They say it, too.

BENJAMIN: I ain't never heard none of 'em say it.

KATHERINE: When did you ever say it to them, Benjamin?

BENJAMIN: Why I gotta say it? Don't I leave here six mornings out-a the week to keep this roof over they heads and food in they bellies? Every time I turn around, they got they hands out for something... dollar for this, dollar for that...

KATHERINE: They'd come to you for other things if they wasn't scared half to death of you.

BENJAMIN: Shit, they ain't got no reason to be scared-a me... I ain't got on'em in a long time.

KATHERINE: It's your ways, Benjamin... you too set in 'em. That's why Joyce and Tom run off.

BENJAMIN: Shit, ain't no "ways" did nothing! That boy run to keep from gittin' a ass-whipping for breaking in my cedar chest and taking all that money... and that gal just wanted to have her way. Naw, I wasn't gonna let her go off with some old hot, tight-britches, snakey bastard making a chippy out-a no daughter-a mine...

KATHERINE: Did you stop it from happening?

BENJAMIN: If you and your mama hadn't put y'awl's big heads together, plottin' and plannin' behind my back to sneak her off, all painted up, maybe I could-a. You shore ain't gonna make no chippy out-a Addie Pearl! I'm gonna see to that! *(A beat)*

KATHERINE: I believe you run these children away on purpose so you won't have to look at the mirror they holding up to you... but you got a big surprise coming when it come to Addie... she ain't the running-away kind. She'll stand her ground 'til the mirror break, and the only way you gonna shut her up is to kill her. Make sure you're prepared to do that. Everybody can see she's your heart... not just because she's named after your dead mama, but because she got ways just like you... with that dev'lish pride that won't bend for nobody! But she's a child and I forgive her. I don't know how much more-a this mess I can take, Benjamin. Let her go to this thing. If you don't want her going with the boy by herself, let Benny Jr. go along to sit between 'em like my mama used to do us...

BENJAMIN: Shit, Benny Jr. ain't got sense enough to pour piss out-a boot! He liable to get to lolly-gagging with a bunch-a thugs and forget all about Addie Pearl.

KATHERINE: Benny Jr. got more sense than he make out. Yeah, he plays the fool around here, but his teachers shore say he's got a good head on his shoulders... and he know how to make money and be slick with it. You just take him aside and give him a good talking to and see if he miss doing what you tell him.

(Benjamin takes a cigar from his shirt pocket, bites the tip off and leaves without responding... but we can see he is trapped in indecision.)

THE REVENGER'S COMEDIES
by Alan Aykbourn

The Characters: Henry Bell (42) a man contemplating suicide, and Karen Knightly (25) a woman contemplating suicide

The Setting: The Albert Bridge, London, midnight, the present

The Scene: When Henry arrives at the Albert Bridge with the intention of throwing himself off, he encounters Karen, a melodramatic young woman with similar intentions.

Midnight. Albert Bridge, SW3. Perhaps a little river mist. Distant traffic, a ship's siren. Henry, a man in his early forties, appears in a pool of street light on the bridge. He is wrapped in an overcoat and scarf. He is hunched and miserable. He stares over the edge, deciding whether to jump. From his expression, it's evidently a long way down. He says a little silent prayer, as though asking forgiveness, and makes to climb over the railing. He is uncomfortably straddled across the railing and in some discomfort when he hears a woman's voice from the darkness.

KAREN: *(Calling)* Help... Help... Please help me... *(Henry stops and listens, rather startled.)* Please help... somebody...
HENRY: *(Calling, tentatively)* Hallo?
KAREN: *(Calling back)* Hallo...
HENRY: *(Calling again)* Hallo?
KAREN: Would you stop saying hallo and come and help me, please? I've got myself caught up here...
HENRY: Oh, right. Hang on, there... Just hang on... *(He starts to clamber back on to the bridge.)*
KAREN: I don't have any option. I've been hanging here for hours.
HENRY: Just one very small second... *(Henry moves to the source of her voice. As he does, so, we make out Karen for the first time. She is in her mid-twenties. She wears a woolly hat and lightweight coat over an evening dress. She is hanging outside the bridge railing. All that seems to be keeping her from falling is the belt of her coat, which has become entangled with the ironwork. Henry reaches her.)* Oh, Lord, How am I...?
KAREN: *(Trying to indicate.)* Do you see? Something's caught - I think it's the belt of my coat...
HENRY: Oh, yes, yes. Look, I think I'd better... *(Flustered)* Look-er... Yes, yes. I think I'd better try and er.... Would you

mind if I - tried to lift you...?
KAREN: You can do what you like - just get me off this bloody bridge...
HENRY: Yes, yes, right... *(He studies the problem.)*
KAREN: Can you see? I think it's my belt...
HENRY: Yes, yes, so it is. I think I'd better get that free before I... *(He starts to untangle the belt.)*
KAREN: Careful...
HENRY: Yes. Only I don't want to tear your coat, you see. If I tried to lift you over as you are, I might damage it... It's a very nice coat...
KAREN: *(Sarcastically)* Well, that's very considerate of you... Thank you.
HENRY: *(Finally freeing the belt.)* Right. There you go, all free.
KAREN: Aaaarh! *(The sudden release of the belt all but causes her to lose her balance and topple over the edge. She grabs at the first available handhold, which happens to be Henry's scarf.)*
HENRY: *(Choking)* Hurrgh!
KAREN: *(Screaming)* Hold on to me, for God's sake!
HENRY: *(With difficulty)* Hould hoo hossible het ho hof hy harf? Hi han't-
KAREN: Don't let go...
HENRY: Hi han't...
KAREN: What!
HENRY: Hi han't heathe...
KAREN: Well, give me something else to hold. *(Angrily)* Quickly, you're so useless... You're so totally, totally useless... What are you doing on this bridge, anyway?
(Henry manages to put his arms under hers and around her middle. Karen releases his scarf.)
HENRY: *(Much relieved)* Ah! Thank you. OK, I'm going to try and pull you over. Ready?
KAREN: Right.
HENRY: And - heave...
(Henry hauls at her. Karen reacts.)
KAREN: Aaargh! Careful!
HENRY: Sorry. It's a question of leverage...
KAREN: Well, could you use another bit of me to lever with?
HENRY: Yes, I'm sorry, I didn't mean to... *(He finds another grip.)* That better?
KAREN: Fractionally. Those are only my ribs.
HENRY: And two-six! Hup! *(He starts to heave her over.)*
KAREN: *(Reacting)* Hah!
HENRY: *(Another heave)* Hip!
KAREN: Hoo!

HENRY: Sorry, is this hurting?

KAREN: No, it's quite nice, actually. Keep going.

HENRY: *(A final heave.)* Hoy!

KAREN: Huf! *(He finally half lifts, half drags her over the railing. Karen finishes sitting on the bridge. Henry regains his breath.)* God! That was terrifying.

HENRY: Close thing.

KAREN: It certainly was. *(She shudders. She looks around her as if searching for someone.)*

HENRY: You all right?

KAREN: Thank you very much.

HENRY: Not at all.

KAREN: You saved my life.

HENRY: Well...

KAREN: I must owe you something...?

HENRY: No.

KAREN: Something. A drink, at least?

HENRY: *(Looking at his watch.)* It's half past twelve.

KAREN: Half past twelve?

HENRY: Yes.

KAREN: *(Angrily)* My God! Half past twelve?

HENRY: Yes.

KAREN: I don't believe it.

HENRY: How long had you been there?

KAREN: Since twenty past eight.

HENRY: Lord.

KAREN: Half past twelve! It's unbelievable. *(Pause)*

HENRY: Well...

KAREN: This is Chelsea Bridge, isn't it?

HENRY: No, this is Albert Bridge.

KAREN: Albert Bridge?

HENRY: Yes.

KAREN: You sure?

HENRY: Positive.

KAREN: Sod it!

HENRY: What?

KAREN: Nothing. *(Another pause)*

HENRY: Er... How did you come to get there?

KAREN: Where?

HENRY: Where you were. Hanging like that? How did you get there? Do you mind my asking?

KAREN: Well, obviously, I was trying to throw myself off.

HENRY: You were?

KAREN: Only I managed to make a complete mess of that, too. Like everything else in my life... *(Suddenly despairing.)* Oh, God... *(She hunches up, tearfully, a pathetic huddle on the*

pavement.)
HENRY: *(Ineffectually)* Oh, come on, now...
KAREN: You can leave me, it's all right. Leave me here. I'm just so pathetic...
HENRY: Look, perhaps I could see you home...?
KAREN: Go away. Just leave me here...
HENRY: I can't do that.
KAREN: I'll be all right. I expect.
HENRY: I can't leave you here like this.
KAREN: *(A little cry of self-pity)* Oh...
HENRY: *(Soothingly)* Sssh!
KAREN: Oh!
HENRY: Please let me... at least get you on your feet. You'll catch your - you'll catch your cold sitting there. *(Karen lets Henry help her to her feet.)* There.
KAREN: *(Holding on to him.)* Thank you. You're very kind.
HENRY: *(Slightly embarrassed)* No, not really. I just-
KAREN: I'm sorry I called you useless . I didn't mean that.
HENRY: No, as it happens you were right. I am a bit useless, really.
KAREN: Yes? Is that how you see yourself? Useless?
HENRY: Most of the time.
KAREN: Well. That makes two of us, then, doesn't it? *(She smiles a little.)*
HENRY: *(Smiling too, despite himself.)* I suppose it does.
KAREN: *(Evidently decides to pull herself together. She scrabbles in her mac pocket and eventually finds a tissue.)* Come on...
HENRY: *(Startled)* Where to?
KAREN: I'll take you somewhere for a drink. Come on.
HENRY: But nothing will be open.
KAREN: I know somewhere that's open. It's all right, it's not far... Do you have your car with you?
HENRY: I don't have one.
KAREN: Mine's parked along there... Come on, we both need something. Unless you've other things you'd sooner be doing?
HENRY: *(Looking back at the river)* Er, no. No.
KAREN: Great. *(Turning and extending her hand.)* By the way. Karen. Karen Knightly.
HENRY: *(Shaking her hand in turn)* Henry. Henry Bell.
KAREN: Splendid. Then follow me, Henry Bell.
HENRY: Where are we going?
KAREN: *(Disappearing into the darkness)* Just as far as the bypass, that's all...
HENRY: Ah. *(As he follows her off, puzzled.)* What bypass?

RUMORS IN THE PALACE
By Enid Rudd

The Characters: Arthur (30's) a prince, and Vivien (18) his young bride.

The Setting: The royal bedroom of a royal palace, the present.

The Scene: Arthur and Vivien are a royal couple suspiciously reminiscent of Britain's Charles & Di. Here, the young bride complains of her husband's thrift.

(The room in the Palace. The stage is dark. The very loud sound of a television show. Telephone ringing. It rings several times. A dog begins to bark. The telephone stops ringing... The dog continues to bark. The light in the room is switched on as Arthur enters in his pajamas and turns on the light. He turns off the VCR. The room is the same. Nothing has changed. Vivien, wrapped in a quilt, is asleep on the couch. A tin of cookies on her lap.)

ARTHUR: Vivien? *(He shakes her gently.)* Vivien? *(He takes the tin of cookies off her lap.)* Darling?
VIVIEN: Hm?
ARTHUR: Wake up.
VIVIEN: What time is it?
ARTHUR: It's two in the morning. You fell asleep in front of the TV. *(He carefully brushes crumbs from the quilt into his hand and into a wastebasket.)* That was my mother.
VIVIEN: Where! Where is your mother!
ARTHUR: On the telephone.
VIVIEN: I got scared. Why is that wretched dog barking?
ARTHUR: The noise woke her up.
VIVIEN: What noise? *(Telephone)* Who's that?
ARTHUR: *(Gets it.)* Yes?... no... no... sorry, Dad. We fell asleep with the VCR on... Mother just called too.. didn't mean to wake up the whole palace..
VIVIEN: Tell him to ask her to send up some heat. *(She has crossed to the fireplace with the quilt wrapped around her.)*
ARTHUR: ...it's Bunty.. she woke up... awfully sorry.. right.. *(Hangs up.)*
VIVIEN: Thee hundred rooms and we have about as much privacy as a monkey in the zoo. Can't you shut that dog up!

ARTHUR: *(Exiting into the bedroom.)* It's all right, old girl. It's all right.. here I am...

VIVIEN: *(Calls in.)* You'll catch cold like that.

ARTHUR: *(Offstage)* Daddy's here.. don't worry.. shhhhh... that's a good girl.

VIVIEN: *(Yelling in)* Why does it have to be so cold? *(She pulls the quilt closer around her.)* I won't get through the winter. I'll die of pneumonia. This fire won't start! *(She bangs down the andiron. Banging from the ceiling. She yells up.)* All right. *(The dog stops barking.)* We might just as well live in a council flat.

ARTHUR: *(Enters, tying a robe.)* I'm used to the cold, I guess.

VIVIEN: All that good, solid, rugged upbringing? Cold showers before dawn and all that.

ARTHUR: I thought we finished fighting.

VIVIEN: Who's fighting? Can you start that fire? It went out.

ARTHUR: Come back to bed. I'll make you warm. *(He hugs her close around the bulky quilt.)*

VIVIEN: Please. Get the fire going, will you?

ARTHUR: That's what I want to do.

VIVIEN: I'm talking about that fire.

ARTHUR: Vivien? I'm sorry. I feel so dreadful.

VIVIEN: Not so dreadful you couldn't fall asleep.

ARTHUR: I adore you.

VIVIEN: Please. Just... don't. All right. *(She pushes him away.)*

ARTHUR: I thought it was getting better.

VIVIEN: Why would you think that?

ARTHUR: Well.. you.. said it was...

VIVIEN: Did I? When?

ARTHUR: ...I thought... well... you...

VIVIEN: Everything here is yours! I'm just looking. Everything. All our wedding and shower gifts are still packed away in crates of tissue paper and straw. Every last one of them.

ARTHUR: I thought we finished all that.

VIVIEN: Even the dog is yours. Look at this room. You wouldn't even know I lived here. And it's so beastly dark. It's always dark. You'd think Dracula lived here!

ARTHUR: I thought we finished all that. I said I was wrong. I said you were right.

VIVIEN: It just upsets me so.

ARTHUR: I was totally wrong. I only thought we'd stay on here until we got our own place. It seemed so wasteful not to use what's here.

VIVIEN: You are cheap. You are tight with money.

ARTHUR: I said I was wrong. Get them. Please. Who cares. Vivien. Do you know what today is?

VIVIEN: I know.

ARTHUR: *(Hugging her close.)* Happy Anniversary. *(They kiss.)* It's only a year. If you married Jack the Ripper you would give him a chance to make things right.

VIVIEN: You think he could?

ARTHUR: If someone had loved and cared about him? *(He removes a small, ring-size, gift-wrapped box from the pocket of his robe.)* Happy Anniversary. *(She doesn't take it.)* Darling.

VIVIEN: Oh God. Oh, Arthur. *(She takes it and kisses him.)* My Billy goat. You make me feel so awful.

ARTHUR: Don't be silly. You can't expect to take two strange people, put them together and not expect a few disagreements.

VIVIEN: It's the ruby ring, isn't it? The one I admired so much. I'm so sorry. *(She smiles as she opens it.)* You are really such a darling. I mean this whole year you've never given me anything except a red rose or a few daisies..

ARTHUR: Vivien...

VIVIEN: ... and fancy barrettes... pill boxes... *(Gay laugh.)* I never met anyone had such a talent for cheap gifts. *(She removes a small pin. Arthur has crossed to the fireplace to fix it.)* ... Is this ... a ...brooch?

ARTHUR: It's papier mache.

VIVIEN: Ah.

ARTHUR: The first anniversary is paper.

VIVIEN: That's right. Leave it to you to remember that... Is that a picture of you?

ARTHUR: Mother, actually... and me.

VIVIEN: *(Staring at it.)* It looks like a souvenir.

ARTHUR: It was given to me by one of the workmen I met when I visited The Workman's Circle. His son made it and he was so proud of it. I thought you would like to have it.

VIVIEN: *(Smiles)* I have a gift for you too.

ARTHUR: I forgot about the ruby ring, Vivien. I just forgot. I could kick myself.

VIVIEN: I'd so much rather have a papier mache picture of you and your mother.

ARTHUR: I could just kick myself. I won't forget again. Next year. That's a promise. *(She hands him a heavy, square, gift-wrapped box.)*

VIVIEN: Happy Anniversary.

ARTHUR: *(Unwraps)* I thought the brooch had an intrinsic value.

VIVIEN: It does.

ARTHUR: You know, Vi, a few flowers always seems to me so

much more romantic than big bunches.
VIVIEN: Of course they are.
ARTHUR: I mean, it's not the gift, is it? It's the thought.
VIVIEN: Do you really believe that, Arthur?
ARTHUR: I do darling. From the bottom of my heart. *(The lid off the box.)* Cue balls.
VIVIEN: With your name on them. See? The Royal Crest?
ARTHUR: Right.
VIVIEN: You have your own stick. I thought it would be nice to have your own balls. *(She's eating another cookie.)*
ARTHUR: You're getting crumbs all over the floor.
VIVIEN: Sorry.
ARTHUR: I can't get the fire started. Come back to bed. *(He embraces her.)* I'll make you warm, old girl.
VIVIEN: Honestly. That's all you ever want to do. We never talk. All we do is fornicate.
ARTHUR: Vivien. Take off this quilt.
VIVIEN: Ask the landlady to send up some heat.
ARTHUR: I can't feel you under all this. Are you in there? *(Hugging her.)*
VIVIEN: Listen. We just had a big row. I know we made up, but I can't turn my emotions on and off that quickly. I'm not like you. I'm not angry. But I don't want to make love either.
ARTHUR: Why not?
VIVIEN: I just told you.
ARTHUR: It's the best way to make up.
VIVIEN: We made up. Now stop it. Please. Let me go.
ARTHUR: You do. You know you do.
VIVIEN: I don't! If I did I'd say so. *(She pulls away.)* Now, just let me go! I really would like to be left alone. *(She gets another cookie. He comes behind and grabs her around again. He pulls her down on the couch.)*
ARTHUR: I love you.
VIVIEN: *(She doesn't struggle.)* Oh, Arthur. Honestly.
ARTHUR: Come back to be bed and we'll snuggle up and I'll make you warm. I'll be your potbelly stove.
VIVIEN: I don't want to play potbelly stove. We made love this morning. We made love after tea. We made love earlier this evening. We made love before our row. Isn't that enough? *(He kisses her.)* I suppose I just don't enjoy it the way you do.
ARTHUR: We'll get things right. You'll see.
VIVIEN: Will we?

76

SAMMY WENT A' COURTIN'
by David Michael Gallagher

The Characters: Karin (30's) a beautiful woman who is a top producer of television commercials, and Sammy (Puerto Rican, 25) a cameraman.

The Setting: A stylish Manhattan apartment, the present.

The Scene: Her feelings of love for younger Sammy have driven Karin to hide in her apartment while she tries to sort them out. Here, Sammy, who is head-over-heels in love with Karin, confronts her at home and forces her to admit her love.

(Karin stands leaning against the door. Sammy slowly stands, facing front. A Pause.)

KARIN: Sammy,...
SAMMY: *(Still facing front.)* Don't be mad.
KARIN: I'm not mad.
SAMMY: What else could I do? You wouldn't answer any of my phone calls. Just that one message left on my answering machine, Karin. And what the hell was that? "Worried about diseases, must end relationship". What?
KARIN: Oh, Sammy...
SAMMY: This is crazy, man. This is fucked-up.
KARIN: *(Moving down to center.)* I know. I needed time. I've been caught up in such a terrible conflict about this, Sammy. I needed this time to sort out what I was feeling. It just happened too quickly. It became too intense too quickly.
SAMMY: Yeah, because it was a long build-up.
KARIN: And I knew that as much as I wanted it, it just wasn't right. I became swept up in it too quickly for it to be real, Sammy. We both did. I was wishing something into being that reality would never support. And I was right. In these two weeks I've come to realize I was right.
SAMMY: Quickly? Quickly? Maybe we never actually connected till the night of the Christmas party, but man, since a year ago, since last February, we been workin' our way to it every day. Come on, Karin.
KARIN: Sammy. Sammy. You are an extraordinarily attractive man. There's no question that I've always found you extraordinarily attractive. Everybody does. You're the most

talked about man in the whole damned office, dear ...
SAMMY: What have we been doing for this whole year? What have we been doing? In the studio...on a shoot... conference meeting, wherever it was, however many people were around us, when we were together we were alone, Karin. You weren't feeling that too?
KARIN: Yes. That was happening. It's your interpretation of what it meant that's off. It was a game, Sammy.
SAMMY: A game?
KARIN: I mean ... it was an adventure for me. After that long period without a man in my life, to feel such a yearning for the male ... it was... it was exciting. It was fun to have that thing going with you. It was like a fantasy.
SAMMY: I'm not a real person to you?
KARIN: Of course you are! Sammy, dear... these two weeks have been really screwed up for me. Really screwed up. You know? I've been so worried about you. I'm sorry, sweetheart. I didn't realize until too late that it was more than just having some fun for you. I assumed we were both feeling the same way.
SAMMY: So did I.
KARIN: I've enjoyed the time we've had together. I want you to know that. You know I absolutely adore you...
SAMMY: Yeah. I know.
KARIN: I have right from the start...
SAMMY: Karin. One year ago today you decked Zena "the reed" Ramsey because she put her hand on my ass. Laid the bitch out flat on your office floor. It was a very impressive moment. I was very impressed. I'm not used to having my honor defended. It meant a lot to me, Karin.
KARIN: Had it coming for twenty years. Dizzy bitch.
SAMMY: Deeply impressed. I'd been at F & M about a week then. I'd scoped out the scene, I'm a pretty quick study. And you know, there were one or two women around that caught my attention. Caught my eye. As for you, I thought you were a hell-of-a-woman up there in your executive office, but pretty much out of my league. *(Laughs)* Till you fought it out for my honor. Then I knew it had to be love. Come on, Karin, this is no fantasy. We really love each other. Okay, I know you told me you were scared. I'm prepared to deal with scared. You want to call it fantasy, Great. Let's just keep the fantasy going, that's all.
KARIN: I can't...
SAMMY: Why not?
KARIN: Look ... why don't you sit down
SAMMY: I'm fine.

KARIN: ...and relax? Okay?

SAMMY: I'm fine.

KARIN: How's your coffee?

SAMMY: I'm fine.

KARIN: Sammy, it won't work. I've thought of it from every angle. Okay? The simple fact is that you are a twenty-five year old...quite young man. I happen to be skidding towards forty.

SAMMY: *(Stepping towards her.)* Kiss me.

KARIN: No! *(Pause)* No.

SAMMY: Twenty-five year old man. Thirty-seven year old woman. I saw it on Movie of the Week last night. Lindsey Wagner-John Stamos. I know exactly how to handle the situation now. I want to kiss you so badly. I want to hold you.

KARIN: Well, you can't. Stay where you are! *(Moving to bar left and pouring a brandy from a decanter.)* I'm not worried about appearances, Sammy. I'm worried about the emotional consequences of such a union. It's not just that you're twenty-five, Sammy. You're also hot as a smoking pistol. I've never seen anybody get hit on as much as you do...

SAMMY: Only you. Only you.

KARIN: I know you're sincere. I know you're caught up in this intensity the same as I am. I trust that you mean what you're saying now. But there are a lot of tomorrows in the sort of commitment you're talking about. I don't mean to be pedantic, but the fact is that tomorrows hold a quite different texture for a twenty-five year old and a thirty-seven year old. Tomorrows are full of lots of tricks and twists and turnings...

SAMMY: It's because you don't believe it yet. You don't believe I really love you.

KARIN: I believe you believe it, goddamnit! But Sammy, I'm sorry, the conclusion I've come to in this self imposed period of withdrawal I've been going through is that I don't really love you. I desired you... but I don't really love you. Darling. Do you want a brandy? You don't drink. Have another coffee.

SAMMY: I still have a cup, thank you.

KARIN: I want you to know that you've helped me enormously. There was a part of myself I needed to reexplore...

SAMMY: So, in other words, when you said: "I love you, Sammy", that last night before your self imposed withdrawal from the world, it was a lie? Just a lie?

KARIN: Well ... I've examined that moment very intently, Sammy. I've heard myself saying those words, and I've had to try to understand why I would say them.... You see? And what I came to realize is that I'd confused love and desire. You see?

SAMMY: You mean you just wanted to fuck me?

KARIN: I ... Yes. I wanted to fuck you.
SAMMY: Okay. I can accept that. I think we can work with that. You still want to fuck me?
KARIN: No!
SAMMY: No? What happened? I suddenly lost all my desirability? No good? Seemed to me we were fucking each others brains out.
KARIN: It won't work now. Won't work now.
SAMMY: Why not?
KARIN: Sammy!
SAMMY: Yeah? *(He takes a folded piece of paper from the inside pocket of his jacket and places it on coffee table. He turns back to Karin.)* I love to fuck. I think you may just be comin' around to the realization that you love to fuck...
KARIN: I *love* to fuck.
SAMMY: Can't argue with that. And I think we should keep doin' it. I think we should keep fucking each other's brains out. I think we should just go ahead and use each other as fuck objects, Karin. Okay? Cause you know what you do to me, and you seem to like the Rivero package okay. Okay! I'm ready to go right now. I mean it. I want to do it! I want to fuck you!
KARIN: Stop it! How many other women *have* you wanted to fuck at Favorsham and MacMillan, Sammy? How many women have you fucked at Favorsham and MacMillan, Sammy?
SAMMY: None.
KARIN: Teresa?
SAMMY: Who?
KARIN: That little redhead in editing?
SAMMY: She's engaged to a guy from my neighborhood, Karin.
KARIN: Cosima. And what about Cosima? The model we used at the Indianapolis 500 shoot?
SAMMY: Cosima? Sheeit. I loved Cosima. She was one of the funniest people I ever met. You should have stuck around longer that night, you'd have come to love her too. You'd have had a really great time, Karin. However, ...I never fucked Cosima. I never made a play for Cosima. The only joining of Cosima and me has apparently occurred only in your mind.
KARIN: Okay. No Cosima. Sammy, you're a hot blooded young man...
SAMMY: Puerto Rican. Hot blooded Puerto Rican. And everybody knows that Puerto Rican men are conquistadors. Wife at home, mistress tucked onto a back street, steady juggling of ladies in and around the work spot. There's a constant rod in a Puerto Rican's jockies, eh Karin? Word!
KARIN: My point is that you have to go nowhere to look for it. It seeks you out. It's there begging you all the time.

SAMMY: I'm a divorced Puerto Rican who has no wife at home; I work much too long and much too hard to even set eyes on a mistress, even if I had one; and I have, and have only had, one focus of attention at my work spot.

KARIN: No one?

SAMMY: No one. After I met you, no one. *(Pause)*

KARIN: What about before that?

SAMMY: Come on! I'm not a saint. I'm crazy about women. I started having dreams about vaginas when I was ten. And I've been with a lot of women, Karin. *(He picks up the piece of a paper he has placed on the coffee table and hands it to Karin.)* Here.

KARIN: What? What is it?

SAMMY: Happy Valentine. *(Karin reads the page and looks at Sammy puzzled.)* It's an official signed document, you'll notice. It says I'm a very clean fellow.

KARIN: *(Turning from him.)* Oh, Sammy...

SAMMY: You tell me you love me one night and the next night I get a kiss-off message on my answering machine? "Worried about diseases, must end relationship"? Happy Valentine, Karin. Okay? Okay?

KARIN: *(Moves to Sammy and kisses him on the cheek, then quickly steps back.)* Would you mind sitting down, Sammy? Just please sit down. *(Sammy sits on sofa. Karin holds up paper.)* Thank you. Thank you, darling. I'm very, very, moved by your... gesture. And thankful. For both our sakes. Please let me assure you, it never crossed my mind that ... *(sets paper down on coffee table.)* Sammy, I have been concerned. Really, it wasn't you, it was just after so long a time without sex in your life, it takes on a sort of leviathan stature when you dare approach it again. And now! Here it looms with a burning dagger in its fist.

SAMMY: We don't have to worry. That's what that paper says. We're okay.

KARIN: Sammy ... *(Crosses to table right.)* Sammy, honestly, hon, it was really a kind of hysterical reaction to ... sex! Sex! As well as a complex series of confusions I've been going through about our ... relationship. I know I sound like a twelve year old, but that's what's happening.

SAMMY: Karin you're crazy about me. You love to make love with me. You love being around me and with me. What's the question? I'm here. I'm safe. What? You wanna go out in pursuit of some more "logical" partner now? Honey. We can work this through. Trust me, baby. *(Pause)*

KARIN: Maybe...

SAMMY: *(Leaping up.)* Yeow!!

81

KARIN: Please! Sit! *(Sammy sits.)* I'm serious. I'm in a terrible state of upheaval here. "Maybe" is maybe. Okay?
SAMMY: Okay.
KARIN: The thing is I'm gonna need more time. I'm certainly not going to make any pivotal decisions till I've understood just what I'm feeling. And. That's that. Time.
SAMMY: Okay. How much time?
KARIN: I can't put a stop watch on this, Sammy.
SAMMY: Okay. So, how do we want to handle this?
KARIN: We've got to avoid intimacy for awhile. You know? I'm going to need just a little distance for awhile.
SAMMY: So, ...how does that break down?
KARIN: No sex.
SAMMY: Aaaaaaaah. Okay. Okay. Just ... hands off? Does that include kissing?
KARIN: Yes! *(She begins a slow cross behind sofa.)* And embracing...
SAMMY: Karin!
KARIN: Sammy! Don't you understand, if we allow this to get physical we'll wind up ... doing it?!
SAMMY: Hey, great.
KARIN: *(Now directly behind him)* Sammy, great for you. Not great for me. You're not seeing my situation very clearly or sympathetically.
SAMMY: Okay. Sorry.
KARIN: That's what I mean.
SAMMY: What? I'm listening.
KARIN: You know damned good and well the effect you have on me. You're a very potent presence for me, my darling. Just the smell of you ... *(She turns and moves to left of sofa.)* Sex is completely out of the question now, Sam. It would only lead to deeper confusion at this time. Trust me about this. I've been working it out with Dorothy. So, ... *(She shrugs.)*
SAMMY: So we go through a courting process now? Getting to know each other more? Okay. I guess we got a whole lot we haven't talked about yet ... why don't we start with dinner tonight?
KARIN: Not tonight. I feel overwhelmed by today...
SAMMY: Okay. Tomorrow night?
KARIN: *(Crossing in front of Sammy to table right.)* I think for the time being we probably shouldn't even date, Sammy.
SAMMY: You mean we can't even go to a movie?
KARIN: No, Sammy. *(Pause)*
SAMMY: And can we even talk to each other about movies? Is that allowed? *(He stands.)* Karin, listen to me, baby, you need to get out of this atmosphere for awhile. Really. Really,

sweetheart. Get dressed. Let me take you out to lunch now. Okay? Irene Dunne and Cary Grant in Leo McCarey's *Awful Truth* is at the Revival Palace today. Let's go. Come on. I won't kiss you. I won't even take your arm.

KARIN: Please sit down, Sam. *(Sitting)* Sam. No, I think we should just go about our business as though this never happened. *(She begins to cross left behind.)* Nobody at work knows about us, so there won't be any pressure from outside. I think we should just ... chill out, that's all.

SAMMY: What?! Sheeit. So if we pass in the halls I'm supposed to, what? Glance away if our eyes should meet? I should go sit in a corner between takes on a shoot? I mean, like are we allowed to engage in a little incidental chit-chat now and again? Or what? *(Leaps up.)* KARIN! Come on! You know something? You're a real asshole, Karin. Yeah. I'm sorry, but yeah. What you really want me to do is hand in my notice at Favorsham and MacMillan, isn't it?

KARIN: No, Sammy...

SAMMY: Because that's the only way you're gonna get what you want. If I just don't exist. You're asking me not to exist, Karin!

KARIN: Sammy ... !

SAMMY: You want me to quit? You want me to just clear out of Favorsham and MacMillan? Okay. You got it, baby.

KARIN: No! That's not what I want!

SAMMY: I'll hand in my notice. I'm gone. I never happened. You got your dream, Karin. Okay?

KARIN: Sammy! Would you please sit down!

SAMMY: *(Sits)* Christ!

KARIN: Sammy ... You know I don't want you to give up your career with Favorsham and MacMillan. *(Directly behind him, she places her hands on his shoulders.)* For heaven's sake. You're going to be a filmmaker. You're training with some of the most gifted people in the industry. The experience you're getting now is invaluable. Invaluable. No, I certainly don't want you to leave Favorsham and MacMillan, Sammy. *(Karin suddenly runs both hands through Sammy's hair and pulling his head back she kisses him on the top of his head. As his hand reaches up to take hers, she swiftly moves away to left of sofa.)*

KARIN: I think that's the key. We should both focus very strongly now on our careers. *(She pours another brandy.)* Do you see what's happening now, Sammy? Because of this turmoil I've been totally unable to deal with work. Here we are in the midst of the biggest, most lucrative campaign F & M has ever launched and I'm a total and complete vegetable. And why? Because of you! This! Do you realize how long and hard I've worked to achieve the position I now occupy? I am now

considered to be one of the finest producers in the business.
SAMMY: You're the best.
KARIN: And suddenly I'm a seventeen year old with a crush on the captain of the football team. This is just too messed up to be real. You see? I know I have a yearning for something in my life now...
SAMMY: Yeah, me.
KARIN: ...But this has become destructive. And that's a clue, you see, to the reality of the situation. Sammy, I feel strangulated by my desire for you. That can't be right. I don't trust what's happening now and I need further time to examine it. Okay? Sammy?
SAMMY: You know ... you're an absolute riot, Karin. Reality of the situation? You know!... for a smart lady you're a fuckin' dumb bitch. What? Are we supposed to go back to day one now and just start over? Only this time we "avoid" falling in love with one another? Karin!, how can you do this to yourself? For ten months you danced around my head till you just couldn't stand it any more, then BOOM!, night of the Christmas party you come rushing into my arms like a crazy woman. Crazy woman. Now *that* was reality, baby. It was also the best fuck you ever had and the best fuck I ever had. But Karin, baby, I can not go through ten more months of foreplay, no matter how great it makes the fuck...
KARIN: Sammy...
SAMMY: No!! Goddamnit, Karin! I've been patient as a saint! Have you thought of me at all? Karin? Do you know what those ten months must have been like for me?! *(Karin crosses before Sammy to table right.)* What about me?!
KARIN: Sammy, I...
SAMMY: Shut up! Now you fuckin' get a grip on it, girl! THIS is the reality of the situation. You and me, here in this room, right now. Goddamnit Karin, our bodies know each other now, we can't go backward. We've been inside each others' bodies. I know your secret place, baby, and you know mine too, don't you? You think we can just look away, pretend it never happened? This moment! You want my body and I know it! Get past your lies, Karin.
KARIN: I can't! I can't! *(Karin moves around back of sofa to left of sofa.)*
SAMMY: *(On his knees on sofa, he physically turns, following her movement.)* Come to me! Come to me!
KARIN: *(At left of sofa)* Sammy! Sammy!
SAMMY: *(Stands)* Hold me, baby. I need you. Please! *(Pause)*
KARIN: The thing is, we've got to give this some time, Sammy...

(Sammy screams and throws himself onto sofa, burying his head.)

KARIN: Sammy? *(Begins to weep.)* Well for heaven's sake, what do you think I've been going through? Of course I've thought of you. I've thought of nothing else. You're in my every last thought! I can't stop thinking of you! Sammy! Sammy! Sammy! Sammy! I feel like I'm going insane!! *(Weeping fitfully)*

SAMMY: *(Stands)* Oh, sweetheart-baby... *(Pause, then he moves toward her.)*

KARIN: NO!!

SAMMY: Aaaaaaaaah!! *(He again throws himself onto sofa, burying his head. Downstairs buzzer.)*

KARIN: It's Clare. *(She moves to buzzer system.)*

KARIN: Clare?

CLARE'S VOICE: Yes ! *(Karen buzzes her up. Sammy stands and moves down center.)*

KARIN: *(Moving down left)* Sammy... *(Long pause)*

SAMMY: At the Christmas party I went lookin' for you through all those rooms at the Fifth Avenue palazzio they hired for the night. I tapped you on the shoulder and I asked you to dance with me. You turned to look at me, Karin... We looked into each others eyes much too long, Karin. You opened the door and you told me to follow, I said, "Right on, lady, you got a date with destiny". All in a look, huh?

KARIN: I was pretty drunk.

SAMMY: You were honest. You took my arm and you walked through that hall of mirrors to the ballroom like a royal duchess. I know you were proud to be with me. I could feel it. Then the dance. That hot, hot dance, Karin. But nothing was more important than that first look. That was it, man. Don't forget, I'm the cameraman. So now you're gonna claim you were too drunk to recall that moment, Karin? Huh? Is that it?

KARIN: *(Softly)* No. I recall that moment, Sammy. Of course it was "the moment". "The Moment". I almost didn't come. I'd just gotten back from the Atlanta shoot. But I'd bought a special dress. I hadn't thought about you the whole while I was away, but when I checked my coat and started up the grand staircase, my only thought was, "I'm going to dance with Sammy tonight!" When you tapped my shoulder I knew who I was turning to.

SAMMY: Hello.

KARIN: Hello. *(She slowly moves to him. An embrace.)* Darling! Darling! *(A deep kiss. Then break, then reunite with passion. Between kisses:)* I love you.

SAMMY: I love you.

KARIN: I love you. *(Upstairs buzzer)*
SAMMY: Hey! *(He laughs.)* Life is so beautiful! My lady.
KARIN: *(Laughing)* Oh, God! You precious man. What am I doing?
SAMMY: Hey! We're together now. Hold on to this. Don't go lookin' for everything that's wrong. Okay!

SERVY -N- BERNICE 4EVER
by Seth Zvi Rosenfeld

The Characters: Servy (20's) a young man on parole and Bernice (20's) the woman he loves.

The Setting: New York, the present

The Scene: When their attempt at cohabitation fails, Bernice decides to go home to her family. Here, she and Servy discuss their future as she gathers her things.

Bernice is alone packing. Servy comes into apartment.

SERVY: What the fuck? What are you doin' here?
BERNICE: Hi Servy.
SERVY: What are you doin' here?
BERNICE: I came to get my things.
SERVY: Oh yeah ... Sorry about your things, you know, I kept them in the closet, I was gonna bring them by your mother's house but I been kinda busy.
BERNICE: I'm sure you're really busy.
SERVY: I been tryin' to catch up on things so that when school starts I'm ready, you know what I'm sayin'?
BERNICE: You're going back to school?
SERVY: Yeah, I been reading up on shit, gonna get me a social work degree jut like my mom's.
BERNICE: You know, I been tryin' to keep busy too. I was supposed to get new pictures done but all my clothes were over here and I couldn't get in and that's why I kept calling ... You never called me back... That's why I showed up. *(Long pause as Servy watches Bernice pack.)* It's a good thing I don't have that much stuff, it never would've fit anyway and there's even less room in my mother's apartment.
SERVY: So you finally went home?
BERNICE: Where else was I gonna go, you saw the way I left outta here, I ran all the way down to East River Park. I'm startin' out into the water and there goes Gail's oldest Deedee, walkin' arm and arm with some young boy talkin' 'bout, "This here is Malik, he's my associate." I said, what y'all got a Limited Partnership agreement?
SERVY: *(Laughs.)* Her associate.
BERNICE: Then I showed up at my mother's house lookin' like somethin' the cat dragged in. Gail and the rest of the kids were

87

lookin' at me like, "Damn, what happened to Dee-dee Bernice."
SERVY: What'd your mother say?
BERNICE: My mother? First thing she said is, "Girl is you eatin' up there in that school?" I proceed to tell her I wasn't in school and she marched me into the kitchen. I knew I was in trouble. I talked so fast and so hard for so long my jaw started creaking.
SERVY: Word.
BERNICE: Talk about a heartbroken woman, Servy. My mother cried for six hours straight. I'm the only good news she gets... Then that night me and Anthony shared the room, we stayed up all night talkin'. He said he don't smoke crack no more, he sells reefer instead. Hey look, he stays off that pipe, I'm happy. He told me, "Bernice, you need to stop frontin'." I told him, " I know that." He said, "Listen to me Bernice, make it easier on yourself, you ain't got to rescue me, or Mommy or Gail, you ain't never asked to be our Saviour they put you in that role. Let all that weight slide off your back, Bernice, all you got to do is be real." I felt myself take a deep breath for the first time in about ten years. He said, " You love Servy, get with Servy."
SERVY: He said that?
BERNICE: That's what he said.
SERVY: So wha'd you say?
BERNICE: I told him to mind his damn business.
SERVY: Word?
BERNICE: I'm just playin', Servy. I'm ready to get outta there.
SERVY: When the going gets tough, Bernice gets goin'.
BERNICE: I never intended to come back here and live with them. I guess we both never intended a lot of things... Maybe you did I don't know.
SERVY: Where you gonna go?
BERNICE: I don't know, I'll find someplace.
SERVY: I know you will.
BERNICE: *(Finishes packing.)* Gotta go.
SERVY: Here's some money so you could catch a cab. *(Servy hands Bernice some money.)*
BERNICE: That's okay. I don't want your money.
SERVY: So you could catch a cab. I'll help you downstairs with everything.
BERNICE: I don't need help.
SERVY: I don't mind.
BERNICE: It's ok.
SERVY: Okay.
(Bernice goes to exit.)
SERVY: Wait.

BERNICE: What?

SERVY: You not gonna take, you know, the plants and shit like that?

BERNICE: I thought maybe you wanted them.

SERVY: I'd prefer if you took everything, you know what I'm sayin', everything you brought you can take out, the plants, the tablecloth, all that shit, I'd prefer if there was no trace of you left in this motherfucker... Nothing personal.

BERNICE: Oh I understand, I understand completely, see the reason I didn't take them to begin with was that we bought them together for this house and I considered them ours, not mine. I don't want them. *(Bernice throws plant out the window.)* Nothing personal. *(Bernice throws tablecloth out, pictures, her bags.)*

SERVY: Bernice stop!

BERNICE: Why? Why? Why should I stop, I don't want to stop! Let's just throw everything out the fucking window- *(Bernice crosses to door.)*

SERVY: They violated me! I'M GOING BACK TO JAIL!

BERNICE: What?

SERVY: Doc told my Parole Officer that I was in Boston, he ain't say nothin' about the jewelry store but I'm supposed to do six months.

BERNICE: Six months.

SERVY: That's right. Doc said, "It's only six months, go to the hearing, do the time." It's only six months, he don't have to do the six months. I'm not goin' back to prison. I'm gonna plan this shit out. I got places to go, people to see, by the time my hearing comes I'll be in the wind. Word to Moms, I ain't goin' back.

BERNICE: Why? What happened to school and-

SERVY: That was lies. It was lies, Bernice, just like everything, it was all fucking lies.

BERNICE: No Servy, no it wasn't, you was-

SERVY: *(Grab Bernice.)* Look at me! I'm like a motherfucker wearing the pants too small for him. He tucks in one side and the seam on the other side breaks, he sews that up puts them back on and the seam in the middle splits. I try. I dress good, say the right things, do the right things, do the right thing, adjust this, fix that, but my real self always manages to bust through and fuck everything up. *(Servy breaks down crying.)*

BERNICE: It doesn't have to be that way.

SERVY: It does.

BERNICE: Listen to me -

SERVY: Go meet some nice motherfucker and live happily ever after! I'm gonna die!

BERNICE: You won't die! Stop it! *(Bernice picks up her bags*

and begins to exit.)
SERVY: I don't wanna lose you. I don't wanna lose you.
BERNICE: I don't wanna lose you neither but Goddamnit Servy...
SERVY: *(Gets himself under control.)* What?
BERNICE: Is this the way it's gonna be forever?
SERVY: I don't know... I don't know, Bernice, I don't know.
BERNICE: I don't know, either.
SERVY: I know.
BERNICE: I know that I wanna wait.
SERVY: No, you don't.
BERNICE: I just wish it wasn't so goddamn hard.
SERVY: Me too.
BERNICE: *(Sits at chair.)* I'll try to wait.
SERVY: I don't trust you.
BERNICE: I don't trust you, neither.
SERVY: See?
BERNICE: What?
SERVY: We don't even trust each other.
BERNICE: So?
SERVY: So how we supposed to make it?
BERNICE: Motherfuckers build bridges, send people to the moon, make bombs that could kill everybody, all we want to do is love each other, right?
SERVY: Shut up.
BERNICE: Right?
SERVY: Yeah.
BERNICE: I think we could do that.

(Bernice and Servy stare out into their individual spaces.)

(LIGHTS slowly fade.)

SIGHT UNSEEN
by David Margulies

The Characters: Jonathan (20's) a young man mourning the death of his mother, and Patricia (early 20's) his girlfriend.

The Setting: Brooklyn, 1970's

The Scene: During his mother's shiva, Jonathan allows his grief to push Patricia away.

(Late afternoon. Spring. Blinds drawn. Jonathan's bedroom in his parents' house in Brooklyn, complete with the artifacts of a lower-middle-class boyhood, the notable exception being a sewing machine. Wearing a vest, suit trousers, and socks, Jonathan is curled up on a bed. His hair is long. There is a tentative knock. Patricia enters. A beat. She whispers:)

PATRICIA: Jonathan? *(She waits, whispers again:)* Jonny? *(She looks around the room, gravitates toward the bookshelf, and begins scanning the titles. After a while, he sits up and sees her looking at a paper back.)* I love your little-boy handwriting. So round. The loopy "J" in "Jonathan," the "o," the "a"s. "This book belongs to Jonathan Waxman." *(Laughs, shows him the book.)* The Man From U.N.C.L.E. I wish I knew you then, Jonny. *(She returns the book to the shelf and continues looking.)*
JONATHAN: What are you doing?
PATRICIA: I love looking at people's books.
JONATHAN: *(Still awaiting a response)* Patty...?
PATRICIA: It's like looking into their brain or something. Everything they ever knew. Everything they ever touched. It's like archeology. Lets you into all the secret places.
JONATHAN: Patty, what are you doing here?
PATRICIA: Only took me two years to get in the front door. Hey, not bad. - Why isn't *Franny and Zooey* at your place?
JONATHAN: It is. I have doubles.
PATRICIA: Oh. *(Pause. They look at one another.)* You look handsome in your suit.
JONATHAN: *(He begins to pull on his shoes.)* Thanks.
PATRICIA: I don't think I've ever seen you in a suit. Have I? I must have. Did you wear a suit at graduation? No, you wore a cap and gown. What did you wear underneath it? Anything?
JONATHAN: What time is it?

PATRICIA: I don't know. *(A beat)* Your dad kissed me. When I came in? He kissed me. On the lips. He's very sweet, your Dad. Said he was glad to see me, he was glad I came. See? He wasn't upset to see me. I told you, you were overreacting. He's always kind of had a crush on me I think. You know the Waxman men and their shiksas. They're legend.

JONATHAN: *(Fixing his shirt.)* I should go back down.

PATRICIA: No. Why? Stay. *(She tries to touch his hair, he moves away.)* So this is where you and Bobby grew up. *(She sits on a bed.)*

JONATHAN: That's right...

PATRICIA: Funny, it's just how I pictured it. Like one of those Smithsonian recreations? You know: those roped-off rooms? "Jonathan Waxman's Bedroom in Brooklyn, Circa 1970." "The desk upon which he toiled over algebra." "The bed in which he had his first wet dream..."

JONATHAN: That one, actually.

PATRICIA: *(She smiles. A beat.)* I loved the oil painting bar mitzvah portraits of you and Bobby over the sofa by the way.

JONATHAN: What can I tell ya?

PATRICIA: Oh, they're great. *(A beat. She sees the incongruous sewing machine.)* Sewing machine?

JONATHAN: She moved it in when I moved out.

PATRICIA: Ah.

JONATHAN: The only woman on record to die of empty nest syndrome. *(She goes to him and hugs him.)*

PATRICIA: Oh, Jonny, I'm sorry...

JONATHAN: *(Trying to free himself.)* Yeah. You know, I really should go back down. My father... *(They kiss, again and again, he's bothered as her kisses become more fervent. Protesting:)* Patty... Patricia... *(She tries to undo his belt.)* Hey! What's the matter with you?

PATRICIA: Lie down.

JONATHAN: Patricia, my father is sitting shiva in the living room!

PATRICIA: Come on, Jonny...

JONATHAN: NO! I SAID! Are you crazy?! What the fuck is the matter with you?!

PATRICIA: You won't let me do anything for you.

JONATHAN: Is this supposed to cheer me up?!

PATRICIA: I want to do something.

JONATHAN: I don't want sex, Patricia.

PATRICIA: I've never known anyone who died before; tell me what I should do.

JONATHAN: This isn't about you. Do you understand that? This is my problem, my... loss, mine.

PATRICIA: But I'm your friend. Aren't I? I'm your lover, for God's sake. Two years, Jonathan ...

JONATHAN: *(Over "for God's sake...")* I thought we went through this...

PATRICIA: I want to be with you. I want to help you.

JONATHAN: You can't help me, Patty. I'm beyond help.

PATRICIA: Don't say that.

JONATHAN: It's true. I am beyond help right now. You can't help me. Your blowjobs can't help me.

PATRICIA: You don't know how I felt not being at the funeral.

JONATHAN: I'm sorry.

PATRICIA: No you're not. I was in agony. Really. I couldn't concentrate on anything all day. Knowing what you must've been going through? What kind of person do you think I am? I wanted to be with you so much.

JONATHAN: So you came over.

PATRICIA: You didn't say I couldn't. You said the funeral. I came over after.

JONATHAN: I meant the whole thing.

PATRICIA: What whole thing.

JONATHAN: The funeral, shiva.

PATRICIA: You mean I was supposed to keep away from you during all this? like for a week? - isn't shiva like a week?

JONATHAN: Patty...

PATRICIA: Do you know how ridiculous this is? Don't you think you're taking this guilt thing a little too far? I mean, your mother is dead - I'm really really sorry, Jonny, really I am - and, okay, we know she wasn't exactly crazy about me...

JONATHAN: I'm so burnt out, Patty... My head is...

PATRICIA: *(Continuous)* Not that I ever did anything to offend the woman personally or anything. I just happened to be born a certain persuasion, a certain incompatible persuasion, even though I'm an atheist and I don't give a damn what religion somebody happens to believe in. But did she even bother to get to know me, even a little bit?

JONATHAN: Oh, Patty, this is -

PATRICIA: It's like I was invisible. Do you know how it feels to be invisible?

JONATHAN: What do you think?, my mother's dying wish was keep that Shiksa away from my funeral?! Come on, Patty! Grow up! Not everything is about you. I know that may be hard for you to believe, but not everything in the world -

PATRICIA: *(Over "in the world -")* Oh, great.

JONATHAN: *(A beat)* Let's face it, Patricia, things haven't exactly been good between us for months.

PATRICIA: What do you mean? Your mother's been sick for

93

months. How can you make a statement like that?

JONATHAN: What, this is a surprise to you what I'm saying?

PATRICIA: Hasn't your mother been dying for months?

JONATHAN: I don't really have the strength for this right now.

PATRICIA: Hasn't she? So how can you judge how things have been between us? Her dying has been weighing over us, over both of us, for so long, it's colored so much...

JONATHAN: *(Over "it's colored so much...")* Look...if you must know -

PATRICIA: What.

JONATHAN: If you must know... *(A beat)* I was the one who didn't want you there. It wasn't out of respect to my mother or my father or my grandmother, it was me. I didn't want to see you. I didn't want you there, Patty. I didn't want to have to hold your hand and comfort you because of how cruel my mother was to you, I didn't want that... I didn't want to have to deal with your display of -

PATRICIA: Display?

JONATHAN: Your display of love for me. Your concern. It was all about you whenever I thought about how it would be if you were with me! I didn't want you there, Patty. I'm sorry. *(A beat)* I guess when something catastrophic like this happens... You get to thinking.

PATRICIA: Yes? Well? *(Pause)*

JONATHAN: I don't love you, Patty.

(He smiles lamely and reaches for her as if to soothe her as she goes to get her bag. She groans, punches his arm, and goes. He stands alone for a long time before moving slowly over to the sewing machine. He clutches a pillow and gently rocks himself as he begins to cry.)

LIGHTS FADE TO BLACK.

94

SPIKE HEELS
by Theresa Rebeck

The Characters: Andrew (35), sincere, quiet, friendly and Georgie (late 20's), volatile, bright. Georgie and Andrew are friends.

The Setting: Andrew's apartment, present

The Scene: Georgie has stopped by Andrew's apartment after work.. She is extremely agitated and angry about her new job. Andrew tries to get her to talk.

ANDREW: Maybe you should sit down and tell me what's going on.

GEORGIE: Yeah, and maybe you should go fuck yourself. *(Pause)* I'm sorry, okay.

ANDREW: Are you okay?

GEORGIE: Yes! No. Christ. I'm sorry, I'm sorry. *(Pause. They stand for a moment in silence. Andrew crosses and puts his arm around her. She leans against him.)*

ANDREW: What happened at the office?

GEORGIE: I don't know. You got anything to drink around here? I mean, could I have a drink?

ANDREW: Do you want some tea?

GEORGIE: Tea? Are you kidding? I mean, is that supposed to soothe me or something? I hate to break the news to you but I really think that that is like, just a myth, Andrew. I think that in reality vodka is far more soothing than tea.

ANDREW: I don't have any vodka.

GEORGIE: Bourbon works too.

ANDREW: I have half a bottle of white zinfandel.

GEORGIE: Oh, Jesus. Make me tea. *(He exits to the kitchen. Georgie crosses, picks up the gym shorts and puts them on. Andrew reenters and sits her on the couch.)*

ANDREW: All right. Now tell me what happened.

GEORGIE: Nothing happened. I mean, it's stupid.

ANDREW: *(Pause)* That's it? It's stupid? You can talk for hours about absolutely nothing. And now all you have to say about something that is clearly upsetting you is, it's stupid.

GEORGIE: I feel stupid.

ANDREW: What are you talking about, you feel stupid? You just walked in here and insulted me for ten minutes.

GEORGIE: That was different. I was mad.

ANDREW: You have to be mad to talk?

GEORGIE: No, come on -- I don't know --

ANDREW: I could make you mad.

GEORGIE: No, you couldn't. You're too nice.

ANDREW: Fuck you.

GEORGIE: Andrew

ANDREW: Fuck you. Come on, Fuck you.

GEORGIE: *(Calm)* Yeah, fuck you too.

ANDREW: Fuck you.

GEORGIE: Fuck you.

ANDREW: Fuck you.

GEORGIE: You look really stupid saying fuck you --

ANDREW: Fuck you. Fuck you! Fuck you.

GEORGIE: *(Laughing, Overlap)* Andrew, stop it. Cut it out. It sounds weird when you say it. You shouldn't talk like that.

ANDREW: You talk like that all the time!

GEORGIE: I'm different. I mean, I know how to swear. You don't. It's like, fuck you. Fuck you. Or, you know, fuck you. It's just - you know, You got to know how to say it.

ANDREW: Fuck you.

GEORGIE: Forget it. You look really stupid. You look the way I look when I try to talk like you.

ANDREW: You've tried it? Really? I must have missed that day.

GEORGIE: Oh, fuck you. You know I can do it; I can be as snotty and polite as anybody and it just makes me look stupid.

ANDREW: Georgie, it doesn't. You just -- look. The English language is one of the most elegant and sophisticated languages on earth, and it will let you be whatever you want. It's poetic and clinical, rich and spare -- it can describe the spirit of God hovering over the face of the deep, or it can explain to you how to change a spark plug. See? The English language is a gift that humanity has given itself to describe the world with grace and wonder, and you can do that. Or you can use it badly and just be what you say you are. You can just be a fucking -- cunt, if that's all you ever --

GEORGIE: UGGH. I can't believe you used that word. Oh, my God. You should see these words coming out of your mouth. It's so fucking weird. I'm not kidding, Andrew. I wouldn't swear if I was you.

ANDREW: Forget it. You want that fucking tea?

GEORGIE: No. I don't want the fucking tea.

ANDREW: You want to tell me what happened?

GEORGIE: Oh, God. It really is stupid. I mean, what do you think happened? He wants to screw me is what happened. *(Pause)*

ANDREW: Could you elaborate on that?

GEORGIE: What, you don't know what that means?

ANDREW: He propositioned you or he tried to rape you or what? You have to be more specific; "screw" covers a lot of ground.

GEORGIE: Well, in his own weird little way he tried both, okay?

ANDREW: *(Pause)* Georgie, don't kid around with me now --

GEORGIE: Just sit down, Andrew. He didn't lay a hand on me, he just -- Look. Last week he tells me we have to talk about my future with the firm so we go out to dinner and he tells me how amazing I am and I could be a paralegal if I keep this up. I spilled my soup, I got so excited. So then he took me home and asked if he could come up, and I said sorry, but I would like to keep our relationship professional. See, I do know how to talk like you assholes when I want to, so you can just stop acting like I'm a fucking idiot with words.

ANDREW: So he propositioned you.

GEORGIE: Last week, that was last week. Yesterday, he had me stay late, right? He says, Georgie, could you stay late and type up some interrogatories. And I say, sure. Then after everybody's gone he invites me into his office and asks me if I know his couch folds out into a bed. So I say I have to get to work, Edward. But he wants to have a debate about the pros and cons of whether or not I should screw him. It was amazing, it went on for 20 minutes. I am not kidding. So I finally said, Edward, I don't have to debate this with you. I don't have to be polite, you know? I'm not going to fuck you. So he says, he doesn't have to be polite either and he could just rape me if he wanted because everybody else is gone and the security guard isn't due until ten. And I stared at him -- and, you know, I could see it in his little lawyer's face; he could've done it. *(Pause)* I mean on the one hand, it was no big deal; I just walked out of the office and took the stairs, cause I wasn't going to wait for any elevator. I mean, I was scared, but I didn't think he was going to do anything because it was pretty clear that in his own sick little mind, just saying it was as good as doing it. What a weirdo.

ANDREW: You went to work today? You went to work after that?

GEORGIE: That job means a lot to me! *(Pause)* What was I supposed to do, just quit and go back to -- fuck, I don't know -- I mean -- I don't want to go back and be a waitress! What was I supposed to do? Quit, because Edward is an asshole? I didn't care, I didn't think he'd he'd try it again! I didn't; I thought that was it!

ANDREW: Wasn't it?

97

GEORGIE: Today, he comes out of his office at about 4:30 and asks me to stay late to type a pleading. And he kinda looks at me, you know? So I said, fuck you, Edward, and threw my pencil at him.

ANDREW: *(Pause)* Why didn't you tell me? Dammit. Why didn't you tell me last night?

GEORGIE: He said something, it was something he said.

ANDREW: He said something *worse?*

GEORGIE: No. No. It was just talk. You know. It was just talk. I just -- I didn't want to make a big deal about it.

ANDREW: It *is* a big deal. It's indecent. It's a big deal. *(He paces angrily.)*

GEORGIE: Andrew. You're mad. I've never seen you mad.

ANDREW: Yes, I'm mad! I'm mad! We'll sue him for harrassment. We'll take him to court.

GEORGIE: What, are you kidding? He'll kill us. He's a really good lawyer.

ANDREW: I don't care. Dammit. Goddammit!

GEORGIE: You want some tea?

ANDREW: No, I -- *(Pause)* I'm sorry. I shouldn't be yelling at you.

GEORGIE: It's okay. I mean he didn't really do anything. It was just talk. Okay? let me make you some tea.

(She goes into the kitchen. Andrew prowls the room angrily for a moment, then picks up the phone and dials. Georgie reenters with the tea.)

GEORGIE: Andrew what are you doing? You're not calling him, are you? Don't call him, okay? Andrew. I mean it.

ANDREW: *(Into phone)* Hello, Jennine? It's Andrew. Is Edward around? Yeah, could you?

GEORGIE: *(Overlap)* Andrew, I'm not kidding. Could you put the -- would you put the fucking receiver down? Oh, FUCK. *(She crosses and pulls the cord out of the wall. They stare at each other for a moment, startled.)* What, did you think I was kidding? Did you not understand that I was saying I do not want you calling that asshole? Do you not understand English?

ANDREW: *(Picks up the ends of the phone cord, angry.)* Have you lost your mind?

GEORGIE: No, I have not lost my mind! What the fuck kind of question is that? I asked you nicely to put the phone down. It was your little macho choice to keep on dialing, so don't go acting like I'm insane. I just don't want you talking to him right now! I don't need you doing some sort of protective male thing here! Just for a minute, okay? *(Pause)*

ANDREW: Okay.

SPIKE HEELS
by *Theresa Rebeck*

The Characters: Andrew (35), sincere, quiet, friendly and Georgie (late 20's), volatile, bright.

The Setting: Andrew's apartment, present

The Scene: Andrew has gotten Georgie, his upstairs neighbor and friend, a job as secretary to his buddy Edward. She has just told him that Edward repeatedly propositioned her. He is furious. She was extremely angry but has calmed down. She tries to calm him down.

GEORGIE: Okay. Let's talk about something else. Here's your tea. Chop those vegetables. Let's talk about - - books. That'll cheer you up.
ANDREW: Georgie - -
GEORGIE: No, come on, you're always beating me over the head to talk about books. I finished the one you gave me. *(She pulls a book out of her purse. They talk nervously.)*
ANDREW: Already?
GEORGIE: It was good; it was a good read, you know? Reminded me of, like, Sydney Sheldon. A lot happened.
ANDREW: *The Iliad* reminds you of Sydney Sheldon. Great.
GEORGIE: Yeah, it would make a great mini series, you know? We should try the idea out on my sister; she's like the expert on junk TV. No shit, she lies around this apartment in the Bronx all day and - - come on, Andrew, help me out here. I'm sorry, okay?
ANDREW: It's okay.
GEORGIE: What else you got? *(She picks up a book from the table. He takes it from her.)*
ANDREW: No, you can't have that. I'm using that.
GEORGIE: Oh, Right. Right! How's your book coming?
ANDREW: It's fine.
GEORGIE: You should let me help you with that. I mean, I'm out of work now. I could come down and plug it into your computer for you. No kidding, I'm fast. I'll type it up for you; you'll be done in a week.
ANDREW: Right.
GEORGIE: I could, I could help! I mean as long as you're going to do this Pygmalion thing, you might as well get something out of it.

99

ANDREW: Do what?

GEORGIE: Isn't that what it's called? Pig something? I heard Edward -- uh -- you know, I heard that guy we both can't stand right now tell one of the partners you were playing this pig game. So I asked Donna about it. Some guy wrote a whole book; I bought it.

ANDREW: George Bernard Shaw.

GEORGIE: Yeah. I mean, it didn't exactly hit me as being the same thing here --

ANDREW: It's not the same thing. It's not the same thing at all. Edward doesn't know shit, okay? *(He takes the vegetables into the kitchen.)*

GEORGIE: *(Calling)* Well -- okay, he doesn't know shit, but I thought there were similarities. And, you know, the whole point of the book is she teaches him things, too, so I just thought --

ANDREW: *(Reenters with washcloth and begins wiping off coffee table.)* It's not the same thing.

GEORGIE: Then what is it? *(Pause)* I mean it. What is this?

ANDREW: What is what?

GEORGIE: This. This. All the dinners and the books and the lessons and the job. What is this, anyway? We been doing this for like, six months or something, you know? I mean -- what's going on here, Andrew?

ANDREW: Georgie. We can take him to court.

GEORGIE: No. I'm not talking about him. I'm talking about this. What is this?

ANDREW: It's friendship.

GEORGIE: Friendship.

ANDREW: Yes.

GEORGIE: You're sure about that.

ANDREW: Yes.

GEORGIE: You get that mad whenever anybody fucks around with your friends, huh?

ANDREW: Yes. *(She looks at him. Suddenly, she crosses and sits very close.)* What are you doing?

GEORGIE: Nothing.

ANDREW: Georgie --

GEORGIE: I'm not doing anything. I'm just sitting next to my friend here with hardly any clothes on.

ANDREW: Come on. Don't do this. Please?

GEORGIE: Just once, Andrew. Don't you want to try it just once? Really. Don't you, kind of.

ANDREW: I don't think a one-night stand is what you're looking for.

GEORGIE: Fine. We'll do it twice. She'll never know.

ANDREW: She's not the one I'm worried about. Georgie -- oh, boy. Look, you're upset about what happened with Edward --
GEORGIE: Do I look upset?
ANDREW: But this isn't going to fix that --
GEORGIE: I don't need to be fixed. Come on, Andrew, let's just do it today. I had a bad day. I'm not upset -- but I had a bad day.
ANDREW: Georgie -- no -- If I-- I would be just as bad as him if I - I'm not going to take advantage of you like that.
GEORGIE: Fuck, yes, take advantage of me. Please. Don't be noble, Andrew. For once, don't be noble.
ANDREW: Georgie, sweetheart --
GEORGIE: Andrew. She's going to be here in half an hour. We don't have a lot of time to talk about this. *(She slides her arms up around his neck. Protesting, he tries to pull her away. She resists and they wrestle for a moment; Andrew finally gets her turned around and holds her in front of him with her arms crossed under his.)* Okay, okay, if you don't want to, just say so-
ANDREW: It's not that I don't want to! *(Pause)* I want to, all right?
GEORGIE: You do?
ANDREW: Yes. Oh, yes. *(He buries his face in her hair for a moment. She waits, uncertain.)*
GEORGIE: Okay. *(Pause)* Are we waiting for something?
ANDREW: It's not that simple.
GEORGIE: Trust me on this one. It is that simple. *(She pulls away; he holds her.)*
ANDREW: Not fifteen minutes ago, you were on a rampage; you were ready to murder me and every other man you've ever met. Now you want to make love?
GEORGIE: Sex is kind of spontaneous that way.
ANDREW: It's not what you want.
GEORGIE: I'm pretty sure it is.
ANDREW: Please, listen to me. Will you please listen? *(She nods. He releases her. Pause)* All right. Nietzsche talks about the myth of eternal return.
GEORGIE: Oh, come on. Don't do this to me --
ANDREW: Thomas Hardy, historical repetition.
GEORGIE: Don't do this to me, Andrew -- we don't have much time here.
ANDREW: *(Overlap)* What history teaches is that people have never learned anything from history. Hegel. History is a nightmare from which I am trying to escape. James Joyce.
GEORGIE: *(Overlap)* This is your fucking book. I don't want to hear about your stupid book now!
ANDREW: You better want to hear about it, because I'm not

talking about my stupid book, I'm talking about your life. Historical repetition. One man treats you bad so you fall in bed with another. God. The system eats up people like you and spits them out like chicken bones; it always has. You end up in dead end jobs, crummy apartments, bad neighborhoods, too many drugs, too much alcohol, meaningless relationships. They don't give you anything to live for, so you live for nothing! I'd see you around the building yelling at the doorman or the janitor, and God knows you were insufferable, but it seemed so clear to me that the reason you were pissed off all the time was because you were just bored. And frustrated. Desperate. And you didn't even know it. I know, you see that all the time on the street, in the subway, and there's nothing you can do about it. Only it makes me sick, okay? What are we doing? We're killing ourselves because -- because we don't believe in simple things, knowledge, compassion. decency -- simple human decency, we don't even understand it anymore! So nothing changes. The rich keep doing it. And the poor disappear; they die, they become peasants. That's what was happening. You were disappearing, and I couldn't stand to watch it.

GEORGIE: What does this have to do with whether or not we go to bed?

ANDREW: I will not become just another one of your lovers. We're both worth more than that.

GEORGIE: I didn't mean --

ANDREW: Relationships *mean* something. People *mean*. You don't sleep with every person you're attracted to; that's not the way it works. And aside from the crucial fact that I'm not about to betray Lydia, who I love, I'm not going to betray you. You want to know what this is? I am not your friend, okay? I am your teacher. And you don't sleep with your teacher; it screws up everything. You don't do it.

GEORGIE: I had a geometry teacher who came onto me in the tenth grade.

ANDREW: Did you ever learn anything from him? *(Pause)*

GEORGIE: Fine. Okay, fine. I mean, I just wanted to sleep with you. I didn't want to threaten world history, you know.

ANDREW: Georgie. It's not that I don't want to.

GEORGIE: No, it's fine, I don't care, I shouldn't of -- I'm no better than Edward, am I?

ANDREW: No. You are.

GEORGIE: What's Lydia like? Is she like you? I mean, is she gentle, like you?

ANDREW: I guess so.

GEORGIE: Edward is so full of shit. You know, he told me -- he told me the reason he came onto me was because you told

102

him to.

ANDREW: What?

GEORGIE: Yeah. I mean, I didn't believe him. Because it was so creepy, and you're not -- I mean, you're so Not That, but it just made me sick to hear it, you know?

ANDREW: *(Pause)* What did he say?

GEORGIE: I don't know. He said you told him I was on the make or something and he should -- you know? Then today when I got here, you said you talked to him, so I thought -- I mean, I didn't want to think about it, but I'm sorry. I just -- I got freaked out. I'm sorry.

ANDREW: It's okay.

GEORGIE: What a creep.

ANDREW: Yeah. *(Long Pause)* It's getting late. We should - get going on this dinner. (He picks up the dishrag and crosses slowly to the kitchen. She watches him for an awful moment.)

GEORGIE: *(Quiet)* Andrew?

ANDREW: What?

GEORGIE: What did you say to him?

ANDREW: What?

GEORGIE: *(Pause)* Oh, no. When I got here you said you talked to him. What did you say?

ANDREW: I said -- I liked you. That was all I said.

GEORGIE: That was all?

ANDREW: Yes! I mean, no I -- of course, we talked about other things, but it wasn't anything -- it wasn't --

GEORGIE: Why are you getting so nervous?

ANDREW: I'm not nervous! I'm trying to remember the conversation. He said -- he wanted to ask you out, and I said I thought that would be okay. I told him you might be -- I told him I thought you might need someone in your life, you seemed -- Look. I thought you were getting a kind of crush on me, so it might be good for you --

GEORGIE: You gave me to him?

ANDREW: No. That's not what I did.

GEORGIE: What the fuck would you call it? Why was he asking your permission to go out with me in the first place? Am I like your property or something and he has to get your permission --

ANDREW: Georgie, no; it was a misunderstanding. He thought there was something going on between us and he just wanted to know --

GEORGIE: Something going on. Some *thing*, huh? Christ, Andrew. I am in love with you.

ANDREW: *(Pause)* I'm sorry. I didn't know.

GEORGIE: You didn't know? How could you not know?

ANDREW: Please believe me, if I had known, I never would have said --

GEORGIE: You never would have said what? You never would have said Go ahead, take her? You never would have said that, huh? I can't believe you. You -- you're just the same as the rest of them, aren't you? *(She picks up her bag and goes to the door quickly, furious.)*

ANDREW: No! That's not -- Georgie, you're upset, you're not being fair, you're not thinking --

GEORGIE: Don't talk to me about fair, just don't even start!

ANDREW: Don't walk out. We have to talk about this, Georgie

(He grabs her elbow. She slaps him hard. They stare at each other.)

GEORGIE: Fuck that, Andrew. You don't like my language, and I don't like yours. I'm sick of talking, you know? You know what I mean? You guys -- for all you know, you don't know shit.

(She exits. Blackout.)

THREE BIRDS ALIGHTING ON A FIELD
by Timberlake Wertenbaker

The Characters: Biddy (30's) a wealthy woman, Mr. Mercer (30-50) a dealer in human organs, and Ahmet (any age) a Turkish organ donor.

The Setting: A doctor's office, the present.

The Scene: When her husband suffers from kidney failure, Biddy endeavors to buy him a new one.

A doctor's office. White walls, an antique bust. Mr. Mercer and Biddy.

BIDDY: I thought I'd come first. And then I can convince him that it will be simple and comfortable. *(Mr. Mercer nods.)* He couldn't stand a machine, you know. He doesn't like- well, the insides of a body, the mess. He's very clean, very private. Very discreet. *(Mr. Mercer nods.)* But if he can just go to sleep and wake up completely well. *(A silence. The doctor looks through some notes, as doctors do.)*
MR. MERCER: I have one coming in that would match.
BIDDY: Oh, that's wonderful.
MR. MERCER: Of course, I would have to see your husband.
BIDDY: Oh, yes. Is it terribly expensive? You see if I paid for it myself, it would - well, the decision would have been made. I have quite a lot of money at my disposal, I was going to buy a painting, but I can do that later.
MR. MERCER: You like art? So do I. I collect antique statuary. And you?
BIDDY: I'm just starting.
MR. MERCER: I have a good contact if you go for the Med.
BIDDY: The Med?
MR. MERCER: *(Points to his bust.)* That sort of thing. Cradle of civilization.
BIDDY: Oh, yes, yes... *(A silence.)*
MR. MERCER: The kidney itself costs two thousand five hundred pounds.
BIDDY: Is that all? I mean - well. But, will it be a good - I mean, at that price...I'd be willing to pay more, if there's a better one going, you know. *(A pause.)* Is it English?
MR. MERCER: I'm afraid not, Mrs. Andreas. You can only get

an English kidney when somebody dies in an accident and then it goes straight to the National Health. The relatives are usually happy to give the organs away. There's a long queue for kidneys and the National Health favours young people, whereas I suppose you could say private medicine favours useful members of society like your husband.

BIDDY: So these - euh - come from...

MR. MERCER: Somebody who is quite happy to give a kidney away, at a price of course. It may not be such a good idea to have someone who lives in this country, in case they change their minds. That would be awkward. Having to get it back. *(He laughs. A silence.)*

BIDDY: Where does the - euh - it come from?

MR. MERCER: We get them from Turkey. But I assure you they come from very healthy specimens. I have a long list, Mrs. Andreas, if you would prefer to wait...but I can't guarantee anything, I just happen to have this one coming in. Today.

BIDDY: Do you have it here? I mean, euh...

MR. MERCER: I have the man over here. He can be operated on in a few days and we will give it straight away to your husband, who should then be able to lead a healthy life for years to come.

BIDDY: This man, he's all right, is he? I mean, he's not a criminal? I'm sorry, I know so little about medicine, I suppose it doesn't matter, it's not the brain, is it? It's just that - Well, yes, fine. I couldn't - euh - meet him? I'd feel better. *(A pause.)* I'm afraid otherwise I couldn't, I simply wouldn't be sure...

MR. MERCER: It's unusual, but I suppose you can, he's in my waiting room. The operation itself is only one thousand, but seven days in hospital, fifteen hundred pounds a night for a private room, that will be - *(He takes out a calculator.)* fourteen thousand. You only need deposit half of that. Nonreturnable if you change your mind as we have to save the room.

BIDDY: I understand. Of course. *(She takes out her cheque book.)* Who do I make it out to? I mean, do I make out two cheques, one for the - euh - ?

MR. MERCER: No, we take care of all that.

BIDDY: It isn't very much for a kidney, is it?

MR. MERCER: It's the going rate. There are lots of them about. *(Mr. Mercer goes to call Ahmet. Biddy looks at the ancient bust. Mr. Mercer comes back in, sees this.)* That comes from Turkey too. But it's unique. And very expensive. There are two more by the same sculptor and my obsession is to find them. Get them. I dream about it at night. Touch it, Mrs. Andreas. *(Biddy touches it.)* You have touched the antique world, the

106

mid-morning of civilization. A sculptor moulded these features more than two thousand years ago, a sculptor who spoke to Plato, who fought Sparta, who knew Alcibiades.

BIDDY: I see, yes. It's very smooth. Doctor, I must ask you one thing.

MR. MERCER: I don't know who the model was, a young soldier I think. Here's Ahmet. *(Ahmet, a young Turk, comes in. He is clearly baffled and does not understand much or any English.)* Ahmet, this is Mrs. Andreas. Your kidney is going to be given to her husband. *(Ahmet nods, smiles, bows.)* You understand? Your kidney. *(Ahmet smiles.)*

BIDDY: It's - euh - very kind of you, I mean, well, we're very grateful.

AHMET: No problem. No problem.

MR. MERCER: And Mrs. Andreas is giving you the money for your mother. The money.

BIDDY: Yes, I hope it's - euh, well - I'm very pleased to meet you. *(She stretches out her hand. Ahmet seizes it and kisses it.)* I hope you don't mind the operation. My husband is frightened. *(She mimics fear by miming cold.)*

AHMET: No problem for Ahmet. Yes. No problem. *(They all smile.)*

MR. MERCER: Good boy. *(Ahmet laughs.)*

AHMET: Yes. Yes.

BIDDY: He's very sweet. *(To Ahmet.)* I hear Turkey is very beautiful. Beautiful. *(She points to her eyes. Ahmet looks in panic at Mr. Mercer, shakes his head and covers his eyes with his hands.)*

MR. MERCER: No, Ahmet, only one kidney. *(He points to his side, ushers him out.)* He thought you wanted his eyes as well.

BIDDY: He does understand what he's doing?

MR. MERCER: Oh, yes, he's signed the form.

BIDDY: Mr. Mercer, when you speak to my husband, please don't tell him the - the - euh - the kidney - is Turkish. You see, he is Greek, and you know, the history of the Ottoman domination, well, he takes it personally. He might reject a Turkish organ.

THROWING YOUR VOICE
by Craig Lucas

The Characters: Doug, Richard, Lucy and Sarah: 4 politically correct yuppies in their 30's.

The Setting: A dinner party, the present.

The Scene: Following dinner, two couples rehash the socio-political climate of the world.

DOUG: *(Overlapping, continuous)* Would you buy coffee from Colombia if you knew - - *(To Lucy)* Where is this coffee from?
LUCY: D'Agostinos.
DOUG: If you knew people had died... culling it.
LUCY: Harvesting.
SARAH: No, I suppose ...
RICHARD: But wait.
LUCY: Culling?
RICHARD: *(Overlapping, continuous)* Wait, wait.
LUCY: Dougie, you always do this. It was so peaceful here.
DOUG: We're not having a bad time. Are we?
SARAH: No.
RICHARD: No.
LUCY: But you're gonna make all the people feel bad. They're gonna go home--
DOUG: No, they're not.
LUCY: --feeling guilty and defiled, sorry they're Americans.
RICHARD: But. I just ... Here's my point.
LUCY: Okay.
DOUG: Okay.
RICHARD: If people were responsible for their own actions alone ...
DOUG: *(To Lucy)* No one's unhappy.
RICHARD: If the soldiers who went to Iraq--
DOUG: I understand.
RICHARD: --were wholly responsible for their going there and I didn't feel any responsibility whatsoever.
DOUG: But you're saying that you do.
RICHARD: Yes, I do. But I'm also--I'm saying that's stupid. Even if I agreed that it was entirely wrong for them to go there which ... I don't know about --
DOUG: You don't.

108

RICHARD: No. But let's say ... I voted for George Bush and I supported the war ... totally ...

DOUG: Okay.

RICHARD: I still ... in an existential way ... don't think I should be responsible for someone else's actions. *(Pause)*

DOUG: Would you invest in South Africa?

RICHARD: I already have.

DOUG: What do you mean?

RICHARD: That's probably where ... I mean, I don't know, that's probably where Sarah's ring is from. I didn't ask when I bought it, I was all of twenty-two.

DOUG: Uh-huh.

RICHARD: But .. I've read that most diamonds, new diamonds come from there. *(Pause)*

DOUG: Well, okay.

LUCY: It is okay, don't say it like that.

RICHARD: I also read that ... people are killed in the diamond mines. Children. It's horrible. And I didn't know. What are we supposed to do.

DOUG: Would you buy ivory?

RICHARD: No. But I also wouldn't throw away *old ivory* if I had it.

DOUG: You wouldn't?

RICHARD: No.

DOUG: Why?

RICHARD: Because I think the damage is already done.

DOUG: But then you're saying there is damage.

RICHARD: No--

DOUG: *(Overlapping)* I caught you! You admit--

RICHARD: *(Overlapping)* No, I'm saying, *if* there's damage, if you're right, which I don't agree with--

DOUG: You do and you don't, you mean.

LUCY: *(To Sarah, quietly, indicating Doug with her head.)* Arlan Specter here.

RICHARD: The damage, you've already paid for the ivory or the diamond or--

DOUG: But if you keep it and treat it as if it's precious, somebody else could sell it someday, thus contributing to the ivory market, thus contributing rather directly to the slaughter of elephants.

RICHARD: Well, I think that's kind of ... a long chain of command.

DOUG: But it is that. You're still in command. You sell that diamond some day, if it's from South Africa--

RICHARD: Oh, come on, look--

LUCY: Doug. *(Pause)*

DOUG: What? *(Pause)*

RICHARD: I think ... when you boycott a nation, the entire economy suffers. Including the poor people. *(Silence. The music has ended.)* And I don't think ... because I buy a diamond

LUCY: *(To Doug, very quietly)* You did this.

RICHARD: *(Overlapping)* I mean, first of all it's the only thing I've ever bought that's worth anything.

DOUG: Fine.

SARAH: *(Overlapping)* Don't get defensive.

RICHARD: I'm not. Have you ever even taken it off, though? In twelve years?

SARAH: No.

LUCY: That's very romantic.

SARAH: And I ... I'm not sure I could get it off now that I'm all swollen.

RICHARD: Well, you may have to when the baby comes, because we're gonna probably need the money.

SARAH: Ohhhh.

RICHARD: I mean ... *(To Doug)* Is that what we should do?

DOUG: No, Richard.

RICHARD: If ... Here. If I'd known for certain ... people had died in the mining of this diamond. A little thirteen year old black girl ... who had to work in the kitchen of some mine ... and she stole a sliver of a diamond to pay for her .. sick ... parents ... and was beaten for it ... beaten to death. *(Pause)* Should I get rid of the diamond? Not sell it because that would contribute to the diamond mine?

DOUG: I--

RICHARD: Should we just ... throw it in the gutter? *(Pause)*

LUCY: I think everybody's--

DOUG: *(Overlapping)* I wouldn't presume to tell you--

RICHARD: Where are your *shoes* from, Doug? Where was this wonderful meal grown? Do you know? Do you check all the labels?

DOUG: No.

LUCY: *(To Sarah, shaking her head quietly)* This always happens. *(Pause. No one moves. Sarah's head makes a sudden, sharp little turn.)* What? Are you okay? *(Sarah nods.)*

Section II

Scenes for
Women

CRIMINAL HEARTS
by Jane Martin

The Characters: Ata (30's) a romantic agoraphobic and Bo (30-40) a burglar.

The Setting: An expensive condo in Chicago, the present.

The Scene: When Bo breaks into Ata's condo, she is surprised to find it empty of all save Ata. As the two women struggle for control of the situation, we can see that they are both in trouble.

ATA: *(Out of sleep)* What? Hello? *(Silence)* Oh, my God. Who's in here? Somebody's in here. Oh, my God. Don't hurt me. Don't kill me. I have eighty dollars, but I don't know where my purse is. I could write you a check. Tell me your name, and I'll write you a check. *(Silence)* I have jewelry, but it's dumb stuff. I was robbed last year, they got the jewelry. You can have my jewelry, though. I'll give you my jewelry and the eighty dollars. *(Silence)* Listen, I'm frightened, I'm very frightened, I'm suppressing a scream here.
BO: Shut up—
ATA: Oh, my God. Oh, my God. You are in here.
BO: Yeah, I'm in here. I want you to shut up.
ATA: I've got a gun.
BO: Bullshit.
ATA: I do. I have a gun. A big gun.
BO: You don't have a gun. I have a gun.
ATA: My husband gave it to me. It's a thirty-seven. Police thirty-seven.
BO: Turn on the light.
ATA: Don't hurt me, I have herpes.
BO: Turn on these lights. I'm counting to three here.
ATA: I can't.
BO: You can't what?
ATA: I have a problem.
BO: So?
ATA: I freeze. I freeze with fear.
BO: Get outta here.
ATA: All my life. My nervous system shuts down. It's called kinetic hysteria. I'm in therapy.
BO: I don't give a goddamn if you're in therapy, turn on the lights!

111

ATA: Don't shoot. Don't shoot. I'll tell you where it is.

BO: What is?

ATA: The switch.

BO: I can't believe this.

ATA: To the left of the door.

BO: What door?

ATA: The front door.

BO: Lady, I don't fuckin' live here, I'm sneakin' around in the dark.

ATA: If you're facing the bed. . .wait. . where exactly are you?

BO: Will you turn on the light!

ATA: *(Begins to make sounds preliminary to screaming.)*

BO: O.K., O.K. I'm below the bed.

ATA: If you could see how I'm shaking, and I'm clammy, I'm very clammy.

BO: And I'm below the bed.

ATA: On a clock, if you're facing the twelve, the door to the living room would be at 8:30.

BO: I'm facing which number?

ATA: The twelve.

BO: To my left. O.K., I'm going. *(Cans kicked over)* What the fuck is this. Are you screwing with me?

ATA: It's nothing. Keep going.

BO: How far?

ATA: Ummm. Eight feet. Well, maybe ten feet.

BO: I'm going to fall over like some little table and kill myself?

ATA: No.

BO: *(More cans)* Damn it. Okay, doorway. Listen, I turn on this light I want no noise. *(She feels around.)* O.K. There is no switch here at any height.

ATA: Left of the door?

BO: Nowhere. None.

ATA: As you come in.

BO: I'm not coming in, I'm going toward! Jesus, okay now. I don't want noise. No noise, You hear me?

ATA: Yes, yes I do. *(Bo turns on the light. The apartment is barren. All furniture gone except the mattress. The walls have been stripped of decoration. Ata is like a squatter in a luxury apartment.)* Don't hurt me, don't hurt me, don't hurt me, don't hurt me.

BO: *(Looking around)* Gimme a goddamn break! What the hell is this? What the hell is going on here? *(Ata opens her eyes. She sees Bo, a burglar in her late 30's dressed in jeans and a black T-shirt. She has a pistol, now pointed at Ata. She has a cast on her wrist.)* Hey, you. . .

ATA: You're a woman.

BO: Yeah, right. Where the hell's the stuff, the goods?

ATA: I'm a woman. We're women.

BO: V.C.R., silver, lap-top, television, videocam, I'm talking negotiables here.

ATA: Women shouldn't shoot each other. Men shoot each other. Women relate.

BO: Stuff, where's the stuff, the goods, the items?

ATA: That's a question, I can tell you that.

BO: Right.

ATA: But, I'm... actually I can't... I'll, I'll tell you where's the stuff, I'd like to, but the gun is making me itch.

BO: You have negotiable stuff, I know that.

ATA: I have stress allergies, I pass out ...I just...you know, out, flat gone. I have a suspect nervous system... Wait! Wait, I know you, I do, yes... oh, God... why do I know you?

BO: Because I've seen your goddamn stuff, lady. I'm not some geek I go in cold, like on the off-chance it could be worth my while, right?

ATA: At the deli? No. No.

BO: Sit there. Don't even blink. *(She moves toward the door leading to the rest of the apartment.)*

ATA: Smoke alarms!

BO: *(After a quick look out the door)* Un-fuckin'-real.

ATA: You were here about smoke alarms, that's right, isn't it?

BO: Yeah. Where's your life, lady? Where's your furniture, for instance?

ATA: We have a relationship. I told you about my marriage. I confided in you. You admired my decor. We exchanged.

BO: I cased you out. Right. Now I'm back for the stuff, O.K.?

ATA: I'm more than an object to you. I'm a dimensional person who feels pain and fear. I'm a woman, I have breasts. Don't shoot me.

BO: Hey! Downstairs I have guy with a truck, get it? He's a professional, O.K.? I'm supposed to hop on down the fire escape, tell him, "Guess what? The bitch has Dr. Pepper and pizza, come on up help me load it out?"

ATA: He did that. He did that. That is exactly... I can't believe you said that. He... he... I was... I went to work... Oh, I'm Ata, Ata Windust. Hi.

BO: Get away from me!

ATA: Sorry, sorry... but, he... I don't know... rented a truck, I'm at work, bam, cleans me out... the apartment, furniture... the stuff.

BO: Who?

ATA: Wib.

BO: Wib?

ATA: My... my, uh... whatsit, whatsit... words. Husband, husband. My husband had the truck.

BO: Your husband is Wib?

ATA: Wib, yes, he's Wib. Was. Well, still is but probably will be was. Husband, I mean. He'll still be Wib.

BO: He took everything but the mattress?

ATA: Mainly, almost. Yes. All of it. Paintings,rugs, corkscrew. *(A sudden rage)* Stop pointing that gun at me! I'm sorry. I'm sorry.

BO: You got jewelry?

ATA: This, this, my wedding ring.

BO: I don't want your fucking wedding ring. I want your jewelry.

ATA: Took it, took it, gone.

BO: Cash?

ATA: Eighty dollars. My purse. There.

BO: Credit cards.

ATA: He canceled them. Well, I have my mother's VISA, but it might be expired.

BO: *(Seeing an object on the floor)* What's this thing?

ATA: It's a battery-operated pencil sharpener.

BO: I oughta fuckin' shoot you for wasting my time.

ATA: *(A blood-curdling scream)* Brent, no!!

(Bo, completely taken aback, whirls around looking behind her. Ata throws herself at Bo, who caught off-guard, is knocked to the floor, they wrestle clumsily.)

BO: Ow! Shit. O.K., Ow.

ATA: Yes, yes, yes, yes, yes...oh, my God.

BO: Hey!

ATA: Yes...

BO: Gimme that. . .

ATA: Yes!! *(Ata, through luck and adrenaline, comes up with the gun.)*

BO: Son-of-a-bitch.

ATA: Yes! I have a gun, I have a gun, I have a gun!

BO: Right, O.K., watch it, watch it!

ATA: You watch it, you watch it. Back. Go on. I could kill you, I could kill you a million times. I could pull this trigger, I could stab you, I could gouge out your eyes, I could eat your flesh!

BO: The trigger...watch the trigger.

ATA: Do you have any idea how angry I am? Deeply, deeply emotionally angry? Coming in here, violating my space? Turning me into an animal? Yes, yes, an animal. That is what you have done to me. I'm a human being not an animal do you understand that?

114

BO: The trigger, the trigger.

ATA: I have problems do you hear me? I have more problems than I should demographically have. And you have pushed me, kicking, screaming, over the edge, and I could cheerfully and without second thought see you bleeding on the floor... is that clear to you?

BO: I get it, O.K., I got it. Look in my eyes here, right? You're pissed off. Good. You should be pissed off, take your finger off the trigger.

ATA: I'm flipped out, do you see that? This is a suprarational state, a fragmentation, a reality-declining-perceptual-veer and you can only pull me out of this by proving to me that you are a human being and you have about three seconds.

BO: The trigger!

ATA: One, two...

BO: Kids. I have kids.

ATA: Their names.

BO: Yolanda, Gitch, Sarah?

ATA: Sarah?

BO: Sarah Claire.

ATA: You have a girl named Sarah?

BO: Yeah.

ATA: I don't want you to have a Sarah. Don't tell me you have a Sarah. I have a Sarah. I had to leave her at my mother's. Oh my God, you have a Sarah. *(She starts to cry.)* I have problems. I have an empathy problem. I hate this. You are making me cry. I'm in control here because I have the gun, is that right?

BO: Yeah.

ATA: All right. I'm in control. This isn't something just happening to me. This is my movie.

BO: Absolutely.

ATA: Tie yourself up.

BO: Tie myself up?

ATA: Fast.

BO: You are fuckin' nuts, lady.

DANCING AT LUGHNASA
by Brian Friel

The Characters: Maggie (38), Agnes (35), Rose (32) and Chris (26); four sisters struggling to make ends meet in prewar Ireland.

The Setting: The home of the Mundy family, Ballypeg, County Donegal, Ireland, 1936.

The Scene: The flavor of daily life in the Mundy household may be sampled in the following conversation occurring in the kitchen.

Maggie makes a mash for hens. Agnes knits gloves. Rose carries a basket of turf into the kitchen and empties it into the large box beside the range. Chris irons at the kitchen table. They all work in silence. Then Chris stops ironing, goes to the tiny mirror on the wall and scrutinizes her face.

CHRIS: When are we going to get a decent mirror to see ourselves in?
MAGGIE: You can see enough to do you.
CHRIS: I'm going to throw this aul cracked thing out.
MAGGIE: Indeed you're not, Chrissie. I'm the one that broke it and the only way to avoid seven years bad luck is to keep on using it.
CHRIS: You can see nothing in it.
AGNES: Except more and more wrinkles.
CHRIS: D'you know what I think I might do? I think I just might start wearing lipstick.
AGNES: Do you hear this, Maggie?
MAGGIE: Steady on, girl. Today it's lipstick; tomorrow it's the gin bottle.
CHRIS: I think I just might.
AGNES: As long as Kate's not around. 'Do you want to make a pagan of yourself?'
(Chris puts her face up close to the mirror and feels it.)
CHRIS: Far too pale. And this aul mousey hair. Need a bit of colour.
AGNES: What for?
CHRIS: What indeed. *(She shrugs and goes back to her ironing. She holds up a surplice.)* Make a nice dress that, wouldn't it?... God forgive me... (*Work continues. Nobody speaks. Then*

116

suddenly and unexpectedly Rose bursts into raucous song:)
ROSE: 'Will you come to Abyssinia, will you come?
    Bring your own cup and saucer and a bun...'

*(As she sings the next two lines she dances - a gauche,
graceless shuffle that defies the rhythm of the song.)*

    'Mussolini will be there with his airplanes in the air,
    will you come to Abyssinia, will you come?'

not bad, Maggie - eh?
(Maggie is trying to light a very short cigarette butt.)
MAGGIE: You should be on the stage, Rose. *(Rose continues
to shuffle and now holds up her apron skirt.)*
ROSE: And not a bad bit of leg, Maggie - eh?
MAGGIE: Rose Mundy! Where's your modesty! *(Maggie now
hitches her own skirt even higher than Rose's and does a similar
shuffle.)* Is that not more like it?
ROSE: Good, Maggie - good - good! Look, Agnes, look!
AGNES: A right pair of pagans, the two of you.
ROSE: Turn on Marconi, Chrissie.
CHRIS: I've told you a dozen times: the battery's dead.
ROSE: It is not. It went for me a while ago. *(She goes to the
set and switches it on there is a sudden, loud three-second blast
of "The British Grenadiers'.)* You see! Takes aul Rosie! *(She
is about to launch into a dance - and the music suddenly dies.)*
CHRIS: Told you.
ROSE: That aul set's useless.
AGNES: Kate'll have a new battery back with her.
CHRIS: If it's the battery that's wrong.
ROSE: Is Abyssinia in Africa, Aggie?
AGNES: Yes.
ROSE: Is there a war there?
AGNES: Yes. I've told you that.
ROSE: But that's not where Father Jack was, is it?
AGNES: *(Patiently)* Jack was in Uganda, Rosie. That's a
different part of Africa. You know that.
ROSE: *(Unhappily)* Yes, I do ... I do... I know that..
*(Maggie catches her hand and sings softly into her ear to the
same melody as the "Abyssinia" song:)*
MAGGIE: 'Will you vote for De Valera, will you vote?
    If you don't, we'll be like Gandhi with his goat.'
(Rose and Maggie now sing the next two lines together.)
    Uncle Bill from Baltinglass has a wireless up his -
(They dance as they sing the final line of the song:)
    Will you vote for De Valera, will you vote?'

117

MAGGIE: I'll tell you something, Rosie: the pair of us should be on the stage.

ROSE: The pair of us should be on the stage, Aggie!

(They return to their tasks. Agnes goes to the cupboard for wool. On her way back to her seat she looks out the window that looks on to the garden.)

AGNES: What's that son of yours at out there?

CHRIS: God knows. As long as he's quiet.

AGNES: He's making something. Looks like a kite. *(She taps on the window, calls 'Michael!' and blows a kiss to the imaginary child.)* Oh, that was the wrong thing to do! He's going to have your hair, Chris.

CHRIS: Mine's like a whin-bush. Will you wash it for me tonight, Maggie?

MAGGIE: Are we all for a big dance somewhere?

CHRIS: After I've put Michael to bed. What about then?

MAGGIE: I'm your man.

AGNES: *(At window)* Pity there aren't some boys about to play with.

MAGGIE: Now you're talking. Couldn't we all do with that?

AGNES: *(Leaving window)* Maggie!

MAGGIE: Wouldn't it be just great if we had a - *(Breaks off)* Shh.

CHRIS: What is it?

MAGGIE: Thought I heard Father Jack at the back door. I hope Kate remembers his quinine.

AGNES: She'll remember. Kate forgets nothing. *(Pause)*

ROSE: There's going to be pictures in the hall next Saturday, Aggie. I think maybe I'll go.

AGNES: *(Guarded)* Yes?

ROSE: I might be meeting somebody there.

AGNES: Who's that?

ROSE: I'm not saying.

CHRIS: Do we know him?

ROSE: I'm not saying.

AGNES: You'll enjoy that, Rosie. You loved the last picture we saw.

ROSE: And he wants to bring me up to the back hills next Sunday-up to Lough Anna. His father has a boat there. And I'm thinking maybe I'll bring a bottle of milk with me. And I've enough money saved to buy a packet of chocolate biscuits.

CHRIS: Danny Bradley is a scut, Rose.

ROSE: I never said it was Danny Bradley!

CHRIS: He's a married man with three young children.

ROSE: And that's just where you're wrong, missy - so there! *(To Agnes)* She left him six months ago, Aggie, and went to

118

England.

MAGGIE: Rose, love, we just want -

ROSE: *(To Chris)* And who are you to talk, Christina Mundy! Don't you dare lecture me-

MAGGIE: Everybody in the town knows that Danny Bradley is

ROSE: *(To Maggie)* And you're jealous, too! That's what's wrong with the whole of you - you're jealous of me *(To Agnes)* He calls me his Rosebud. He waited for me outside the chapel gate last Christmas morning and he gave me this. *(She opens the front of her apron. A charm and a medal are pinned to her jumper.)* 'That's for my Rosebud,' he said.

AGNES: Is it a fish, Rosie?

ROSE: Isn't it lovely? It's made of pure silver. And it brings you good luck.

AGNES: It is lovely.

ROSE: I wear it all the time - beside my miraculous medal. *(Pause)* I love him, Aggie.

AGNES: I know.

CHRIS: *(Softly)* Bastard.

(Rose closes the front of her apron. She is on the point of tears. Silence. Now Maggie lifts her hen-bucket and using it as a dancing partner she does a very fast and very exaggerated tango across the kitchen floor as she sings in her parodic style the words from "The Isle of Capri".)

MAGGIE: "Summer time was nearly over;
Blue Italian skies above.
I said, "Mister, I'm a rover.
Can't you spare a sweet word of love?"

(And without pausing for breath she begins calling her hens as she exits by the back door:) Tchook-tchook-tchook-tchook-tchook-tchook-tchook-tchookeeeeee

(Michael enters and stand stage left. Rose takes the lid off the range and throws turf into the fire.)

CHRIS: For God's sake, I have an iron in there!

ROSE: How was I to know that?

CHRIS: Don't you see me ironing? *(Fishing with tongs)* Now you've lost it. Get out of my road, will you!

AGNES: Rosie, love, would you give me a hand with this *(Of wool)* If we don't work a bit faster we'll never get two dozen pairs finished this week.

ESCAPE FROM HAPPINESS
by George F. Walker

The Characters: Nora (50's the off-center matriarch of dysfunctional family and her three daughters: Elizabeth (30's, Mary Ann (20-30) and Gail (20's).

The Setting: The worn down kitchen of an old house in the east end of a large city, the present.

The Scene: When Gail's husband is beaten up by thugs, the sisters gather at their mother's house and their conversation reveals their fear and hatred of their father as well as their inability to communicate.

(Mary Ann and Elizabeth appear at the screen door.
MARY ANN: Is he gone?
GAIL: Yes.
ELIZABETH: Go check.
GAIL: I just did. He's gone to his room. For the night.
ELIZABETH: Go make sure.
MARY ANN: Go make sure he's not listening at his door. That he's actually going to bed.
GAIL: No.
ELIZABETH: Go check, Gail.
MARY ANN: We're not coming in until someone goes up there and tells us he's in his bed.
NORA: Please, Gail. We need them to come inside. We need to talk together as a family. We can't talk about the things we need to talk about through the screen door.
ELIZABETH: Look, we're not staying out here indefinitely. We're leaving.
MARY ANN: She's right. We're leaving. Or we're coming in. But we're only coming in if someone actually goes up there and checks him out.
NORA: *(To Gail)* Please, dear.
GAIL: Unbelievable. *(She goes out.)*
NORA: This should only take a second. How are you both?
ELIZABETH: Fine.
MARY ANN: I'm okay, Mom.
NORA: How's your daughter, Mary Ann?
MARY ANN: She's great, Mom. She missed you. She said to give you a kiss. She said, 'Give gwamma a beeg kiss.' She said, 'I miss gwamma. I want gwamma.'
ELIZABETH: Shut up!

120

MARY ANN: That's what she said.
ELIZABETH: She said 'gwamma'?
MARY ANN: Yeah.
ELIZABETH: Well, she's four years old. Teach her how to say it properly.
(Gail comes back.)
GAIL: He's in bed. he wants split pea.
ELIZABETH: He wants what?
GAIL: Soup. He likes soup. That's basically all he likes.
NORA: You can come in now. *(They come in. Elizabeth heads for the telephone. Takes a pad from her briefcase. Punches in her code. Writes down her messages.)* Will you make his soup for him, Gail?
GAIL: That's what I'm doing, Mom. That's why I opened the cupboard. That's why I took out this can.
NORA: *(To Elizabeth)* Junior usually makes his soup. But Junior- But, well, Junior ... You better tell them, Gail.
GAIL: I told them already, Mom. I called them and told them. That's why they're here.
MARY ANN: Where's your daughter?
GAIL: Upstairs. Asleep. Where's yours?
MARY ANN: At home. What do you mean? She's at home, of course. She's asleep, too. What do you mean, Gail? What were you getting at?
GAIL: Nothing. Relax. You asked about mine. I asked about yours.
NORA: That's what sisters do. They ask each other things. It's great. I always feel great when you're all together asking each other things. Telling each other things. I can't tell you how it makes me feel.
GAIL: Sure you can. It makes you feel great.
ELIZABETH: How come Dad only eats soup? Is he getting worse?
GAIL: Yeah.
MARY ANN: Has he seen a doctor lately?
NORA: Now, why would Gail want to talk about that. Talk about a man who, to be kind about it, may or may not be her actual father, when her actual husband is lying in the hospital fighting for his life.
MARY ANN: His life? *(Elizabeth hangs up the phone.)*
GAIL: No. He's all right. He's going to be all right. Broken arm. Ribs. Cuts and stuff. Mom, why do you do that? Make outrageous exaggerations like that.
NORA: To get attention, perhaps. To bring the truth into focus. To provide a starting point for conversation. Something to be agreed with or disagreed with. To get things rolling.

121

Something like that. Tea anyone? Sit down. Everyone sit down. Except you, Gail. You just continue making the man upstairs his soup. And make sure you serve it at just the right temperature. I know you will, though. I know you deeply respect his needs. *(To Mary Ann)* She deeply, deeply respects his needs ... for some reason.

MARY ANN: She feels sorry for him, Mom.

ELIZABETH: Yeah, Mom. She's like you that way. She has sympathy for the diseased and dying.

GAIL: He's my father.

ELIZABETH: So what? He's my father, too. And do you see me taking care of him? I'd like to throw him off the fucking roof.

MARY ANN: You see, Mom, we all feel our own way about him. Elizabeth hates him. I'm afraid of him, and Gail feels sorry for him. And that's okay. It has nothing to do with you. It's not directed at you. Any of it.

NORA: He's in my house. He eats my food. Uses my furniture. And my bathroom. Occasionally sleeps in my bed.

GAIL: By accident.

NORA: So she says. But, well, I'll give her that one. That one is too distressing to discuss in detail. We'd have to explore the darkest part of human sexuality.

ELIZABETH: We can have him moved out, Mom.

MARY ANN: We can find a home for him.

NORA: You'd go to all that trouble? And expense? You're wonderful people. So compassionate. To extend yourself so badly for a total stranger.

ELIZABETH: Mom, please.

NORA: I know. I know. That man upstairs says he is your father. And you all have a tremendous inner need to believe him.

ELIZABETH: And you have a need to not believe him. We respect that, Mom.

MARY ANN: We agreed to that, Mom. We agreed to let you not believe. And you agreed to let us believe.

NORA: But from an historical perspective, Mary Ann-it's hard. You see, historically, your actual father deserted us and left us in a wretched hole of poverty and debt. And then ten years later a man just ... showed up. The man upstairs. Why? Whoever he is, why is he here? It's a simple question. But the answer could be historically terrifying. It scares me. I can't sleep. I'm thinking of taking pills. Lots of pills.

GAIL: Oh, stop it. You're fine. You don't see him much. You never talk to him. You can deal with it. He stays. I want my kid to know her grandfather. I want her have roots.

NORA: Okay. Forget it. I'm fine ... if she says so-

ELIZABETH: *(To Gail)* Whatya mean roots? She doesn't need roots from that jerk. He's her grandfather, but he's slime.

MARY ANN: Anyway, she's got us. We're her roots.

GAIL: You're never here.

MARY ANN: We're here.

GAIL: You sneak in at night for a few minutes. Give Mom a hug, then piss off. When's the last time you saw Gwen?

MARY ANN: Who's Gwen?

GAIL: Gwen's my daughter's name, you asshole.

MARY ANN: Please be nice to me. I've made so much progress in the last few months. I'm a much stronger, more independent person. But I believe my strength and independence are entirely dependent on people being nice to me. So does Clare.

GAIL: Who's Clare.

ELIZABETH: Her therapist.

MARY ANN: My friend ... My therapist and my friend. Mom. I have something to tell you.

GAIL: Not now. *(To Elizabeth)* Please don't let her get started.

MARY ANN: I have knowledge. It's important knowledge, and I want to share it with my mother. With you too, Gail.

GAIL: No. Look. I guess you guys have forgotten why I called you. We're in a bit of trouble here. You know. Junior. The crooks. The cops.

ELIZABETH: Don't worry. I'm looking into it. I've called my contacts on the police force.

NORA: I thought everyone on the police force hated you, dear.

ELIZABETH: Most of them do, I guess. Ignorant, Neanderthal bastards can't take a little constructive criticism.

NORA: *(To Gail)* Elizabeth has recently been publicly critical of the attitudes and practices of the police in several sensitive areas.

MARY ANN: We know, Mom.

GAIL: She's a first-class shit-disturber.

MARY ANN: We're all real proud of her.

GAIL: Right. But now we've got to-

ELIZABETH: Don't worry. When I've got time I'll call my contacts back. See what they found out.

MARY ANN: Mom. Gail.

GAIL: When you've got time?

MARY ANN: Gail. Mom. Listen. I have to share this knowledge with you. I've always shared my knowledge with you. All of you.

ELIZABETH: And that's what's made us the people we are today.

MARY ANN: Elizabeth is a lesbian.
ELIZABETH: What?
MARY ANN: You're a lesbian. And you're proud of it. And I'm proud of you for being proud. And now Mom and Gail can be proud of you, too.
ELIZABETH: Mary Ann, what are you doing?
MARY ANN: I'm outing you.
NORA: What, dear?
MARY ANN: I'm outing her. She's been in the closet. I'm helping her get out. She's a lesbian. Say it loud and clear. She's a lesbian. She's a lesbian! Clare told me to do it. Someone did it to Clare, and it was the best day of her life. So I'm doing it to you. Elizabeth. You're a lesbian. You have sex with women. Lots of women. Lots and lots of women. Right?!
ELIZABETH: *(To Nora and Gail)* Let's talk about Junior.
NORA: We went to see him in the hospital.
GAIL: There were two cops guarding his door. I mean, come on-they think he's some kind of criminal mastermind.
NORA: I'm worried, Elizabeth. The beating was unprovoked. Junior was alone here. They broke in and beat him for a reason Junior doesn't know.
ELIZABETH: Or isn't telling.
GAIL: He doesn't fucking know. Okay? We got that straight? We can move on from that?
ELIZABETH: Yeah. Okay. He doesn't know.
MARY ANN: *(Pointing at Elizabeth.)* Lesbian!
ELIZABETH: Look, what's your problem.
MARY ANN: It won't work unless you admit it. Admit it, and let us all hug you and love you. Lots and lots and lots.
ELIZABETH: If I admit it, do you promise not to hug and love me lots and lots and lots.
MARY ANN: Whatever.
ELIZABETH: Okay.
MARY ANN: Say it.
ELIZABETH: I'm a lesbian.
MARY ANN: Tell Mother.
ELIZABETH: Hey, Mom. I'm a lesbian.
NORA: I know, dear.
ELIZABETH: She knows.
MARY ANN: She knows? For how long?
ELIZABETH: Forever, you silly cow. You're the only one in this family who didn't know.
MARY ANN: Why? Why am I the only one who didn't know? Why? Tell me.
ELIZABETH: Guess.
MARY ANN: No. Tell me. Why didn't you tell me? How come

Clare had to tell me?

ELIZABETH: Your therapist told you I was a lesbian?

MARY ANN: Yes. Clare told me. She says you're famous in lesbian circles. You're a famous lesbian. She told me to be proud of you. So I am. Not that I wasn't before. But now I am, too. But more so.

ELIZABETH: Why? Why more so?

MARY ANN: Because it was hard.

ELIZABETH: What was hard?

MARY ANN: Being a lesbian.

ELIZABETH: Get another therapist. One who will concentrate on your problems.

MARY ANN: Wasn't it hard?

ELIZABETH: Your life's falling apart. You've been a basket case for almost twenty years, and you sit around talking to your therapist about me ... Amazing ... Now tell them. Stop talking about me, and tell Mother and Gail what's new with you.

MARY ANN: Not yet.

ELIZABETH: Tell them. Or I will. And I won't make it all sad and gooey like you will.

MARY ANN: I'm leaving my husband.

GAIL: Again?

MARY ANN: I have to. I'm at a crossroads. How many times does a person come to a crossroads?

GAIL: If they're like you, about every three months.

NORA: What about your daughter? Is she with Barry?

MARY ANN: Larry. Yeah. He loves her. He'll be good to her. He understands my needs. He understands me.

GAIL: Great. Maybe he could explain you to us.

ELIZABETH: He doesn't really understand her. I asked him once. Actually, I begged him. I begged him to explain to me what makes her tick. He just shook his head and whistled. And then he made the sound of a loon.

MARY ANN: You should talk to Clare. She could explain me to you. She explained me to me ... Okay. This is the thing. I'm a kindred spirit of all the victims of the women's holocaust. A once powerful gender-species decimated by the religious patriarchy because they were terrified of their feminine strength.

GAIL: What the hell is she talking about? And why is she talking about it now!

ELIZABETH: *(Smiles. To Mary Ann.)* A witch. Are you saying you're a witch?

MARY ANN: I would have been a witch if the witches hadn't been decimated. *(To Nora)* The way it is now, I don't belong anywhere. I'm at a crossroads, though. I'm ready to belong somewhere. And the thing is, I've always admired Elizabeth so much. Elizabeth has always been my strength. So I'm thinking maybe I'll become a lesbian, too.

ELIZABETH: You see, that's why I never told you. I knew you'd pull some kind of wacky shit like this. This is not something you choose.

MARY ANN: I think you might be wrong. Clare showed me some statistics.

ELIZABETH: All right. It's something you shouldn't choose. I made a choice. But all your choices are wrong. So you shouldn't choose!

MARY ANN: That's not fair!

GAIL: (Suddenly bangs the pot of soup down on the stove, hard.) Okay! That's it. That's enough! I mean, come on. Junior's in the frigging hospital. And there are cops swarming all over our lives here.

NORA: Mary Ann. I don't like saying this, but you leave me no choice. You could go to hell and rot there for eternity if you don't stop deserting that child of yours.

MARY ANN: I'm not deserting her. I'm at a crossroads!

GAIL: (Bangs the pot.) Hey! Shut up! Shut the fuck up! I didn't call you here to listen to this garbage!

MARY ANN: It's my life!

GAIL: Your life is a joke! (She starts to bang the pot over and over again.)

ELIZABETH: Okay!! Okay!! That's enough!! I haven't got much time I've got three court appearances tomorrow, a letter to the editor I have to write, and a poor, sick bastard I'm trying to get committed! I'm very, very busy! Let's deal with this Junior thing, whatever it is.

GAIL: You're always very, very busy. I'm just asking a little advice from you. If you can't spare the time to help your family, get the hell out!

ELIZABETH: Listen, kid. Watch your attitude. I'm here, aren't I?

MARY ANN: And so am I!

NORA: But that could be a mistake, Mary Ann. You're here. But is there somewhere else you should be instead. Perhaps somewhere in the vicinity of the innocent, little child you brought into this world.

MARY ANN: Please, Mom. Don't keep doing this. You have no right to say those things to me.

(Gail throws her arms up. She goes to the table. Sits. Puts her head down.)

ELIZABETH: She's your mother. She's just expressing an opinion.

THE EVIL DOERS
by Chris Hannan

The Characters: Susan (15) a self-obsessed heavy metal fan, Tracky (15) her best friend, and Agnes (30-40) Tracky's alcoholic mother.

The Setting: Glasgow, the present.

The Scene: When Agnes, an alcoholic, makes a rare public appearance, she is greeted by the ungracious Susan, who wastes no time in reminding Agnes of an embarrassing incident. The scene evolves into a frustrating confrontation between mother and daughter.

Enter Agnes Doak. She's still young, thirty-six, and when she can be bothered she cares about how she looks, or worries about how she looks. Considering she's come from her work, and considering she went to her work in an alcoholic blackout, she looks good. The initial impression - clothes and accessories - is of individuality - interesting splashes of colour - though a keener eye might see that this effect is partly accidental. The second impression is that of a worrier. The way she seems to be carrying too much stuff, coat, bag, shopping, etc. And as she anxiously checks her appearance, she notices a scorch mark on her new good cream-coloured coat which she's never seen before. Just when she's got herself presentable, she panics. Drink. Into the shoulder-bag, out with a wee quarter bottle of whisky, takes a ladylike mouthful, then another, and puts it back. Susan enters.

SUSAN: Mrs. Doak. It's me. Tracky's pal. Susan.

AGNES: Susan. Oh I never recognized you, darlin'. Susan?

SUSAN: Oh Mrs. Doak, I can't tell you how I feel! I don't think Tracky approves but *(Tracky!):* she's not very in touch with her feelings. Because he's utterly gorgeous. And he really like listens to me, which is, because you know what men are like: they listen to you for about fifteen seconds and then they think you're dead self-centered.

AGNES: Susan?

SUSAN: Susan MacAlindon. I saw you last Saturday. Remember? That was the night you set yourself on fire.

AGNES: *(Mildly indignant)* Nobody mentioned that to me.

SUSAN: I smothered the flames with your new good coat.

AGNES: Oh well ... I won't hold it against you. (Use an old

127

blanket next time, will you, pet.) - It's Sammy I'm looking for, have you seen him?

SUSAN: You're pure voodoo, Mrs. Doak, how did you know Mr. Doak was here?

AGNES: I phoned him.

SUSAN: Aw.

AGNES: Has he fallen out with me? I had a wee night last night - *Tracky's* pal, of course I know you! (What am I thinking about?) - and when I woke up this morning I was at my work (Belvider Hospital?) What a fright I got, waking up with my plastic gloves on! - and I must've been hard at it because the toilet pan was shining.

(Tracky enters.)

TRACKY: Mammy! Susan! What are you doing here?

AGNES: I've come to make it up with your Da. Will you be in for your tea, darlin'? I got some chinky ribs at the butcher's, your favourite.

TRACKY: Give the drink a chuck, Ma, will you?

AGNES: I will, darlin'. I have. That's what I came to tell your Da. I've stopped. No way: this carry-on?: and a memory like a ditch ... no idea what ...

TRACKY: *(To Susan)* If you're looking for Tex- I just seen him with a toolbox. Oh don't worry - I didn't talk to him.

SUSAN: It's not what you think, Tracky. What's so bad about that, I only want to bring two people together - she's got contacts in the music biz so think twice before you go and judge people because what about the time you lumbered me with Mongo Robertson -

AGNES: (School), Do they not teach you join your sentences up?

SUSAN: - and then Mongo called me a lezzy.

AGNES: It's like a pile-up on the motorway.

SUSAN: - just because he tastes like antiseptic? - so *that's* why I'm going. *(i.e. 'this explains my exit to look for Tex'. And she exits.)*

AGNES: Barbecue sauce. You like that, don't you?

TRACKY: Oh Mammy.

AGNES: It's you I get it for.

TRACKY: Did I used to be nice? Likes of, when I was wee. Was I nice then?

AGNES: What kind of question's that? All wee girls are nice.

TRACKY: Tell me then.

AGNES: Tell you what?

TRACKY: Tell me ... (About me.)

AGNES: ... (About you) ... You used to have a lovely pink all-in-one babysuit, I remember that. (Is that what you mean) You were a wee doll. They say all wee girls suit pink, of course, but then you had the fair hair too.

TRACKY: That's a lie! - did I?

AGNES: Yes! - did you not know that? - Then when you got up a bit, when we ever went out holidays, you were a terrible, terrible thoughtful wee girl - is that the time? - soon as you got money first thing you thought was to get your Daddy a present. Oh you loved your Daddy! Every day for a fortnight, we'd lie back on the beach and you'd go off and come back with something else.

TRACKY: What like?

AGNES: Oh for goodness sake, Tracky ... a lot of rubbish likely. You were only eight. - How did you, sleep OK last night? *(Beat)*

TRACKY: See if my Daddy asks you for money, don't give him it, right? Because he's got to face facts.

AGNES: What facts?

TRACKY: Just. He wants to think everything always turns out good in the end. Well it doesn't.

(Tracky goes, leaving Agnes mystified.)

INFIDELITIES
by Richard Zajdlic

The Characters: Linda (20-30) and Jenny (20-30), two women awaiting the return of their army husbands.

The Setting: A home in England, the present.

The Scene: Linda and Jenny discuss the upcoming return of their military husbands.

Jenny's house: Jenny sitting quietly. The doorbell buzzer sounds. Jenny jumps, startled.

JENNY: Christ. *(The doorbell sounds again.)* Little bastards. *(The doorbell sounds again. It rings a third time and stays pressed.)* Right. *(She opens the door.)* Just sod off, will you!
LINDA: *(Entering)* Sod off yourself, you cheeky cow.
JENNY: Linda! Sorry, I -
LINDA: Get in, will you! It's pouring-
JENNY: It's these kids. They keep ringing. I didn't think.
LINDA: Not your forte, is it.
JENNY: What are you doing here, anyway?
LINDA: Oh, that's nice. I'm doing you a favour, that's what. John phoned. They're going to be late. About an hour or so, he thinks.
JENNY: Oh. Right.
LINDA: He called me a few minutes ago. Been trying for ages, he said. Sure. And I'm Mel Gibson's love-toy.
JENNY: 'Least you got a call.
LINDA: Some problem of logistics they have to sort out at the barracks, apparently.
JENNY: Logistics?
LINDA: Oh. I don't know. Like as not he's got his fat nose in a pint at The Harrow. Savouring his last moment of freedom. Plucking up his courage to meet me.
JENNY: Yes.
LINDA: He always said the real war was living with me. That's why he became a soldier, he said. If he hadn't been trained to fight he'd never have lasted. Well, six months in Belize should've toughened him up.
JENNY: Bri hated it. He said in one of his tapes -
LINDA: Tapes?

130

JENNY: Yeah, you know, cassettes. Telling me what he's doing. What it's like.
LINDA: Bloody gorgeous, John says.
JENNY: It's lovely to hear his voice. If you close your eyes, you can imagine he's right next to you. Holding you close. *(Linda sticks her fingers down her throat and pretends to throw up. Jenny laughing.)* Oh, piss off. It's nice. It is! It was Bri's idea anyway. The tapes. Makes us feel less lonely in a way.
LINDA: John never feels lonely. Only when he's at home.
JENNY: That's horrible.
LINDA: I'm a horrible person.
JENNY: No, you're not. Not all the time.
LINDA: Ooh, you bitch!
JENNY: Bitch! *(They laugh.)* Didn't John write?
LINDA: Twice. Both times telling me what a great time he was having and how he didn't want to come home. Bastard.
JENNY: You love it really. Make me coffee, you.
LINDA: What did your last slave die of?
JENNY: Not doing what she was told.
LINDA: White, no sugar?
JENNY: Two sugars.
LINDA: Uh-Uh. Diet.
JENNY: I don't care. I want two sugars.
LINDA: I thought you wanted to be slim and beautiful for the big day.
JENNY: Big day. Big deal.
LINDA: *(With relish)* Big sex session!
JENNY: I wonder if they'll have changed at all?
LINDA: John won't have. Same socks as the day he set off.
JENNY: No. Changed. Different. That scares me sometimes.
LINDA: What?
JENNY: That when Bri comes back, all those new things he's done, people he's met - I get scared that he'll come back changed and that what we had won't be the same anymore.
LINDA: Don't be stupid.
JENNY: I'm not.
LINDA: It's been six months. It's bound to be a bit awkward at first.
JENNY: Linda?
LINDA: Yes? *(Pause)* What?
JENNY: I'm nervous.
LINDA: It's okay.
JENNY: I don't know why. I don't know what I'm going to say.
LINDA: You won't be doing much talking!
JENNY: I wish he wasn't in the army. When he's away, I get so lonely. I sit here, wondering what he's doing. Wondering if he's

131

thinking about me. If he's missing me.

LINDA: Tell him that.

JENNY: You know, last time, when he came back from Cyprus. It was like we had to get to know each other again. Like strangers almost. And really shy. We both were. So shy we ...

LINDA: What?

JENNY: We didn't even make love at first. We just fell asleep holding hands. When we woke up that way the first morning, I don't know why but I cried. Bri thought something was wrong but there was nothing wrong I just cried. *(Pause)*

LINDA: I envy you.

JENNY: Why?

LINDA: I don't know.

JENNY: I do. It's because you're a lot shallower than I am.

LINDA: You bitch! *(They laugh.)* You make the coffee, scumbag.

JENNY: Where are the girls?

LINDA: Round at their grandma's. For the rest of the day and night. So John's got no excuses. We can do it where we like and be as loud as we like. I quite fancy the kitchen table myself.

JENNY: Excuses?

LINDA: Oh, yeah. I mean, he used to be like a man possessed. I never even had time to say hello before I was dragged upstairs. Mind you, that was it, no action replays. If you missed it the first time ... but now, I have to drag him! Tell him how big he is. How wonderful. Yawn.

JENNY: You told me you loved it.

LINDA: I do. It's getting him started though. After that, well, when you're into it you can think about who you like, can't you? *(Laughs)* And believe you me, I'm not thinking about him.

JENNY: No?

LINDA: No. Are you joking? What's exciting about your husband? Well, do you? Think about Bri?

JENNY: Yes.

LINDA: Always?

(Jenny thinks, then grins and shakes her head. They both laugh.)

132

THE MISSOURI TRILOGY: PIE SUPPER
by Le Wilhelm

The Characters: June, Lavinia and Lelafaye, three young women assigned the task of snapping beans for the pie supper (17-21).

The Setting: The home of Mavis Clines in the Missouri Ozarks, summer, 1959.

The Scene: Lelafaye and June are moving to California. Lavinia is so desperate to join them that she'd do or say just about anything.

LAVINIA: I hate shelling peas. Give me the beans and let me do that for awhile.
LELAFAYE: I do wish you's coming to California, Lavinia.
LAVINIA: I'm going. I'm going one way or the other. Wait and see.
LELAFAYE: Maybe you and I could get in the movies. That's what I plan on doing.
JUNE: How could you two become actresses?
LELAFAYE: Why not?
JUNE: You don't know nothing about it.
LELAFAYE: What's to know? You just got to be pretty.
JUNE: That isn't all. You have to act. Remember all them lines.
LELAFAYE: I can do that. And I'm pretty. Don't you think I'm pretty enough to be an actress, June?
JUNE: Of course you are, Lelafaye.
LELAFAYE: If I make it in the movies, it'd be great. Can you imagine all the kids at the drive-in, sitting there having their Coca Colas and popcorn and doing what they do at the drive-in. *(Laughs)* And I'm on the screen. Can you imagine their faces?!
JUNE: If you do get in the pictures, I hope you can do something like "The Footprints of Jesus". Tha'd make Mom and Dad proud.
LAVINIA: I saw that. Momma took me to see that.
JUNE: Unhun. Maybe you can play Mary, the mother of Jesus.
LELAFAYE: Rather be Mary Magdalene.
JUNE: She's a bad woman.
LELAFAYE: Jesus forgave her. Told her not to sin anymore. She'd be fun to act.

LAVINIA: *(Oddly)* Wonder what would happen if someone got pregnant by an angel nowadays?

LELAFAYE: What?

LAVINIA: Got pregnant like Mary did.

JUNE: I don't think that'd happen, Lavinia.

LELAFAYE: I wouldn't want some angel telling me I was going to have a baby. Oh I want to do romantic movies. My dream is to do a love scene with Tab Hunter. Can you imagine that. He's a big, strong man. Wish we had men like that around here.

LAVINIA: He's on the cover of that movie magazine.

LELAFAYE: I got that one. Got them broad shoulders. Can you imagine doing a love scene with him? If I do, if I get in the pictures, I'll let Junie be my helper. Do my hair and help me with my fancy dresses.

JUNE: I'm not staying in California long. I'm going to get a job. Save money and come back here. I don't care if it rains or not.

LAVINIA: What do you want to come back here for?

JUNE: I like it here.

LAVINIA: There is a chance I might be going to California. Mother might be sending me out there with you all.

JUNE: Your mom would never let you go out there alone.

LAVINIA: Might.

LELAFAYE: How do you figure?

LAVINIA: I haven't had my time for the last two months.

JUNE: What?

LELAFAYE: Are you sick?

JUNE: Do you think -- Lavinia, you aren't going ... are you with child?

LAVINIA: Shh. *(Whispering)* You've got to promise not to tell.

JUNE: I didn't even know you's going out.

LELAFAYE: Have you gone to the doctor?

LAVINIA: No.

JUNE: Sometimes you miss. It don't mean you're pregnant cause you miss. I'm real sorry, Lavinia.

LELAFAYE: Who's the dad?

LAVINIA: I'm not sure.

LELAFAYE: *(Aghast)* You're not sure?

LAVINIA: God. God is the father of my baby.

JUNE: What?

LAVINIA: It's the truth. God's the father of my baby.

LELAFAYE: Huh?

LAVINIA: Like we was talking about a minute ago. Like with Mary. He came to me in the form of an angel.

JUNE: It's blasphemous to make up something like that. It's a

134

wonder we don't have hellfire and brimstone right now.

LAVINIA: I'm not making it up.

LELAFAYE: Oh, no one's going to believe that. No one. My God.

JUNE: Lelafaye, don't take the Lord's name in vain.

LAVINIA: It's the truth!

LELAFAYE: Lavinia.

LAVINIA: It is the truth. I swear it. I swear it's the truth. He came to me in the form of an angel. I never felt anything like it in my life.

LELAFAYE: What did it feel like?

LAVINIA: Like being in the presence of the Almighty God. It's like how you feel when you ask Jesus to save your soul and he comes into your body and makes you pure. It was like that. Only more. Much more.

LELAFAYE: What happened?

LAVINIA: Huh?

LELAFAYE: What did this angel do to you? How did he get you pregnant?

LAVINIA: He didn't do anything nasty. Just looked at me. Didn't say a thing. Just looked at me and when he looked, I knew that I was with child.

LELAFAYE: What did he look like?

LAVINIA: Handsome. Really handsome.

LELAFAYE: Yeah?

LAVINIA: Sort of looked like Tab Hunter. But all golden. Like Tab Hunter only better looking.

JUNE: Lavinia, you'll burn in hell for telling something like that.

LAVINIA: It's the truth.

JUNE: If it's true, you tell me why would God choose you. You're no better than anyone else.

LAVINIA: I thought about that.

JUNE: And?

LAVINIA: I figure God probably knows I should go to California. So he made me pregnant so Mom would send me away cause she'd be ashamed of me being in the way.

LELAFAYE: *(Understanding)* That ain't going to work, Lavinia. You tell that story about the angel coming, only place you'll get sent is to the insane asylum. That's where you'll go.

LAVINIA: I'm telling the truth. The God's truth.

LELAFAYE: Well, if you are, you better hope that kid of yours performs miracles. Cause if he don't, no one is going to believe you.

LAVINIA: You believe me, don't you June?

JUNE: No, Lavinia, I don't believe a word of it.

135

LAVINIA: I'll swear it's true. Swear it on a stack of Bibles.
LELAFAYE: Don't do that, Lavinia.
LAVINIA: I did see an angel. In my room. And I haven't had my time for two months. It's the God's truth.
JUNE: Shh. They'll hear you.
LAVINIA: Promise not to tell.
LELAFAYE: I wouldn't tell that story to anyone.
LAVINIA: June.
JUNE: Me, either. Shh.

MOVING
by Lee Klacheim

The Characters: Megan (23) a young woman contemplating abortion, and Diana (21) her best friend.

The Setting: A small apartment in New York, 1970.

The Scene: Affluent Diana has selected to strike out on her own. When Megan helps her to move into her tiny new apartment, she confesses that she is pregnant.

One room (two if you count the kitchen as a room) apartment in New York's Upper West Side. It is an old railroad flat. Not in the best of shape. It has just been carelessly repainted. The kitchen has old fixtures, a few cabinets, a bathtub, covered to be used for counter space. Windows looking out of the airshaft. Bleak. The room is filled with cardboard boxes. Signs of someone moving in. Also pieces of furniture in odd places. A table. Chairs. A nice wicker chair, which stands out in its crispness. Mattress, box spring, and a bed headboard are leaning against the wall. Bathroom door to bathroom off. Through the front door comes Megan Shea an "ample" young woman followed by Diana Schmidt, pretty, slight .... She carries a large box, as her glasses keep slipping off her nose. Megan sets her box down. Stands there to catch her breath. Opens the box to see what was inside. Pulls out one, two, three, four throw pillows. Then ... reaches in ... and pulls out a small palm plant. Puts it down.

DIANA: How many times have we moved this plant?
MEGAN: *(Comes over to look at it closely.)* Well, the first time was when I moved in with Peter after school.
DIANA: No! We moved you into that place on 110th Street first. Then we moved it to Peter's. Then you gave it to me because Peter didn't have any light.
MEGAN: *(Looks around at dark place.)* I don't think the plant's gonna do too well here.
DIANA: I'll get a "grow-lite". It'll be fine.
(Suddenly a blast of fire engine sirens . .. and truck sounds. They both stand ... frozen.)
MEGAN: Does noise affect plants?
DIANA: Oh, Meg. It'll be fine.
MEGAN: Did you know about that???

DIANA: It'll be fine, your plant will be fine!

MEGAN: I'm not worried about the plant. Can you live with that noise?

DIANA: It's just when there are fires.

MEGAN: Do you know how many fires there are near 113th and Amsterdam?

DIANA: How many things can I think about when I'm finding an apartment. This is my first apartment. I thought about location. And ... and .. room ... and ... light ... and quiet. *(She looks.)* So I got a small, dark, noisy apartment.

(They both laugh. Meg gives her a big hug.)

MEGAN: Congratulations! You saw my first apartment.

DIANA: It wasn't as bad as this.

MEGAN: Your floor is straight.

DIANA: *(Looks again.)* It's awful, isn't it.

MEGAN: It's not awful! It's not.

DIANA: What would you call it?

MEGAN: It's ... poverty. Millions of poor people live like this. How were you to know? *(Diana just shakes her head.)* I don't understand why you didn't get something better. If your mother knew you were living like this ... she'd have the check in the mail today.

DIANA: Oh noooo. Not my mother. She's big on self sufficiency.

MEGAN: What's the sense of having money if you don't use it?

DIANA: She uses it on herself. She feels it's bad for her children's character if they spend money they didn't earn. *(Laughs to herself.)* My mother never earned a cent in her life. It's her philosophy. If my father were alive ... and saw this place ... he'd take me by the hand ... drag me down to a substantial looking building in a safe neighborhood, pay the rent, and give me a blank check for anything else I might need.

MEGAN: Your mother should see this place. She'd change her philosophy.

DIANA: She'd never come here.

MEGAN: Well, maybe it's all for the best ... *(She looks around.)* Heyyy .. lookee here. A bathtub in the kitchen. A friend of mine had one of these on the Lower East Side. *(She lifts the lid.)* Must be weird bathing in the kitchen. You could use it for other things.

DIANA: My mother would fill it with rhododendron leaves.

MEGAN: You have a bathroom?

DIANA: Just a closet with a toilet.

MEGAN: *(Opens the door, looks.)* Geeze, that's even too small to take a shit in. I'll bet you can't even open a magazine in there.

DIANA: And there's no ventilation.

MEGAN: Do you plan to use it much? *(They giggle.)*

MEGAN: Why didn't they put the toilet out here, too? Whoever designed these places must have said ..."Ahh, it's for poor people ... they don't give a shit. Put the toilet where they can't use it!" Y'know, good design is as cheap as bad design!

DIANA: The windows are nice.

MEGAN: The windows?

DIANA: They remind me of a Hopper painting. The big windows, the moulding ...

MEGAN: *(Looks)* Oh, yeah. That's a plus.

DIANA: Megaaan ... you're supposed to be making me feel good about this.

MEGAN: Come onnnn. We all live like this. What's the big deal.

DIANA: I wanted my place to be special.

MEGAN: It is special. *(She steps on a roach.)*

DIANA: Oh no!

MEGAN: You didn't expect it to be that special! *(We hear a car horn beep repeatedly.)* Oh, God ... *(Runs to window, opens it and shouts.)* Be right down! I forgot about Peter. I'll run down.

DIANA: You might as well go with him. Thank him again for me ... he was a Godsend.

MEGAN: Nooo, I'll help you unpack. Be right back. *(She exits.)*

DIANA: *(Alone in room ... just looks around, shakes her head and lets out a deep sigh,)* Oh, God ... *(She then goes to a cardboard box to get to work. Opens it ... her eyes light up, as she pulls out a turntable phonograph. Puts it down. Pulls out speakers. She is excited. Looks around for a plug. She plugs it in. Plugs in speakers. Then ... looks frantically for box of records, opens a few boxes, then sees one marked "records" big as life.)* Smarty! *(She opens it, goes through it and pulls out a record. We hear the bagpipes and flutes and Eastern European folk music. Diana stands, takes a deep breath and proceeds to fling herself into a Yugoslavian folk dance. Megan enters, watches a second. Diana sees her and beckons.)*

DIANA: Come on ... join in!

MEGAN: You bet!

DIANA: Come onnn ... I'll show you the steps ...

MEGAN: Thank you, no!

DIANA: It's easy .. come on.

MEGAN: We have a lot of unpacking to do!

DIANA: Just one dance.

MEGAN: You dragged me to that folk dance class once ... and I made an ass of myself ... now ...

DIANA: You did not! You were terrific.

MEGAN: My boobs are too big to do those dances. It hurts.

DIANA: Yugoslavian women have enormous breasts.

MEGAN: Did you ever ask them if they hurt?

DIANA: That dance used to be just a dance for the men. But ... during the Second World War ... most of the young men were off fighting ... so, the women had to fill in. And they learned it ... and it became a dance for men and women.

MEGAN: No kidding.

DIANA: I mean ... women were never allowed to dance the men's dances ... it just shows how cultural cornerstones can change very rapidly because of something ... like a war ... and then ... you know ... it doesn't change back. Now, this is accepted as a dance of both men and women. And I'll bet if you ask a Yugoslavian about it ... they don't know why.

MEGAN: You'd have to ask an American anthropologist.

DIANA: I think it's interesting.

MEGAN: Oh, yes!

DIANA: Do you know, that in Yugoslavia .. the peasant women always walk in front of the men? You know why that is?

MEGAN: The men like to look at them.

DIANA: No, come on.

MEGAN: That's a good reason!

DIANA: During the War ... the roads were covered with land mines. So the women ...

MEGAN: ... walked ahead ... Terrific. Remind me not to go out with any Yugoslavian men.

DIANA: It's not a political thing. They don't dislike women.

MEGAN: Oh, no ... they just feel they're expendable.

DIANA: But it's not political. It's cultural. It's practical. The men are more necessary ... to ... to ... farm...to fight the wars ... so the women can afford to be risked, so that the society as a whole will continue.

MEGAN: Couldn't they send their dogs in front?

DIANA: Oh, Megan!

MEGAN: If a husband of mine ever asked me to walk in front of him to test for land mines ... I know what I'd do!

DIANA: You don't know what you'd do in another society.

MEGAN: Listen, women are second class citizens here, it doesn't mean that I have to put up with it!

DIANA: I don't want to get manipulated into a political discussion .. I just ...

MEGAN: Well, I don't want to get intimidated into a Yugoslavian folk dance!

DIANA: OK! You don't have to dance!

MEGAN: Thanks!

DIANA: Ohhh! *(Takes the needle off the record.)* Some day, Miss Shea ... I am going to teach you to dance. You don't know how freeing it is!

MEGAN: I don't need freedom. I need discipline. I have thirty-six pages of a novel at home in my refrigerator. If I wasn't so free, I'd have two hundred and thirty-six pages.

DIANA: What's it doing in your refrigerator?

MEGAN: It's in case of fire. It's fire proof. It's also there every time I want a Pepsi .. saying ... "Write me! Write me!"

DIANA: You indulge yourself. That's the problem. You could discipline yourself. You could be neat. You could be prolific. You just think you deserve to spoil yourself. It's a Catholic thing. I know a lot of Catholics like that. Their whole childhood is spent towing the line ... they leave home ... wham. Now I'm gonna do it my way.

MEGAN: Nuts. I was a slob Catholic. Never hung up my clothes. Late for Church. Spilled ice cream on my communion dress. I was this way before I knew what religion was. It's in the genes.

DIANA: Oh, Megan!

MEGAN: Everything doesn't have a sociological reason! Jesus! Let's unpack. *(She moves to a box, starts unpacking.)*

DIANA: *(Just looks at her.)* You OK?

MEGAN: Yeah. Let's get this done.

DIANA: *(She goes to Meg.)* Hey. Something's wrong.

MEGAN: Nothing's wrong. I just don't ... sometimes you exhaust me.

DIANA: Sometimes you exhaust me.

MEGAN: Fine. Let's unpack and lay off each other. *(Diana moves away .. stops. Starts to unpack. Megan bringing out a cup, drops it, breaks.)* Shit!

DIANA: *(Runs to her ... reaching for the broken cup.)* Don't worry about it! It's not ... *(Picking up piece)* too valuable.

MEGAN: Swell..

DIANA: My mother has closets full. *(They rise, each with some pieces in their hands. Diana nods to an empty box, they dump pieces in. Diana turning to go, she takes Meg's hand.)* Meg...

MEGAN: *(She just stands ... finally looks at her.)* What do you wanna know first?

DIANA: What do you want to tell me first?

MEGAN: First ... I think it's over with Peter.

DIANA: Oh, Meg.

MEGAN: Second. I'm pregnant. I've got an appointment for an abortion on Friday.

DIANA: Ohh, Megan ...

MEGAN: *(She crosses away ... looks out dirty window.)* Oh,

141

great. There's an old man over there flashing at me. Just what I need! *(She opens window.)* Creep!

DIANA: *(Joins Meg at the window.)* He's Puerto Rican. He doesn't understand.

MEGAN: He understands "creep!"

DIANA: I don't think he's flashing at you. I just think he undresses in the window.

MEGAN: Is that a Puerto Rican cultural custom?

DIANA: He was there when I saw the place. He's old. He doesn't know he's standing in a window.

MEGAN: Does he know his pants are down?

DIANA: Megan! I don't care about that man ... I wanna know about, Peter!

MEGAN: I told you ... I think it's over.

DIANA: Is it because you're pregnant?

MEGAN: No. He doesn't know.

DIANA: He doesn't know? Why not?

MEGAN: I didn't tell him.

DIANA: Why not?

MEGAN: Because, I don't want him to feel guilty about our breaking up. My being pregnant has nothing to do with us!

DIANA: *(Shakes her head and moves off, turns.)* What does it have to do with?

MEGAN: Me. I'm pregnant. I got pregnant. It wasn't a joint decision. It was an accident. So, I don't see why he should have to know. He doesn't want it. I don't want it. So ... the decision about it is made. Why should I bring it up and have it mess up the decision about us. Got it?

DIANA: Yes ... What ... what about the two of you?

MEGAN: I don't know ... Peter's a sweet ... lovely man. I just think maybe the thing's run its course. We were babies when we met. I was nineteen. He was twenty. It's been four years. We've grown. Maybe we've outgrown each other.

DIANA: Can you be more specific?

MEGAN: Well, he doesn't make me walk on land mines ...

DIANA: Megaan!

MEGAN: He's not enough-for me, now. I'm not a nineteen-year-old Barnard sophomore. I'm a twenty-three year-old waitress! With a thirty-six page novel in her refrigerator. Things aren't as easy as they were when all I had to think about was going to class occasionally and getting my papers in late. I gotta think about making a living. I gotta think about achieving something. I gotta think about what I want to do out there. I gotta deal with a lot of the shit that I looked forward to dealing with in the most naively, romantic way imaginable. I imagined that waiting on tables to help pay the rent might be a bit tedious

... but I didn't imagine that every waitress job I had, I'd have to fight off another lecherous boss.

DIANA: Did you tell Peter about all these ... bosses?

MEGAN: Sure.

DIANA: And.

MEGAN: The first time ... he was ready to go out like Lancelot and slay the son of a bitch. By the third time ... he just laughed. Hell, the problem isn't those creeps. I can deal with that. There's always another two weeks somewhere else ... The problem is I wanna move on. Peter was great for going on Peace marches with. And picnics to the Cloisters. But, he just disappears when I have real world problems. Vietnam he can deal with. Me ... is a problem. *(She wanders away, again to the window. Stops. Looks.)* I see what you mean. The man is cooking without his pants on. You think he's senile ... or just gets his jollies doing everything that way?

DIANA: Megan ... come on! *(Going to her.)*

MEGAN: Come on, what?

DIANA: Is it really unsalvageable? It's just ... Peter's such a sweetheart.

MEGAN: He is a sweetheart. But I'm past my sweetheart stage. *(Moves away, again.)* I think I'd like to fall in love with an adult.

DIANA: Don't you think maybe the pregnancy has ... distorted your feelings. You know, I think you should tell him. By not telling him, you're taking all the responsibility yourself. How can he be an adult if you don't give him the chance to be responsible?

MEGAN: This didn't happen yesterday. This has been going on for some time! *(Stops back at box.)* You want to put the dishes up there?

DIANA: No, no, no ... Let's just unwrap them and stack them. I wanna wash them all ... and I've got to scrub the shelves .. and line them with paper ...

MEGAN: This cup looks clean to me.

DIANA: It is clean to you.

143

THE SHALLOW END
by Wendy MacLeod

The Characters: Becca and Teresa, two rather morbid 13 year-old girls.

The Setting: A public swimming pool, the present.

The Scene: The ennui of summer vacation is here felt quite keenly by Becca and Teresa as they lounge at the community pool.

BECCA: He made me sit on the bench with these dorky 8 year olds. Did you see? I nearly died.
TERESA: It's just because he likes you.
BECCA: Oh sure.
TERESA: He does.
BECCA: He's in college.
TERESA: Six years difference. Big whoop. Monica's father married a woman 23 years younger than him.
BECCA: Poor Monica.
TERESA: She's really pretty. She wears a hairpiece.
BECCA: Monica hates her.
TERESA: Monica has an Electric complex.
BECCA: What's that?
TERESA: Honestly Becca, you are such a'tard.
BECCA: Why's Addie talking to Marjorie?
TERESA: She wants to meet the kid with the heart condition.
BECCA: What if they fall in love and he dies? That would be so romantic.
TERESA: I wouldn't want a boyfriend with a heart condition.
BECCA: Why not?
TERESA: What if you want to break up with him?
BECCA: I thought she liked Jerry.
TERESA: She may like Jerry but I doubt he likes her. She's a brain. Brains don't get boyfriends. They get A's.
BECCA: She says he looks at her all the time in 6th Period.
TERESA: She sits near the window. I sort of can't wait for Addie to go to Vermont.
BECCA: Same.
TERESA: I mean she's really nice and everything but she's too critical.
BECCA: I know.

TERESA: She's so judgmental.

BECCA: I know.

TERESA: She's about 10 pounds overweight too. She's approaching Marjoriehood. It's cause she eats all the time. She gets a Slurpee every day.

BECCA: So do I.

TERESA: That's different. You're super-thin.

BECCA: I'm flat.

TERESA: I'd much rather be flat than heavy.

BECCA: Me too.

TERESA: Would you rather be crucified or have your face smeared in dog doo?

BECCA: If I had to.

TERESA: Of course if you had to, you're not gonna do it for fun.

BECCA: What kind of dog doo?

TERESA: What kind of dog doo?

BECCA: No, what kind of doo? I mean, is it like diarrhea?

TERESA: Yes, yes it's diarrhea!

BECCA: Oh my God! Crucifixion!

TERESA: You are such a'tard.

BECCA: Why?

TERESA: Crucifixion kills you.

BECCA: Well how long would the doo be on my face?

TERESA: An hour.

BECCA: Well, you didn't say that.

TERESA: Did you think it'd be on there forever?

BECCA: I didn't know!

TERESA: Well you should get all the facts before you make your decision.

BECCA: I'll never have to make a decision like that.

TERESA: Unnhuh. My Dad says life is filled with tough choices. I'll give you another one.

BECCA: I'll give you one.

TERESA: Oh all right.

BECCA: Would you rather live in the lint filter screen of the dryer or be the Tidy Bowl man?

TERESA: That is so retarded.

BECCA: Why?

TERESA: Neither of those are bad things.

BECCA: Yes they are!

TERESA: But they're not gross.

BECCA: All right. You do one.

TERESA: All right. Would your rather have a sharp pencil puncture your ear drum or drink urine?

BECCA: Whose urine?

TERESA: Becca!
BECCA: What?
TERESA: Does it honestly matter whose urine?
BECCA: Well is it my urine?

(Blackout)

STAR DUST
by Elizabeth Gould Hemmerdinger

The Characters: Diana (40's) a well known actress, and Cordelia (20's) a disturbed young woman.

The Setting: An old house on the coast of Maine, the present.

The Scene: Cordelia arrives at Diana's summer house, which has recently been listed for sale, and claims to be a potential buyer. As their conversation progresses, it becomes clear to Diana that Cordelia is both mentally unbalanced and dangerous.

DIANA: *(A chill runs up her spine.)* Damn this storm! My family's out sailing and just look at the state of that sea. They're good swimmers, but still ...

CORDELIA: Lucky for me ... I get you all to myself. *(Picks up a photo of two pre-teenagers.)* They'll be fine.

DIANA: Yes, well. I'm always quick to worry. Sorry. Tea's a great idea!

CORDELIA: You do have bathrooms, right? Sometimes people hide things in the water tank behind the toilet.

DIANA: You don't find weird people like that living up here. But we do have three bathrooms, counting the one down here.

CORDELIA: Then, of course, if you knew, it wouldn't be a secret, would it? Do you have English Breakfast?

DIANA: Tea? Why don't I check? *(Diana goes into the kitchen, where we can see her clattering around, making tea. Cordelia paces the floor, as if she might be measuring "feet".)*

CORDELIA: This place in Tenant's Harbour? It used to be my aunt's, but these people who bought it? Turned it into an inn? We used to spend Thanksgivings there, you know, touch football and treasure hunts. When this letter came from a lawyer -- I thought it must be a, you-know, message -- and it was time to get myself up here make some decisions.

DIANA: Lemon? Sugar?

CORDELIA: What's a big check for, anyway, but shelter? *(Jumps)* What was that? Out the window? A car? A racoon? They carry rabies, you know. No, it was nothing, never mind. Do you get scared?

DIANA: *(In the kitchen)* What? Me? Here? Nooo.

CORDELIA: Then why do you want to sell?

DIANA: Time to move on. All the fixtures and faucets are original. But three or four years ago they hooked us up to town water. It's been a big improvement.

CORDELIA: Want to do scenes from your movies? You can be you. Usually I do you, but hey! this is an exception.

DIANA: *(Comes out of the kitchen, bringing two mugs of tea.)* Wouldn't that be fun? But I can't leave this room halfpapered, can I?

CORDELIA: It must be very hard for you to sell the house you grew up in. I can just picture you, learning to ride a bike in the back road, making s'mores on the flagstone walk with a handsome Uncle.

DIANA: *(Troubled)* S'mores? How do you know?

CORDELIA: Isn't that one of those Maine things? *(Sips her tea)*

DIANA: You make it sound positively idyllic, as if I gambolled, carefree, in the glen, or fen, or whatever they call the backyard in a fairy tale. *(Cordelia lights a cigarette, inhaling deeply. Diana seeing the cigarette.)* That cigarette!

CORDELIA: What?

DIANA: Put that cigarette out! *(Moves to grab the cigarette, Cordelia cringes, so Diana demurs.)* Please. Two years of scrubbing and fumigating the smoke smell will be down the tubes.

CORDELIA: "Smokesmell," that's good! Your mother was probably smoking right here when you took those first little steps.

DIANA: I'm not kidding. One of the things you cannot do here is smoke. I don't even have ashtrays.

CORDELIA: Okay, okay. *(Takes a big draw, then goes out on the porch to exhale. She looks around and then throws the cigarette over the rail.)* Smokesmell's all gone.

DIANA: It gets in the upholstery, in the wood, everywhere, and wreaks havoc with my throat. *(Quietly)* There are rules in this house -- while it's still mine.

CORDELIA: Okay, okay. *(On the porch, looks over into the sea.)* Long way down.

DIANA: You can see the rocks at low tide.

CORDELIA: Have you noticed any strangers lurking around?

DIANA: Only you.

CORDELIA: HaHa!

DIANA: No, I didn't mean it that way.

CORDELIA: I am serious. Have you been paying attention? I mean, anybody could have walked right in here. I'll check. *(Starts off through the house.)*

DIANA: *(Grabs her arm.)* I think you probably want a house that's less secluded. Millie's got a lot of other listings.

CORDELIA: I knew you didn't want me here. Can't you see the headlines? "Celebrity Brush-Off!"

DIANA: Are you from one of those tabloids?

CORDELIA: Oh, sure. I do a perfectly normal thing and she unloads on me!

DIANA: I'm sorry. I didn't unload anything.

CORDELIA: I don't know what you'd call it, but all I do is innocently light one little cigarette, perhaps the two millionth one smoked in this house, and you blow it all out of proportion. Mmmm, nice pun. Oh, DeeDee, I'm very disappointed.

DIANA: *(Sharply)* Why did you call me that?

CORDELIA: It's a nickname, is all.

DIANA: Don't call me that.

CORDELIA: Sorry. Hey. I'd be nervous, too, if I was up for a big part. What is it, two years without work?

DIANA: You've been reading that supermarket trash.

CORDELIA: I don't like supermarkets.

DIANA: Not working has been my choice. But I'm going to start rehearsals on Tuesday morning. Big musical. Big part.

CORDELIA: I want you to like me.

DIANA: I'm sure I would ... I'm just so involved.

CORDELIA: I can't leave. I've got to stay here. *(The telephone rings and Diana moves to answer it.)* Don't touch the phone. *(Ring. Diana stops and stares at Cordelia.)* Seriously, don't touch the phone!

DIANA: How absurd! That's the dockmaster, calling to say my family is safe. *(Picks up the phone. The telephone emits a peculiar sound, then a huge bolt of lightning flashes across the sky and ricochets off the mirrors in the house. Glass tinkles. Cordelia shrieks in fear, falls to the floor, then creeps to a hiding place.)*

CORDELIA: *(Panicked)* Hide me! Help me!

DIANA: *(Slams down the receiver.)* Dead! It never fails! Four drops of rain and you're incommunicado in this place. *(Noticing Cordelia's behavior)* That was only lightning.

CORDELIA: Only lightning? Lightning is as big as Nature gets. This is bad, DeeDee. No kidding, I hate storms. *Please*, don't throw me out there. Please let me stay.

DIANA: *(Stopping in her tracks)* Wouldn't you really rather come back another time?

CORDELIA: *(Laughing)* Because I hate lightning?

DIANA: You don't want to buy this house, do you? *(Thunder, Lightning, Pelting Rain)*

CORDELIA: *(Cringing)* You do get low marks for the weather. *(Diana closes the doors to the porch, then goes into the kitchen, where she finds her purse and digs around in it. Rain pelts down. Lightning flashes.)*

DIANA: If you need money for the cab and the bus ticket -- wherever you're going -- I'll give it to you, gladly.

CORDELIA: I didn't come here as an extortionist! *(Cordelia contemplates a box on a shelf from afar, then approaches to examine it more closely, picks it up to stuff it in her handbag while she talks -- but it opens and plays "Pennies From Heaven". Fascinated, she stops and starts it.)* You think I have no feelings; you think you can say anything to me. So what if I *am* flawed? *(Too late to get it in her bag, regretfully returns music box to it place just before she would be caught.)*

DIANA: *(Returning, she jiggles the car keys.)* What I'm going to do is drive you into town. Right now.

CORDELIA: Did I forget to tell you? I noticed when I was coming in, but I guess I forgot to say: your tires are flat. All of them. Slashed. Terrible.

DIANA: My what! *(Rushes to the backyard door, throws it open. Lightning and rain flood in. She slams the door.)* Flat! Slashed! We're stuck here! You did that! *(Lightning and thunder so fierce that even Diana cringes.)*

CORDELIA: I never!

DIANA: What the hell do you want?

CORDELIA: Oh, babe, I want a lot of things. Among them to be chums with you.

DIANA: By slashing my tires! That's not exactly Dale Carnegie behavior.

CORDELIA: Don't think you're going to win friends accusing me, either.

DIANA: I'm imagining this. *(Backing up towards the backyard door.)* I'm going to look again, and the car will be intact, and you will not be here.

CORDELIA: You are blowing this way out of proportion, DeeDee. *(Diana stops in her tracks, stiffens and glares.)* Okay, okay. I won't. Never again. Your mother called you that.

DIANA: That is *not* what my mother called me.

CORDELIA: When you were little.

DIANA: *(Bristling)* It's what's Arny Valerina called me on the school bus, *not* my mother.

CORDELIA: Touchy subject!

DIANA: As a matter of fact, yes. He sang this mean little song.

CORDELIA: Sing it.

DIANA: No.

CORDELIA: Come on, please.

DIANA: *(Profoundly uncomfortable)* I couldn't; no. I'm going to find where Bob put the snow tires. I'm sure I can change them. No big deal, right? *(Lightning)*

CORDELIA: *(Cringing)* Okay, okay. That's why the lightning happened! They're angry at Arny about that mean song. The stars. I have this theory that thunder storms are caused by those sun spots, you know? Where an explosion of hydrogen gas rips the Sun's surface. It causes all kinds of bad reactions. Have you ever been on a mental ward in a thunder storm?

DIANA: Why do you want to know?

CORDELIA: I didn't think so.

DIANA: Tea all gone?

CORDELIA: I'm not leaving by land, no matter what. And it's miles to go early for my boat to arrive. You don't see a Canadian Patrol boat, do you?

DIANA: *(Finds the binoculars, scans the horizon.)* I'd *know* that they were safe if I'd answered the phone on the first ring. It takes no time to get here from the dock. They've gone for a movie, that's what it is. *(Announcing)* My family will be here any minute. And so will Millie. Anyway, you mean the Coast Guard.

CORDELIA: No, I don't at all. I can assure you I know what I mean. I don't trust the Coast Guard. No, it's the Canadian boys I want. I suppose you're dying to know what I'm talking about.

DIANA: No! .. yes, I am. *(Phone rings.)* Thank God, it's working again! *(Goes for the phone.)* That's Bob!

CORDELIA: DON'T TOUCH THE PHONE!

(Phone rings. Lightning Flashes. Telephone makes peculiar sound as Diana picks it up.)

DIANA: I dislike shouting. Bob! *(The phone is dead.)* Oh, no!

CORDELIA: *(Quietly, though she stalks Diana)* I know somebody who died. She was talking on the phone when lightning struck. She was *fried*. You were very lucky just now. DON'T TOUCH THE PHONE. So, Okay?

DIANA: Okay, okay.

CORDELIA: Okay. You can see how nature makes a simple gizmo act weird, right? Just think what it does to your receptors. That's why I can't remember... *(The wind kicks up and creates a repetitive banging outside.)* What's that?

DIANA: Must be the door to the garbage shed. *(Walking toward the backyard door.)* It happens all the time.

CORDELIA: *(Pushing Diana away from the door.)* Forget the garbage. What are you gonna do, double-dog-dare Nature? *(Locking the backyard door, she laughs.)* Have you got a screw loose?

DIANA: *(Getting free.)* You want to hurt me, don't you?

CORDELIA: Relax, I *love* the house!

DIANA: I have young children. *Why* do you want to hurt me?

CORDELIA: Why should I?

DIANA: Why do you want to scare me?

CORDELIA: *(Finds this all hilarious)* Why shouldn't I?

DIANA: Have I done you any harm?

CORDELIA: Who wants to know?

DIANA: Where do you come from?

CORDELIA: *(Serious)* One of those stars.

DIANA: Kind of a long walk, wasn't it?

CORDELIA: Think of the odds! A star emits a tiny cosmic particle, in another age from the very depths of space, that spins through the Milky Way. Where's the right place for me to be? Mount Shasta? Montreal? Mars?

DIANA: Where do you want to go?

CORDELIA: Back to the place where I was germinated. I blew down to earth by mistake and the guys on my star have been trying to get me back since I was mytoplast. You start out as this little neutrino, lolling around in a cloud of interstellar gas? Suddenly, the whole thing collapses, like gravity pulled it in tight, tight, tight. Me? I miss the little hook, and whoosh, I'm blown down to this sorry planet. I don't belong here, but God knows, I'm trying. *(Diana checks her watch, looks out at the water anxiously.)* What are you looking for?

DIANA: The boat.

CORDELIA: How do you know about the Canadian Patrol?

DIANA: I meant Bob's boat. There it is! I see it! Tall mast? See? The children will be exhausted. I've got to get down there. I'll run. I don't need the car. Want to come? I do a lot of jogging.

CORDELIA: Bad for the ovaries. The bridge is out.

DIANA: Nonsense! It's gone out, what? three times in my whole life.

CORDELIA: The tide was rising when I came out here. I barely made it across, myself. And with this rain. And the full moon.

DIANA: *(Defeated)* No!

CORDELIA: It's one of those extra-high tide days ... You probably even know the name of this little trick of You-know-who. Does Millie have an amphibious vehicle?

DIANA: No.

CORDELIA: Ah, well. That accounts for the lack-of-Millie. Poor thing. I hope she had the sense not to tempt the current. It was *very* strong. Best for us to wait it out. Trust me.

DIANA: Yes, well.

CORDELIA: Do you trust me?

DIANA: Trust is a Girl Scout concept. Can we get back to your destination?

CORDELIA: If only I could. I came here because I need your help.

DIANA: So it's not the house. And you're not a lapsed astronaut. No, wait, I get it. You're very good. A great audition. You really got me going. Whoa! I'll give you some phone numbers in Hollywood. Private numbers. Cellular phone numbers of agents who are never in - - to anybody. You're good!

CORDELIA: Someone *is* after me.

DIANA: No one's after you!

CORDELIA: She's an evil person, and she knows I know her secrets, and so I'm here to ask for shelter.

DIANA: Here!

CORDELIA: We're going to need all the help we can get. No kidding.

DIANA: You're right. *(Reaching for the phone.)* But - - no phone.

CORDELIA: Now do you see what I mean?

DIANA: How do *you* call for help? Is this something I ought to remember from STAR TREK?

CORDELIA: Typical! Bob's not here when we need him. So, where are his guns?

DIANA: NO GUNS. We have no guns here. At all.

CORDELIA: But he hunts.

DIANA: How do you know...?

CORDELIA: Lucky guess. It's the wilderness up here.

DIANA: With a Ralph Lauren outlet down the road?

CORDELIA: Still, Bob hunts.

DIANA: The guns are at his friend's house. No guns in this house.

CORDELIA: Another rule. Tight ship. Okay, okay. We'll have to use our ... superior intelligence! That ought to be a comfort.

DIANA: Have you been to the police?

CORDELIA: No police! They are beings without vision. I did the best I could to cover my trail, but we won't know until I'm on that boat. Settled?

DIANA: Well, then.

CORDELIA: *(Jumps to the window.)* I was sure I lost the kid who was tailing me. It wasn't easy, but what is? I've done the best I could, but I'm no longer responsible. I wish this rain would stop so I could hear my instructions.

DIANA: You've got a big problem.

CORDELIA: Welcome to my world. Good thing we locked up. *(Furtively looking out the back door window.)* Aren't those eyes, glinting near the car? They're too high up to be racoon eyes.

DIANA: What's really going on here? I want you to call it off!

CORDELIA: I'm here to protect you.

DIANA: If somebody's after you, coming here is no way to protect me.

CORDELIA: Relax, will you. I've got this friend? Important guy - - really big - - with the Canadian Coastal Patrol. Soon as he can get the boat in close, I'll be on my way. I am going far,

far up into Canada, somewhere where there is no electricity, where I can get my signals. Do you see how it's all falling into place? The boat, this house, you and me. *(Pulls her hard.)* Don't stand near the window!

DIANA: I'll give you anything if you'll just go away.

(Lightning lights the sky and reveals the porch furniture buffeted by the wind and rain.)

CORDELIA: *(Cringes)* I'm not going out in that storm, even with your secrets. All that freewheeling electricity jams my receptors, gives me vertigo.

DIANA: *(Taking control)* Any problems with my head, I go right for the Advil.

CORDELIA: No! *(Remembering her manners)* Thank you. Anyway, I've got to find out the secret before I go. I knew it once, but now there's all this interference.

DIANA: Sometimes hunger makes my head buzz. Would you like to try some milk and cookies? Xanax? Prozac?

CORDELIA: I DON'T want any drugs -- ever again. Is that clear?

DIANA: Crystal clear.

CORDELIA: The only thing that ever works is looking at my collection.

DIANA: So you're a collector, too? Me? I never pass up a flea market. Okay. Why don't you show me your collection? As soon as Bob gets here, I'll make you a nice big sandwich, and brew you a thermos of English Breakfast tea -- I'll give you every tea bag I've got -- and then Bob will drive you to the bus station in his car. Listen. I think I hear the car ...

(Diana moves toward a switch near the backyard door.)

CORDELIA: DON'T TOUCH THE LIGHTS!

DIANA: *(Pulls her hand away, as if nearly electrocuted.)* Not the lights!

CORDELIA: You're signaling her! You're in on the conspiracy to kill me -- to keep me from bringing all your secrets back to my star.

DIANA: I have no secrets.

CORDELIA: Everybody's got secrets. What about that DeeDee song? That's a secret, isn't it?

DIANA: It's a private, little pain, that's all, nothing cosmic that some distant civilization needs to know about. *(Angry at Bob.)* Bob will be back from that boat very soon, and then everything will be all right.

CORDELIA: One second after midnight, and it's not my birthday anymore. *(Sobs)*

DIANA: Is your collection in your bag? Why don't you show me what you've got in there.

CORDELIA: *(Clutching the bag to her breast.)* Everything's got a story. It's no good just showing you these things without telling you all the stories, and I don't have much time.

DIANA: Anyway, we can get started. You talk, and I'll wallpaper. See? Nice? *(Picks up the glue brush and attempts to resume her task.)*

CORDELIA: *(Stops crying.)* Okay. *(Rummages around in the handbag.)* Oh, look, right on top. Here's the Glenn Close meat cleaver. And it's not just a movie prop, either. No, Glenn used it often for picnics between takes. I know because my friend, Juanita? Who lives in Kansas City? Traded for it with the prop girl. When I got it, it still had fake blood and caked brie cheese on it. But I've used it so much, that shit's all worn away. It's got excellent balance -- you could do lobotomies with it. Okay. You go.

DIANA: What?

CORDELIA: You tell a story now, about someone famous you worked with.

DIANA: No. Really.

CORDELIA: That's how it works; you've got to.

DIANA: Ah!

CORDELIA: And it's got to have a lump of matter to improve the drama. Something I can take away with the story. *(Sits down with childlike expectation.)* Something like that box of music there.

DIANA: A plain old story isn't enough?

CORDELIA: No, it isn't. It's got to be about the object that you're going to trade.

DIANA: I can't give you my music box.

CORDELIA: Why not?

DIANA: I've had it since I was a child.

CORDELIA: Perfect! What's the story?

DIANA: There is no story! I've got other stuff that has good stories. How about this figurine? Look, he's a cute little farmer boy.

CORDELIA: He's too alone. It's got to be about something I want.

DIANA: I don't want anything in exchange. You can just have him. *(Met with silence, she hardens.)* That's the offer, take it or leave it. *(Diana pretends to be absorbed with gluing. Cordelia is silent, expectant and very fidgety, eyes never leaving Diana; then she taps her fingers on the couch. Diana can't stand the tension.)* All right! How about this frog. It's beautifully carved.

CORDELIA: *(Not interested)* And about someone I know.

DIANA: It's got a great story. You know Jimmy Coco, right?

155

(Cordelia warms a bit.) Good! We were on location in Panama City, years before they took out Noriega, in "Two for the Future."

CORDELIA: You were in that jungle; sweat's pouring off your face. Lloyd Richey's in the other helicopter ... *(As Diana, sighting an imaginary machine gun.)* "Steady, Ray, this one's for the Colonel." *(Shoots the imaginary gun.)*

DIANA: Lloyd finds me in his gun sights: his hand tightens on the trigger...

CORDELIA: I want to know about the lump of matter. *(Settles down)*

DIANA: It was a Sunday, and we had the day off. The locals told us there was a fiesta in some little town. We borrowed a car. You have to understand that Jimmy was a very funny man... *(Cordelia begins to doze. Diana rattles on, watching Cordelia slump down.)* ... So we come upon this very old guy carving frogs from dry tree fungus. Jimmy picks this frog and kisses it and ... *(Diana tiptoes carefully and noiselessly toward the phone. The phone rings.)*

CORDELIA and DIANA: DON'T TOUCH THE PHONE! *(Cordelia shoots upright, totally alert. In a flash, she registers the situation and jumps between Diana and the phone, brandishing the meat cleaver.)*

CORDELIA: Didn't I warn you? No phone calls.

DIANA: It was that weird ring, again. It always goes on and off in a storm. But now it's dead. See? Nature's on your side.

CORDELIA: *(Cries)* How can I ever trust you again? *(Brandishing the meat cleaver.)* LIAR! LIAR! LIAR!

DIANA: Okay, this is bad.

CORDELIA: Does Betty Bacall lie? Does Stockard Channing lie? Here I've picked you out from a *very* rich list of actresses and look at the gratitude I get?

DIANA: I'll give you thirty seconds to leave - -and not another word about missed signals and microchips.

CORDELIA: Worshipping at the feet of false idols, we are poor, lost sheep.

DIANA: You are trespassing, young lady, and you have upset me. In a major way. I have had enough!

CORDELIA: *(Suddenly sympatico)* I definitely sense we're, you know, bonding? You're not receiving your signals, either.

DIANA: *(Going for broke)* What the hell. *(Picks up the phone.)*

(Cordelia gives the meat cleaver a mights swing and cuts the phone cord, leaving the cleaver imbedded in the table.)

CORDELIA: Damn AT&T! Damn Actor's Equity, too!

Section III

Scenes for Men

.

ASCENSION DAY
by Michael Henry Brown

The Characters: Nat Turner (African-American, 30) a slave on the verge of rebellion, and Putnam (11) the liberal-minded son of a plantation owner.

The Setting: Virginia, 1831

The Scene: Following his first escape, Nat Turner returns to the plantation and resumes his slave duties. Here, he encounters young Putnam Moore, a colorblind youth who treasures Nat's friendship.

Nat enters stage left where sits a barrel of water with a ladle in it. Nat is exhausted and sweaty. Nat dips the ladle and drinks. Then he goes up to the tree and almost collapses as he sits. Enter young Master Moore, a white boy of eleven. He enters, and upon seeing Nat he dashes for the tree.

PUTNAM: Nat!...Nat! *(Nat does not go to slave posture. He looks up and smiles.)*
NAT: How ya be, Massa Putnam? *(Nat is standing now. The man and the boy obviously want to embrace, but something stops them.)*
PUTNAM: I don't believe it... I don't believe it.
NAT: Here I is in de flesh...
PUTNAM: You're right in front of me and I still don't believe it. *(Putnam closes his eyes.)* Pinch me, Nat... so that I know it isn't a dream.
NAT: Well, Massa Putnam, I can only doos dat if'n you orders me... *(Putnam's eyes remain closed.)*
PUTNAM: As your lawful and rightful owner, I order you to pinch me...if you don't obey you get thirty.
NAT: Thirty, suh?
PUTNAM: The roughest, toughest, punishment any master can give a slave. Thirty. Thirty days of washing E.T. Brantley's underclothes .
NAT: Even afta he come from town drinkin', Suh?
PUTNAM: Even more so... 'cause then his drawers are sure to be pissy. *(Nat gets to his knees.)*
NAT: Okay, Massa... Ise'll do anything, jest don't doos dat...even de whip is betta den dat... *(Nat looks around to make*

157

sure that nobody is looking, then he pinches Putnam. Putnam jumps, slightly startled. He gives Nat a mean look. Nat cowers. Putnam giggles. Nat joins him.)

NAT: Youse a learnin', Li'l Massa.

PUTNAM: Am I?

NAT: You sho'ly is.

PUTNAM: Suppose I don't want to..

NAT: Yo' Daddy wouldn't take lightly to it...

PUTNAM: Suppose I want to free you?

NAT: Yo' Papa...

PUTNAM: My papa's dead...

NAT: You new papa, Massa Travis...

PUTNAM: You mean my Mama's new husband.

NAT: Not so new anymo', Suh.

PUTNAM: Stop it, Nat, I'm already angry at you .

NAT: Fo' what, Suh?

PUTNAM: For coming back.

NAT: Youse not glad to see me, Li'l massa?

PUTNAM: Ol' Rabbit, Grab it Travis is always right. And you made him right again by coming back. Now he's walking around like a rooster with a pig iron stuck up his butt.

NAT: Massa Travis is a smart man, Suh.

PUTNAM: I think we both know better than that Nat...Now my Mama, she's dumb enough to believe that...but not you and me, Nat...

NAT: Mrs. Moore... I mean Mrs. Travis...

PUTNAM: Hmmmph!

NAT: She not dumb, she jest in evahlastin' love.

PUTNAM: Looks more like everlastin' stupidity to me. *(Putnam laughs. Nat follows.)* Mr. Travis is a carriage maker not a farmer. I can run this farm better than him and so can you. Everybody in the county knows he's going to ruin my daddy's farm, Mr. Ol' Rabbit, Grab it, Travis ! *(Pause)*

NAT: How be school, Massa Putnam?

PUTNAM: Boring... Except for history.

NAT: Dat always be yo' favorite thing.

PUTNAM: You, know, I can never get over the courage of our founding fathers. Like General Washington at Valley Forge...All of those soldiers freezing in the snow...some of them didn't even have shoes...

NAT: But dey went on and won de war, Suh.

PUTNAM: They were so down, Nat. How did they do that?

NAT: Deys all rallied 'round de leader. General Washington...he be a great leader. People will folla a great leader who be strong no matta how bad things will be.

PUTNAM: Did you read about General Washington when you

were little? *(Pause. Nat goes to slight slave posture.)*
NAT: All I reads is de Bible, Li'l Boss.
PUTNAM: That would get boring... General Washington, Cornwallis... and your favorite Napoleon... you must have read about them. *(Nat goes to deeper slave posture.)*
NAT: No, Suh...
PUTNAM: But you told me about their great battles long before my teacher did.
NAT: Dat jest come thru de years hearin' white folk talk 'bout dem, Suh.
PUTNAM: Oh, Like Brantley?... Nat... you never treated me like a child before. You're talkin' to Putnam, Nat.
NAT: Ise talkin' to my Massa.
PUTNAM: When I grow up...when I'm twenty-one...this land will be all mine...
NAT: Dat be de natrified truth, Suh.
PUTNAM: And that's when I'm going to free you and your Mama.
NAT: Dat be a long way off, Suh, you'll git smart an' change yo' mind...
PUTNAM: I've thought about this a long time. You are too smart and too good to be a slave. Where are you going, Nat?
NAT: Thirsty...want to fetch some watah...
(Putnam dashes to the water barrel, dips the ladle and returns to Nat.)
PUTNAM: Well, don't just stand there, take it.
NAT: Suh, I be de slave.
PUTNAM: It's just water, Nat...
NAT: Now you listen here, Massas don't bring slaves watah...
PUTNAM: You're my friend, Nat. And anyway, I'm going to free you.
NAT: Lil' Boss, you don't let slave or white man see you like dis. *(Pause)* Youse gittin' too big...I reckon we caint be like dis no mo'...
PUTNAM: Like What?...Like what, Nat?
NAT: Yes, Suh, it be 'bout dat time. *(They exchange looks, Nat looks around. Then he takes the ladle and drinks some water. Putnam takes it back from him and drinks from the ladle. Putnam smiles.)* Dat not be funny, Li'l Massa.
PUTNAM: It wasn't supposed to be funny, Nat. I was thirsty. *(Putnam goes and puts down the ladle in the barrel. Nat sits down slumped against the tree. Putnam returns.)* See, I'm like my daddy, I'm a man of my word. When I'm twenty-one, I am going to free you and your Mama. I'll even give you money to get Cherry and your children from Mr. Niles Reese.
NAT: Suh, how you gonna run de farm...

PUTNAM: Don't worry, Nat, even with you and your Mama gone, I'll still have fifteen slaves... And by then some of them will have had children... so I figure I'll have another seven to ten slaves by then... So don't you worry, Nat. My farm will be fine.

(Silence)

NAT: Yes, suh, Ise almost forgot 'bout dos Isa leavin' behind.

(Lights Fade)

BRAVO, CARUSO!
by William Luce

The Characters: Enrico Caruso (40-50) the great tenor, and Mario Fantini (40's) Caruso's dresser.

The Setting: Caruso's dressing room in the Metropolitan Opera House, Christmas Eve, 1920.

The Scene: While awaiting the evening's performance, Caruso entertains reporters in his dressing room. Here, he and his faithful dresser, Mario, describe their first meeting.

CARUSO: *(To Mario)* Mario, where are you when I need you? Do you think I could sing, if I work as you do? Can you stare at the ceiling and dream and the work will do itself? By Bacchus, what are these I have around me? Statues? *(Winking at reporters)* Mario he has been my valet for seventeen years.
MARIO: *(Hurt)* Eighteen, Commendatore.
CARUSO: Seventeen, eighteen. He know I make fussy now and then. Is nothing. He's a fine fellow, Mario. *(To Mario)* If I holler at you, it's because I'm nervous, eh?
MARIO: Si, is all right, Commendatore.
CARUSO: A railway station porter in Milano when first we meet, eh?
MARIO: Si.
CARUSO: *(To reporters)* I like the way he carry my bags. Proud, efficient. So, I say, "What is your name, my friend?"
MARIO: Mario Fantini. *(Caruso indicates his cigarette.)*
CARUSO: *(To Mario)* Mario, per favore.
MARIO: Si, Commendatore. *(Rummages through his pockets and finds the matches.)*
CARUSO: *(To reporters)* So, I say, "Mario Fantini, how would you like to come and work for Caruso?"
MARIO: *(Lighting cigarette.)* Si, Commendatore. When?
CARUSO: "Mo." I say. That is all. He come the next day.
MARIO: *(Lighting the cigarette.)* The same day, Commendatore.
CARUSO: *(To Mario)* Same day, next day. Put out the inhalator, Mario.
MARIO: Si.
CARUSO: *(To reporters)* A French steam inhalator.
MARIO: Swedish.

CARUSO: *(To Mario)* French, Swedish. *(To Reporters)* Mario recently marry a pretty brown-eye girl by name of Brunetta Di Federico. But I have prejudice for married servant. No man can serve two master. But they were engaged for nine year, so what you gonna do? I finally give consent, to please my wife. I say to her, "Doro, tell Mario he can get married. But I don't want to see no hair and hide of Brunetta. And tell Mario, no babies." *(To Mario)* Right, Mario? No babies? In Napoli there is old saying, "Niente piccerille." No babies.

MARIO: No babies? *(To reporters)* In Napoli?

CARUSO: Si. Prometteme, niente piccerille.

MARIO: *(To Caruso)* Si, Commendatore.

CARUSO: Ripete cu' me. Niente piccerille.

CARUSO & MARIO: Niente piccerille.

CARUSO: Ancora.

CARUSO & MARIO: Niente piccerille.

MARIO: *(To reporters)* Give him another nine years. He change his mind.

CARUSO: Bene. You get more cold cream I ask for?

MARIO: *(Finding it.)* Here, Commendatore.

CARUSO: Va beene. *(To reporters)* Loyalty like that of little brother. In Napoli there is other old saying.

MARIO: Oh, boy, they got a lotta saying in Napoli.

CARUSO: "Nu fratello e scelta e chiu forte e nu parente."

MARIO: A brother of choice is stronger than kin.

CARUSO: Have your heard it said? It is truth. I have no friends, though.

MARIO: *(To Caruso)* No, please ...

CARUSO: No, no, not really. Not intimate. I must wear the mask for the public, make face, play the clown.

MARIO: *(To reporters)* The Commendatore he shake the great tassel of the curtain when he gonna make a bow, and he make a people laugh at Caruso.

CARUSO: Si. People who say they love Rico, they stream into the Hotel Vanderbilt every day ask for me.

MARIO: Last week a man rush down the corridor to the apartment door. I stop him. "May I help you?" I say to the man. *(To Caruso)* You be the man, Commendatore. *(Pause)* May I help you?

CARUSO: *(As crazy man)* I have come to save the miserable, tormented soul of Enrico Caruso from burning in the everlasting fires of hell.

MARIO: That's very good.

CARUSO: *(Modestly)* Grazie. *(Resuming as crazy man)* I am Jesus Christ, the King of Heaven and Earth.

MARIO: Still you gotta make an appointment.

CARUSO: Too many people want to see Caruso.

MARIO: *(To reporters)* At stage door every night is the crowd.

CARUSO: *(To reporters)* Ai me, the crowd.

MARIO: I hear them whisper. "There he is. He is shorter than I thought. And what a fatty! Now I can go home to bed."

CARUSO: But always the applause and the handshake.

MARIO: Hundreds wait to see and flatter and touch and kiss.

CARUSO: Si, and to ask favores.

MARIO: I remember how a little old man with white hair stand quietly at the door, tears streaming down his face. "Signor Caruso," he say, " I love you."

CARUSO: *(Caruso walks to the screen and examines the costume just ironed by Mario. To Mario.)* Be sure to iron this, Mario. Is all wrinkled. E chiu brutto do diavolo.

MARIO: *(Peering at it.)* But, Commendatore, I already .. si.

(He hastily exits to retrieve the ironing board.)

DOWN THE FLATS
by Tony Kavanagh

The Characters: Fran (25) a young man flirting with life as a petty criminal, and Henry (24) his partner in crime.

The Setting: A flat in Dublin, the present.

The Scene: Fran and Henry have just returned home after having committed a robbery. As they divide the stolen money, they discuss various aspects of their profession.

We hear the sound of a police siren down the flats. Fran and Henry burst in the front door, the lights go up. Henry has a small leather money bag in his hand. They both look out the window at the cop car, down the flats.

FRAN: Look'a the head on tha coper... Holy Mother'a Jaysus I'm glad tha fuck did'ent get his hands on us...

HENRY: *(Pause)* Fuck... There must be some'tin wroung whit his head?... He must of been'in born whit one those head's God Love Him... Ya know wha I mean...When the oul head is swelled like.

FRAN: Well were do you think he got it from? He did'ent sent away for the fuckin thing... Where all born with head's. *(Henry walks over to the table and sits down he takes a knife from his pocket and rips open the bag.)*

HENRY: Do ya know how he reminds me of... What's your man's name now... Ya know him... Ya know the fuckin eiggit... The fella how does be in the story book's... The fella on the wall.

FRAN: *(Pause)* Humpty...Dumpty...

HENRY: That's how it is...Humpty fuck'in Dumpty...Jaysus I'm glad he did'ent catch us...I'd say heed have no mercy on ya... *(He pulls a wad of twenty's from the bag. He smells the money.)* Money...Money..Money... *(Fran walks over to him. He takes tens and twenty out of his pocket and throws them on the table. Speaking as he does so.)*

FRAN: Yeah...Could you imagine if he hit you with tha head...It's like a fuckin Cannon Ball....

HENRY: Where did you get tha from?

FRAN: Henry, I can smell money...fuckin smell it...you know I naver leave an office till its clean.

HENRY: *(counting the money)* I wonder will it be a BIG mortal Sin?

FRAN: Wha? *(Straightening out the money.)*

HENRY: Robb'in an Undertaker... I mean I naver robbed an' Undertaker before...I tink I'd get worried like...Ya know that's way I did'ent want to do it...I don't think God is goin to like tha...

FRAN: *(Pause)* No... You can rob'an Undertaker it's all right... Sure they rob people all the time?

HENRY: Do'dee...the fucks...

FRAN: Christ it cost more to live now...Then it does to die... no I mean it costs more to die now then it does to live....

HENRY: Your right there...Ya know when I was watchin your man' when you were in the office.?

FRAN: Yeah...

HENRY: I tell ya I could'ent believe wha he was doin to tha poor oul crap...

FRAN: Wha poor oul crap... Wha are you talkin a'bout?

HENRY: The dead Gezzer he was workin on...I could'ent believe wha he was doin...That fuck of an Undertaker. I mean the oul fella looked allright to me...he was just lying there like ya know...He was dead...he looked like he was sleepin... he did'ent look so bad... nore he did'ent look to good...he was kind'a pale lookn thats all...

FRAN: Course he was fuckin pale lookin...he was fuckin dead was'ent he...Thats the way your suppost to look when your bleedin dead.

HENRY: I know you are...Thats wha I'm saying...But your man was in ther puttin a smile on the poor fucker face.

FRAN: Holy Fuck...

HENRY: Yeah... *(Seems disappointed)* I all ways thought people died with smiles on their faces...but they don't...Them fuckin undertakes put them on.

FRAN: Good Jaysus Wha...

HENRY: Yeah... Then you know what he was doin... Bleeding disgusting...

FRAN: Wha... What was he doi... Don't tell me...

HENRY: No... He was'ent doin that for Jaysus sake...fuck I'd a gone in and murder'ed him if he doing the like'a tha... no it was'ent tha... it was worse even...

FRAN: Wha?....Wha was it?

HENRY: He was puttin make up on the poor man face...can you belive tha...lip stick an all I tell ya...

FRAN: Holy jaysus...

HENRY: I wonder way they do tha...I mean wha do you need a smile on your face for...and make up on your mug when your fuckin dead...I tell ya he looked like he was goin dancein...it bleedin disgracefull I think...

FRAN: The world is a madhouse...a madhouse...fuck them

undertakes...right how mush?

HENRY: Six hundred bang on...not bad for a days pay wha?

FRAN: We're professionals, ain't we? Professionals have to be paid well...

HENRY: Yeah...When ya come to think of it, we are professionals....

FRAN: Thats right Henry...PC'S thats wha we are.

HENRY: *(Henry looks at him)* PC's...Wha that?

FRAN: Professional Criminals ...That's our trade...

FASTING
by Bill Bozzone

The Characters: Emmett (60) a man who has just lost his toe, and Frank (57) a man nervous about his class reunion.

The Setting: A beach house, summer, the present.

The Scene: Emmett and Frank have just arrived at their beach house and Emmett is surprised by Frank's decision to fast in order to lose weight for his high school reunion.

In the darkness, the voice of a Radio DJ.

DJ: *(Voice.)* ...which would make this the hottest June 30th on record. *(Beat.)* But let me tell you something, my friends. I'm gonna be bringing you the coolest music this side of the Alaskan pipeline. So just kick back, chill out, pop a top, and toast the weekend before it toasts you. *(Then intro bars of Freddy Cannon's "Palisades Park" play.)* Ten before nine at 94-point-five, WTOY. New Jersey's original summer oldies station! *(The DJ has nailed it perfectly. Freddy Cannon's lyrics begin as soon as the intro is done.)*

FREDDY CANNON: *(Voice.)*
"Last night I took a walk in the dark,
a swingin' place called Palisades Park,
to have some fun and see what I could see -
That's where the girls are! -"
(The song continues, then fades as the lights rise on stage. June. Mid-morning. Saturday. Sounds of traffic mingle with sounds of the beach. The rear deck of a beach house on the New Jersey shore. The deck itself is primarily redwood; a railing runs on both sides and steps lead down to the ground below. A sliding glass door which leads into the beach house stays open, the sliding screen is currently closed. A round aluminum table, with umbrella, sits in the center of the porch. To one side of the table, a padded chaise lounge. To the other side, a matching padded deck chair. Two matching stack tables on the outsides of chaise and chair. Set on the stack table next to the chaise, an almost empty glass of iced tea. On the stack table next to the chair, a 1950 high school yearbook. Also, a cane by the foot of the chaise. There's a gas grill, its cover closed, pushed off to one side.

Inside, the interior of the bungalow is in darkness.

Emmett, 60, looks through the high school yearbook. He wears shorts and an Hawaiian print shirt. He stands, using the back of the chair for support, on one foot. On his raised foot Emmett wears a white cotton sock and an open-toe sandal. On the other foot, the matching sandal. He also wears a watch. After a moment, Emmett returns the yearbook to the stacking table. He picks up a second book, examines it. The title: FASTING FOR YOUTH.

FRANK: *(Off. Into phone.)* No, no. It's right on the beach. It's impossible to miss. Route 35 south and if you see a sign that says Captain Jack's Clam Hut, you know you've gone too far... Okay, fine. We'll see you then. *(Emmett hears Frank hang up the phone. He puts down the book and tries to make it back to the chaise, but he's too late. Frank comes out on to the deck. He's a large, powerful-looking man of 57. He wears swim trunks and thongs. He carries a glass of ice water. Frank stops when he sees Emmett off the chaise.)* Emmett... *(Emmett freezes.)*

EMMETT: *(Innocently)* What?

FRANK: You're supposed to rest. That's why we're up here. You heard Dr. Ramanan as well as I did. Stay off that foot for at least a week. *(Emmett sighs, returns to the chaise on one foot. Frank sits in the chair.)* It must be 95 degrees inside that house.

EMMETT: Did I tell you? Did I say if you rented a unit without air conditioning we'd suffer?

FRANK: It's high season, Emmett. It was this or nothing. *(Pause)* At least we have a piano.

EMMETT: How useful.

FRANK: It very well could be. We might make friends with someone out here who plays. We could invite him-or-her in. It could be very nice. *(Pause)* How's your toe?

EMMETT: I wish people would learn to say something a little more creative. Not just you, everybody. The people I work with at the bank. "Have you noticed a weight loss?" "Can you still kick a football?" Something. Anything besides, "How's your toe?" *(Pause)*

FRANK: So how is your toe?

EMMETT: It's gone, Frank, that's how it is. It's laying in some wastebasket in St. Luke's Hospital. Let's be realistic.

FRANK: Okay, how's your stump?

EMMETT: You're a real comedian, Frank.

FRANK: And it's "lying" in some wastebasket. Not "laying."

EMMETT: Is this what I have to look forward to? Sweltering in the sun for seven days while you correct my grammar?

FRANK: I'm sorry. When you teach remedial English for as long as I have it becomes a habit. *(Pause)* And don't think I didn't notice that you're not using your cane.

EMMETT: I hate my cane. It makes me feel like I should be standing outside a circus tent pointing at freaks. *(Pause)* To tell the truth, I don't even know why we came down here. *(Short pause)* Look around you. Smell around you. It stinks. There's medical waste all over the beach. If we stare at the water long enough, we'll probably see my old toe wash up.

FRANK: Emmett...

EMMETT: Besides. We could have just as easily sat around at home, with cable.

FRANK: You won't "sit around" at home, Emmett. That's just the problem. You're up and down every five seconds. *(Short pause)* I might also point out that you were the one who suggested coming here. Not I. You were the one intent on watching the sunset on the ocean.

EMMETT: Can we at least take a walk along the beach?

FRANK: No.

EMMETT: You can carry me on your back while I hold both our noses. *(Frank refuses to respond. After a moment.)* Then at least tell me who was on the phone.

FRANK: No one.

EMMETT: You gave instructions to "no one" on how to get here?

FRANK: Emmett, please...

EMMETT: Fine. I'll just lie here. *(Beat)* Or "lay" here, whichever's grammatically correct. *(Short pause)* I won't ask about the phone, I won't ask about the book, I won't ask about anything. *(Frank looks over.)*

FRANK: *(After a moment)* What book?

EMMETT: The book on fasting. *(Frank points to the book on the stacking table.)*

FRANK: This book?

EMMETT: That book. Yes.

FRANK: You'll only get upset.

EMMETT: I won't get upset.

FRANK: *(After a moment)* Okay. *(Beat)* I was thinking of fasting for the entire week we're up here.

EMMETT: *(After a moment)* You what?

FRANK: I was thinking of going without food.

EMMETT: Entirely?

FRANK: Completely.

EMMETT: Which would explain why you didn't have breakfast when we stopped.

FRANK: I didn't have breakfast, Emmett, because I'm fat. Look

169

at me. I'm grossly overweight.

EMMETT: Nonsense. You have a heavy bone structure. That's all. It's hereditary.

FRANK: They're the same bones I had in high school, Emmett. When I weighed 60 pounds less. *(Pause)*

EMMETT: So you're going to fast.

FRANK: Only water. A gallon a day.

EMMETT: And you're going to ride that ridiculous exercise device you dragged along.

FRANK: Correct.

EMMETT: And that way you'll look trim and svelte for your 40th reunion next weekend.

FRANK: At this point I'll settle for looking human.

EMMETT: You look fine, Frank. You may not be the 17-year-old full-back who ran down the field at Lancaster High, but you look fine.

FRANK: It's a very healthy thing to do. It says so right in the book. People have been fasting since time began.

EMMETT: Which would mean to me that people have also been passing out since time began. Have you considered that? A water-bloated man flat on his face while I hop to the phone and try to call 911?

FRANK: Nobody's going to pass out. *(Pause)* I knew I should have gone to the other reunions. That way they'd have seen me change with time.

EMMETT: It's beyond me why you even want to go now. Bunch of middle-aged charlatans milling around like overdressed cattle. *(Pause)* Do yourself a favor. Forget the fasting. We'll go to your reunion, we'll eat like pigs, the following day we can take a ride to Gettysburg. *(Pause)*

FRANK: I was thinking of going by myself, Emmett. *(Emmett stares over.)* It's kind of a long ordeal. I don't think it's good for you to be on your bad foot that soon.

EMMETT: Maybe I could stand by the punchbowl like a flamingo.

FRANK: I think you should fully recuperate and then we can think about doing something together.

EMMETT: I understand. You're ashamed of me.

FRANK: I am not ashamed of you.

EMMETT: You'd rather your high school class doesn't know I exist.

FRANK: I just want to go to this thing and enjoy myself.

EMMETT: Which you can't do if I'm there. *(Pause)*

FRANK: There's nothing wrong with reliving past glories.

EMMETT: Did I say there was?

FRANK: I was quite a football player in those days, I was active

among the student council, I was very popular.
EMMETT: This wouldn't by chance have anything to do with Gilbert Ridnick. *(Frank looks over.)*
FRANK: How did you know about Gilbert Ridnick?
EMMETT: He's in your yearbook. With the corner of the page folded down. "To Frank. Remember Grant, Remember Lee. The hell with them. Remember me. Gilbert Ridnick."
FRANK: He played center on the football team. He was my best friend all through high school.
EMMETT: Strange you never mentioned him.
FRANK: *(Smiles)* He used to have this car battery in a wooden box with a crank on the side. It had tow cables and a meter on top. *(Beat)* And what you would do is take hold of these cables while somebody turned the crank. And the meter would register how much voltage you could take.
EMMETT: Why in God's name would you do that?
FRANK: It was fun. We were very competitive.
EMMETT: And as far as you know, Gilbert will be there?
FRANK: As far as I know.
EMMETT: You think he'll bring his battery?
FRANK: Will you please be serious? *(Pause)*
EMMETT: I'd love to find where they pulled that quote from. *(Frank looks over.)* The one under your picture. In the yearbook. *(Pause)*
    "The wisest man could ask no more of Fate
      Then to be simple, modest, manly, true..."
FRANK: James Russell Lowell. *(Mock laugh from Emmett.)* I was 17, Emmett, I thought it was quite appropriate. *(Pause. Emmett sits back.)*
EMMETT: So tell me. What happens if you don't lose the weight?
FRANK: If I don't lose the weight, I don't go.
EMMETT: Exactly how much tonnage are you planning on shaving off?
FRANK: I don't know. Twenty pounds anyway. *(Pause)* So how was breakfast?
EMMETT: Wonderful.
FRANK: You had what? A soft-boiled egg?
EMMETT: A soft-boiled egg done to perfection, toast with strawberry preserves, and freshly squeezed orange juice. *(Pause)*
FRANK: It must be the sea air. I've never been so hungry in my entire life.

FLAUBERT'S LATEST
by Peter Parnell

The Characters: Felix (30's), a novelist and Colin (20's) a dancer/choreographer.

The Setting: The garden of a country house in Western Connecticut, mid-summer, the present

The Scene: Here, two lovers share a few moments alone before dinner.

(The garden of a house in the country. The kitchen of the house opens onto this garden through doors that are now open. A summer afternoon. At Rise, Colin is rehearsing to the strains of a Mozart string quartet coming from a small tape player beside him. His concentration is intense. In between the strains of the Mozart, a typewriter can be heard pounding, off. After a few moments, the typewriter stops. Felix enters from the kitchen. He states at Colin for a few moments, then goes to the flowers and stares at them. Colin continues to practice his movements, pretending to be only mildly aware of Felix. Felix moves to another flower bed, examines it. Colin doesn't break his concentration.)

COLIN: Are you working, or taking a break?
FELIX: What?
COLIN: Are you working, or ...
FELIX: I'm working.
COLIN: Good. Then I won't ask.
FELIX: Won't ask what?
COLIN: How it's going?
FELIX: Are *you* working?
COLIN: Mmn-hmn.
FELIX: Doing justice to Mozart? Satisfying the Terpsichorean muse?
COLIN: What?
FELIX: Terpsichore. The goddess of dance.
COLIN: Ah.
FELIX: At least it isn't *Don Giovanni.*
COLIN: What isn't?
FELIX: The Mozart. That you're doing justice to. Because nobody can do justice to that. It's perfect as it is. Flaubert once

172

said the three finest things God ever made were the sea, *Hamlet* and *Don Giovanni*. And on the fourth day, He rested.

COLIN: I thought on the fourth day, He made Flaubert.

FELIX: No. Not *all* Flaubert. But enough.

COLIN: Shit.

FELIX: What's the matter?

COLIN: My ankle again.

FELIX: Didn't Howard tell you not to - -

COLIN: I know, I know. I'm fine, so long as I don't break my concentration. *(This last meant for Felix. Colin has stopped and gotten a towel. Felix looks at him a little sheepishly.)*

FELIX: Sorry.

COLIN: I take it it isn't going well?

FELIX: What isn't?

COLIN: The muse you're trying to do justice to.

FELIX: What makes you say that?

COLIN: Oh I don't know. Maybe the fact that you were staring at the nasturtiums as if you were going to strangle them.

FELIX: I wasn't staring at them. I was watching them *grow*. And is that what they are? Nasturtiums? Since when do you know so much about gardens?

COLIN: I took care of one. Three years straight in sleepaway camp. For the head of the place, a kindly old lady named Mrs. Shaw.

FELIX: The other campers must have loved you. Tended a garden *and* wore a dance belt at the age of twelve.

COLIN: I'll have you know I was also the best ball player in my age group.

FELIX: Such a jock. You're the jockiest dancer in Alan's company, that's for sure. Except for Adrian.

COLIN: Adrian's straight, give me a break.

FELIX: We know this definitely?

COLIN: We know this definitely.

FELIX: *(Sighs)* Oh, well. There goes another invitation to a long weekend in the country.

COLIN: As if you were ever serious. You know you can't stand being with my dancer friends for more than a couple of hours.

FELIX: Modern dancers. Such scintillating conversationalists.

COLIN: Why do you always differentiate?

FELIX: You're right. They're not exactly deconstructing Tolstoy over at ABT. *(Pause)* Did you see the *Times* this morning? There's another article about Paul Bremer's new book. Although Claire called to tell me Michi Kakutani is giving it a bad review tomorrow. Also, she thinks his movie deal fell through.

COLIN: And why does that make you happy?

FELIX: Because! A twenty-two year old Columbia student living at the St. Regis? He writes one novel, it makes the big time, and what's he doing? Having dinner with Michelle Pfeiffer! The kid's never even read *Beowulf*!

COLIN: That's no reason to wish *your* lack of success on somebody else.

FELIX: *(THUNDEROUS)* I am not *unsuccessful*!

COLIN: I was only quoting *you*!

FELIX: When did I ever say - -

COLIN: Last night, in the middle of dinner.

FELIX: Oh, I was drunk. You can't ever listen to me when I'm - - besides, *I'm* allowed to say that, nobody else! One critically well-received novel, published five years ago, is not unsuccessful. Then I was still in *my* twenties, and I *deserved* an article about myself. *(Pause)* Jesus. Three years and I'm still on the same book ...

COLIN: You told me Melville took five years to finish *Moby Dick*.

FELIX: Yes, but wasn't he stuck at sea with all those foretopmen? He didn't have *time* to write. Besides, nobody wants to read books like that anymore. Nobody wants to *read* books it takes somebody three years to write. Frankly, nobody wants to read books, period. They all want to go to the ballet, where everything is beautiful.

COLIN: To tell you the truth, I'm getting a little sick of City Ballet. All those pretty boys tipping around, pretending to be straight.

FELIX: Now, Colin, here's where we part company. Give me Balanchine over Mark Morris any day. I'm sorry, but *Viennese Waltzes* makes me genuinely happy.

COLIN: Well, I'm glad to hear that something does ... *(Colin has moved to Felix and begun to massage his back.)* Feeling better?

FELIX: Mmm.

COLIN: You haven't been stretching.

FELIX: I know.

COLIN: You're going to turn flabby.

FELIX: I've already turned.

COLIN: No you haven't.

FELIX: Look at me. I'm starting to go gray. My hair is falling out. I'm thirty-three years old. Flaubert already looked like an old man when he was thirty-three.

COLIN: Are you trying to emulate him in *all* things?

FELIX: Not in that!

COLIN: Well then, you have to listen to me. You have to do as I say. If you want, I'll knead your body. Do you want me to

174

knead you?

FELIX: Wouldn't it be better if I kneaded you?

COLIN: Why? I'm kneaded all day long.

FELIX: Yes, but by all the wrong people! *(Colin begins to grab Felix. They embrace. Felix reacts.)* Not here.

COLIN: Why not?

FELIX: People can see.

COLIN: What people? There's nobody around. It's the middle of the afternoon.

FELIX: Schoolchildren on their way home from school.

COLIN: It's Sunday.

FELIX: Farmers, tilling the land.

COLIN: There are no farmers tilling near here. They'd have to be spying at us through binoculars on top of a hill.

FELIX: Do you remember *Shoah*?

COLIN: How could I forget it? You dragged me in the pouring rain to see it.

FELIX: Remember the Ukranian farmers kidding about the fellow whose field was next to Treblinka? How he pretended not to hear the screams. And the other farmers kept laughing, "Yeah, but sometimes he had to look up, his field was on top of a hill, he must have *seen* something, you can't just farm looking *down* all the time..."

COLIN: You certainly know how to put a damper on things.

FELIX: I'm sorry.

COLIN: Don't you like fooling around anymore?

FELIX: Of course I like fooling around. It just takes too much energy.

COLIN: Oh, Pardon me! Is it that, or something else?

FELIX: It's *that* Colin. Did you know that ejaculating one ounce of sperm is more exhausting than losing three liters of blood?

COLIN: Where did you read that?

FELIX: In Flaubert's letters! In 1859, he wrote to his friend Ernest Feydeau and told him not to exert himself on women, but on words! "Save your priapism for style and fuck your inkwell!"

COLIN: Great! So your Flaubert was a closet reactionary!

FELIX: No, not at all! It's just that, at certain key times, writing and sex were one and the same! Writing *was* sex. It required the same passion, the same -- *(Grabbing book)* Look, here, after he starts *Salammbo*, listen to what he writes ... *(Reads)* "An erection has finally been obtained, by dint of whipping and manustrupating myself! Let's hope that climax will ensue!"

COLIN: If that's true, then why did you tell me you usually jerk off before you start to write?

175

FELIX: Because I get excited! It's the same response! I start getting involved, and all of a sudden my mind is racing, my blood is boiling, and I'm hard, or semi-hard. I want to whip it out, but do I?

COLIN: Yes! I've seen you!

FELIX: Where?

COLIN: In the apartment. Once. After you thought I'd left. I stayed behind and ...

FELIX: Impossible, I never do it at the desk.

COLIN: *(Laughs)* You don't?

FELIX: No. I go look at pictures. Or turn on the VCR.

COLIN: You're such a voyeur.

FELIX: And you're not?

COLIN: Uh-uh. I *like* getting what I want.

FELIX: And you think I don't?

COLIN: Obviously not.

I HATE HAMLET
by Paul Rudnick

The Characters: Andrew (30's) a popular television actor, and Barrymore (40-50) a ghost.

The Setting: A brownstone apartment in New York, the present.

The Scene: When Andrew is offered the role of Hamlet in a New York production, his subsequent anxiety summons the ghost of John Barrymore. Here, these two very different actors discuss method and romance.

ANDREW: You're ... him.

BARRYMORE: AM I?

ANDREW: You're ... dead.

BARRYMORE: You know, occasionally I'm not truly certain. Am I dead? Or just incredibly drunk?

ANDREW: You're ... Barrymore.

BARRYMORE: Yes. Although my father's given name was Blythe; he changed it when he became an actor, to avoid embarrassing his family. Your name?

ANDREW: *(Still completely unnerved.)* Andrew. Rally. It's really Rallenberg. I changed it, to avoid embarrassing ... the Jews.

BARRYMORE: *(Surveying the premises.)* Behold. My nest. My roost. *(Indicating where things had been, perhaps with musical cues.)* A grand piano. A renaissance globe. A throne.

ANDREW: You're dead! You're dead! What are you doing here?

BARRYMORE: Lad - I'm here to help.

ANDREW: Wait - how do I know you're ghost? Maybe you're just ... an intruder.

BARRYMORE: *(Toying with him.)* Perhaps. Cleverly disguised as Hamlet. *(Andrew slowly sneaks up on Barrymore. He touches Barrymore's forearm. Barrymore is very nonchalant.)* Boo.

ANDREW: But - I can touch you. My hand doesn't go through.

BARRYMORE: I'm a ghost, Andrew. Not a special effect.

ANDREW: But ... ghosts are supposed to have powers! Special powers!

BARRYMORE: I just rose from the dead, Andrew. And how

177

was your morning? Now shall I truly frighten you?
ANDREW: *(Not impressed)* I'm not afraid of you.
BARRYMORE: Shall I cause your flesh to quake?
ANDREW: *(Very cocky)* You couldn't possibly.
BARRYMORE: Shall I scare you beyond all human imagination?
ANDREW: Go ahead and try.
BARRYMORE: In just six weeks time, you will play Hamlet.
ANDREW: *(Screams, Genuinely terrified.)* Oh my God, you really are him, aren't you?
BARRYMORE: John Barrymore. Actor. Legend. Seducer. Corpse.
ANDREW: So- it worked. The seance. Felicia, her mother - she brought you back, from over there.
BARRYMORE: Not at all. You summoned me.
ANDREW: I did?
BARRYMORE: As a link in a proud theatrical tradition. Every soul embarking upon Hamlet is permitted to summon an earlier layer. From Burbage to Kean to Irving - the call has been answered.
ANDREW: Wait - you mean you're here to help me play Hamlet? Because you did it?
BARRYMORE: Indeed.
ANDREW: Okay. Fine. Then the problem's solved. Because I'm not going to play Hamlet. No way. So you can just ... go back. To ... wherever.
BARRYMORE: I'm afraid that's not possible.
ANDREW: Why not?
BARRYMORE: I cannot return, I will not be accepted, until my task is accomplished. Until you have...
ANDREW and BARRYMORE: Played Hamlet.
BARRYMORE: Precisely.
ANDREW: *(Completely floored)* Oh no. Oh my God. You mean, if I don't go through with it..
BARRYMORE: Then I'm here to stay. Within these walls. Trapped for all time, with a television actor.
ANDREW: Well, excuse me - I happen to be a very good television actor! And I don't need any dead ham bone to teach me about anything! Even if I were going to play Hamlet, which I'm not, I could do just fine! All by myself!

(Barrymore glares at Andrew. He removes a small leatherbound copy of Hamlet from a pouch on his belt, and tosses it to Andrew.)

BARRYMORE: Very well then. Hamlet. "To be or not to be."

ANDREW: That happens to be the speech I did at my auditions. And I got the part. *(Andrew tosses the copy of Hamlet back to Barrymore.)*

BARRYMORE: Proceed. *(Barrymore reclines full length on the couch. Andrew, very full of himself, decides to show Barrymore a thing or two. He strides in, and turns his back. He hunches over.)* Yes?

ANDREW: I'm doing my preparation.

BARRYMORE: Your ... preparation.

ANDREW: Yes. My acting teacher taught me this. Harold Gaffney.

BARRYMORE: Harold Gaffney?

ANDREW: The creator of the Gaffney technique. Act To Win. I can't just do the speech cold, I have to get into character. I have to become Hamlet. I'm doing a substitution.

BARRYMORE: A substitution?

ANDREW: I'm thinking about something that really happened to me, so I can remember the emotion, and recreate it.

BARRYMORE: And what are you remembering?

ANDREW: It's a secret. Otherwise it won't work. Be quiet, I'm going to act.

BARRYMORE: Why do I feel we should spread newspapers about? I'm sorry, I shall be silent. Out of deep respect. Road closes - man acting. *(Andrew turns, and moves D. facing out. He makes a small snuffling noise. He loosens up his shoulders, like a prizefighter shadow-boxing. He makes a few faces; he is being ultra-naturalistic, very Method. He makes an ungodly howling noise, then slaps his own face. He repeats this. Barrymore watches all this, appalled.)* You know, Andrew, I am dead, and I shall be for all eternity. But I still don't have all day. *(Andrew begins again. After a few lunges, he begins to speak. His forehead is furrowed with intensity; his speech patterns are reminiscent of a Brooklyn tough guy, in the Brando / DeNiro mode.)*

ANDREW: To be ... nah. *(He paces. A thought occurs.)* Or ... not ... to ... be. That, that is the question. Whoa. Whether ... *(He holds up a hand.)* Whether 'tis nobler ... huh ... in the mind, right ...

BARRYMORE: Wrong.

ANDREW: What?

BARRYMORE: No.

ANDREW: What "No?"

BARRYMORE: No.

ANDREW: No, what? No you disagree with my interpretation, no my interpretation wasn't clear, no you think I'm totally horrible?

BARRYMORE: Yes.

ANDREW: I'm horrible?

BARRYMORE: At the moment. What were you doing?

ANDREW: I was internalizing the role. I was finding an emotional through-line.

BARRYMORE: Why?

ANDREW: Why? So the character will come alive! So I'll achieve some sort of truth! *(Barrymore rises, aghast.)*

BARRYMORE: Truth! Your performance - the pauses, the moans, all that you clearly consider invaluable - it's utterly appalling. We must never confuse truth with asthma.

ANDREW: What?

BARRYMORE: I understand the impulse, God help me, I lived just long enough for the introduction of truth into the modern theater. As I recall, it accompanied synthetic fibers and the GE Kitchen Of Tomorrow.

ANDREW: Oh - so you just want me to ham it up.

BARRYMORE: I beg your pardon?

ANDREW: Hamming. Mugging. Over the top. Too big. Too

BARRYMORE: *(With a grand gesture)* Barrymore?

ANDREW: Well, you did have the reputation. As someone ... larger than life.

BARRYMORE: What size would you prefer? Gesture, passion - these are an actor's tools. Abandon them, and the result? Mirror reality. Employ them, with gusto, and an artist's finesse, and the theater resounds! I do not overact. I simply possess the emotional resources of ten men. I am not a ham; I'm a crowd! Andrew, who is Hamlet?

ANDREW: A prince?

BARRYMORE: A star.

ANDREW: What?

BARRYMORE: A star. The role is a challenge, but far more - an opportunity. To shine. To rule. To seduce. To wit - what makes a star?

ANDREW: Talent? *(They exchange a look.)* Sorry, I wasn't thinking.

BARRYMORE: A thrilling vocal range? Decades of training? The proper vehicle? *(He shakes his head, no.)* Tights.

ANDREW: Tights?

BARRYMORE: Tights. Where are you looking? Right now?

ANDREW: I am not!

BARRYMORE: Of course you are! The potato, the cucumber, the rolled sock - this is the history of Prince Hamlet.

ANDREW: You mean - you padded yourself?

BARRYMORE: Unnecessary. Even for the balcony. *(Pause, as he gazes upward.)* The second balcony.

ANDREW: So Hamlet should be ... horny?

BARRYMORE: Hamlet is a young man, a college boy, at his sexual peak. Hamlet is pure hormone. Ophelia enters, that most beguiling of maidens. Chastity is discussed.

ANDREW: Please, don't joke. Not about chastity.

BARRYMORE: Why? What?

ANDREW: I can't talk about it.

BARRYMORE: Oh dear. Your beloved? A problem?

ANDREW: A nightmare. Five months.

BARRYMORE: What?

ANDREW: Nothing.

BARRYMORE: Truly?

ANDREW: Necking at the Cloisters. Picnics on Amish quilts. Sonnets.

BARRYMORE: Not... sonnets.

ANDREW: Yes. And I've been faithful. Totally. It's unnatural. Do you know what happens when you don't have sex?

BARRYMORE: No.

ANDREW: Thanks.

BARRYMORE: But why?

ANDREW: Why her, or why me? Deirdre won't have sex because ... she's not sure. Because she's the victim of a relentlessly happy childhood, which she fully expects to continue.

BARRYMORE: And you?

ANDREW: Me? Why do I put up with all this? Why have I begged Deirdre to marry me, practically since the day we met? Because, in the strangest way, she's the most passionate woman I've ever met. Because when she sees a homeless person, she gives them a fabric-covered datebook. Deirdre's just ... she makes me think that love is as amazing as it's supposed to be. She's romantic, which means she's insane. I know I love her, because I want to strangle her. Does that make sense?

BARRYMORE: Of course, A virgin goddess.

ANDREW: Please - don't encourage her.

BARRYMORE: She is to be treasured, and honored. I have known few such women in my sensual history. Perhaps only five hundred. They are the most adorable saints. But ... there are ways.

ANDREW: *(Eagerly)* What?

BARRYMORE: No. It would be unthinkable.

ANDREW: What?

BARRYMORE: I could never condone such Casanova-like tactics. Such Valentino mesmerism.

ANDREW: Such Barrymore deceit.

BARRYMORE: *(Mortally offended)* Cad.

ANDREW: Yes?

BARRYMORE: Knave.

ANDREW: Please?

BARRYMORE: Hamlet!

ANDREW: No! Stop with that.

BARRYMORE: Hamlet, to cunningly expose his father's murder, feigns madness. To perfect the pose, he must spurn his beloved, the fair Ophelia. She is undone.

ANDREW: But doesn't she kill herself? I don't want to hurt Deirdre.

BARRYMORE: You'll be merciful.

ANDREW: No, that would be dishonest.

BARRYMORE: You would prefer, perhaps, some form of therapy? Continued discussion? What is the present-day epithet "communication?" That absolute assassin of romance?

MY SIDE OF THE STORY
by Bryan Goluboff

The Characters: Gil (40-50) a man fearing the end of his marriage, and Aaron (25) his son.

The Setting: The bathroom of a luxury apartment in New York City, the present.

The Scene: Aaron discovers his father drunk in the bathroom. Gil informs him that he believes his wife is having an affair. When Aaron defends his mother, the following discussion ensues.

AARON: Tell me what happened...

GIL: I found myself outside this restaurant. They're sitting in the window. She's smiling like high school...I'm sweating behind this bush, hiding.. .Finally, I went inside... *(Gil takes a deep breath.)* I went up to the table. They were shocked to see me. They sounded like the record was on the wrong speed - excuses, excuses, excuses. I didn't hear a word. They shut up. I didn't know if I was gonna smash his face or scratch her skin off or...I reached over onto his plate and picked up this huge piece of steak and I - (*He shows Aaron how he tore the steak to pieces right in front of their faces. It is a strangely violent and vicious act, especially with the vigor that Gil pantomimes it.)* Ripped it apart. Blood splattered everywhere, on my shirt, in your mother's face...It was weird, I don't know why I did that... The restaurant was silent, I mean, nothing...And I came to. Just snapped out of it. Regained control. Your mother was crying, wiping the blood off her face. And I ran out of the restaurant, I ran for blocks...Thinking "Sucker, sucker, sucker, you shoulda known..."

AARON: Jesus Christ, that's crazy. That's a crazy thing to do. But you didn't really hurt anybody, right?

GIL: I'm so stupid -

AARON: Just calm down, talk to her. I'm sure she has a reasonable explanation-

GIL: *(Not listening to Aaron.)* I shoulda known. I mean, she was depressed so long and I couldn't help her. I tried, but I'm not Carl fucking Jung, you know? Then all of a sudden she's peppy as cheerleader, out of the house all the time. *(He hits himself in the head in mock amazement.)* Come on, Gil, figure it out!

AARON: You liked her better in the bed, crying?

GIL: At least I knew where she was...

AARON: Dad, the depression had nothing to do with you, that's why you couldn't help. It was a time of life she was going through.

GIL: How the fuck do you know what was going on between us? Jesus Christ! You were in Santa Fe with your friends, free as the wind, the night it really came down, the night I knew we were in real trouble... *(Gil takes a big swig of tequila.)* Last year's anniversary - She made an effort you know? First time in months she was out of her bathrobe. There was something good in her eyes. We started kissing on the couch. It had been so long it felt new. Your mother's a great kisser when she surrenders to it-

AARON: Dad-

GIL: I was rubbing her shoulders, kissing her ears, I know just what she likes, I'm telling you. I was going straight to dreamland-

AARON: Come on, Dad, I-

GIL: Then I touched her breast, soft, like I would pet a kitten and she just burst into tears. Believe that? I said, "what did I do wrong? What did I do?" I really didn't know. I couldn't figure it out...

AARON: Dad, I don't think we should talk about this-

GIL: Why not?

AARON: That's my mother we're talking about, not some woman you're trying to bang.

GIL: After 31 years of marriage, they're still women we're trying to bang...

AARON: Gee, that's romantic...There's gotta be more to it than that...

GIL: What time is it? *(Gil looks down at his wrist, but his watch is not on.)* I can't find my watch. What time is it?

AARON: *(Aaron looks at his watch.)* It's ten fifteen.

GIL: I feel like I've been waiting for that Goddamn woman all my life. No more of this shit.

AARON: What are you going to do when she gets home?

GIL: Don't worry about it.

AARON: You're not gonna touch her, Dad. Not while I'm in the house.

GIL: *(laughs at Aaron.)* You make one trade on the stock market and you think you're fucking Superman... I'll do whatever I want.

AARON: You won't hurt her-

GIL: *(A sudden flash of rage)* Have you ever been hit in the

face, hard, once in your shit soft life? You learn that in your "progressive" private school? I used to fight my way to school... *(Aaron is staring at his father, deciding if he wants to fight him.)* You think you got fire in your balls? *(Aaron looks down at the floor. The challenge has not been taken.)* I didn't think so... *(There is a silence between them.)*

AARON: Man, you make me sick sometimes-
GIL: Watch how you talk to me-
AARON: Like you're the moral minority of one in this house. How about you, Dad? Have you ever had an affair?
GIL: Why are you protecting her like this?
AARON: I asked you something-
GIL: We're talking about her.
AARON: How 'bout it, Dad?
GIL: That's an inappropriate question.
AARON: Inappropriate? You've been grilling me about Mom like fucking Baretta. I wanna know about you.
GIL: Just because you're working your way through the entire Wall Street typing pool doesn't mean I've been unfaithful to my wife...Not every man's like you-
AARON: You turn everything on me, don't you, Dad?
GIL: You make me laugh. You think you're such a cocksman. What are you, 25? When I was your age, I was changing your shitty diapers, couldn't find your little thing with a tweezers-
AARON: Yeah, well, I haven't had any complaints-
GIL: You think they're gonna tell you to your face? *(Aaron doesn't answer him. Gil offers his son the tequila bottle.)* Take another drink. We haven't had a drink together since your Bar Mitzvah. You got sick in the bushes on Manishevitz wine. Lightweight.
AARON: I was thirteen years old! I'm not gonna argue with you. You're looking at a lightweight. You're right. *(Aaron takes an enormous swig of tequila.)* Don't be surprised if I eat the fucking worm!
GIL: Alright, Aaron!
AARON: You gonna answer my question now? About the other women? *(Gil doesn't say anything.)* Nothing,huh? I remember in the old place in East New York, I was just a little kid, you came back from somewhere and Mommy found a hair on your clothes or something. Unbelievable fight! You tore the bannister off the wall chasing her up the stairs. I was afraid you were gonna kill her.
GIL: Did I kill her?
AARON: Obviously not.
GIL: Did we get divorced?

AARON: No.

GIL: You have your answer...

AARON: What about you and David Goldsmith? All those "business trips" to the Bahamas? You guys are a legend in the office. "You shoulda seen the killer tear into that little filly..." Ha ha ha... How do you think that makes me feel to hear that shit?

GIL: It's a joke! They're blowing it up. *(Pause)* You didn't tell your mother, did you? *(There is an embarrassed silence.)* Why are you attacking me like this?

AARON: Why are you attacking me?

GIL: Let me explain something to you, Aaron. I met your Mom when I was 14 years old and I married her at 18. Do you really think I've never touched another women in my entire life? Can you really expect that? I've got red blood same as yours.

AARON: Doesn't Mom have red blood, too? After 31 years?

GIL: It's different-

AARON: How is it different?

GIL: You know something, you better tell me!

AARON: I don't know anything Goddamnit! It's sick and - It's sad that you don't believe your own son. Shit, man...

GIL: You know what I think? You're right. Your mother and I should both be free to do whatever we want. I'll live my life like you- It's a smorgasbord of women out there I can get 'em all. I'm rich, I still got my looks left. You see how those young secretaries flirt with me. That Janice is always braiding my ponytail. Sandra's always looking at my car. I still got it. We'll fuck other people, then your mother and I will meet after for cigarettes and sexy banter, O.K.? Sound good? *(Suddenly stricken.)* What the hell time is it?

AARON: *(checks his watch)* Five minutes after the last time you asked me...

RIPPLES IN THE POND
by *Jon Shirota*

The Characters: Hitoshi Harada (40's) a Japanese businessman, and Ohara (40's) a Japanese-American Internal Revenue Agent.

The Setting: The offices of Harada Enterprise, Los Angeles, 1960.

The Scene: When the officious Ohara pays a visit to Hitoshi Harada with the intention of auditing his books for the IRS, he is prepared to press criminal charges of tax evasion until the two men discover that both their lives were irrevocably altered by their experiences in WWII.

HARADA: American women are becoming more and more educated. - -And, independent.
OHARA: They're beginning to run the country.
HARADA: When I go Princeton University graduate school before war, not too many women go college...
OHARA: So. You went to Princeton?
HARADA: You go Princeton, too?
OHARA: Me? Los Angeles City College. - -Look, Harada, I've got another appointment in the valley. Let's get back to business.
HARADA: Yes. Of course.
OHARA: All right. Let's try again... Who'd you pay the commissions to?
HARADA: Oh, yes. Commission... I...was just thinking... What if Mr. Ohara not allow deduction?
OHARA: If the commissions weren't legitimate business deductions I'm going to have to disallow them. What I want to know is who received them.
HARADA: Even if deduction not allowed?
OHARA: It's taxable income to whoever got it, one way or another.
HARADA: So na
OHARA: Look, Mr. Harada, you can get in big trouble for conspiring to obstruct justice.
HARADA: *(Pause)* Mr. Ohara say he was in Guam during war?
OHARA: Now what the hell does Guam have to do with this?
HARADA: Please... I...want explain...
OHARA: Harada! I'm not going to listen to any more of your

goddamn shit! You either tell me or I'm leaving!

HARADA: Yes. I tell you.

OHARA: *(Beat)* Well!

HARADA: I...was in Guam, too.

OHARA: *(Looks at him)* During the war?

HARADA: *(Nods)* ... And after war...

OHARA: You went back there after the war?

HARADA: I...did not leave until 1948.

OHARA: 1948? The war was over in 1945.

HARADA: I...did not know.

OHARA: That the war was over? *(Now realizing)* Oh... one of those guys...

HARADA: After big final battle, my men and I, we stay in cave. We...thought of surrendering. Then, Americans come, throw grenade. Only three of us survived. We...now realize Americans not take prisoners. We escape into jungle.

OHARA: What the hell you guys expect? A royal treatment after what you did to us? My friend, Kiyoshi Yonemura, was killed there.

HARADA: Many of my friends killed there...

OHARA: Kiyoshi was killed by...one of your fanatics while trying to stop Japanese women and children from jumping off a cliff. The...same women and children you guys indoctrinated that it's better to die than to be captured by...barbaric Americans.

HARADA: Ah, so data...

OHARA: That very same day, a naked Japanese soldier comes in surrendering, lifts his arms and drops two grenades, killing everyone around him. You goddamn right we stopped taking prisoners.

HARADA: Senso was senso...

OHARA: War is war all right... Anyway, what does all this have to do with your tax return?

HARADA: Yes. I tell you ... While in jungle, the other two men die of wounds. All the years I live alone, I thought war still on. Whenever I see American soldiers, I move deeper and deeper into jungle. Then, one day, just at sunrise, I see American soldier coming toward me with rifle. Before...he can shoot me, I...shoot him.

OHARA: You killed him?! Three years after the war ended?!

HARADA: I...did not know.

OHARA: How..did you find out?

HARADA: Few minutes later when I sure no one else around, I go to him. Like myself, he is a Captain. Just before he die, he look up at me. "Why?" he say. "Why?" His rifle, I notice now, is not Army rifle. It is hunting rifle. When I go through his wallet, there is a picture of him taken at Mt. Fuji. It...is dated 1945.

OHARA: Jesus Christ... *(Beat)* What did you do then?

HARADA: I...surrendered.

OHARA: And, they let you go?

HARADA: There was a trial. Because U.S. Army not want further strain in Japanese-American relationship trial not public. I had a very good lawyer. An American Major, Harold Simpson. He...convince everyone that I, indeed, did not know war was over. Therefore, what I did was act of war.

OHARA: *(Pause)* The commissions... What...does all this have to do with the commissions?

HARADA: It...is money I am giving to Captain's wife and four children.

OHARA: *(Looks at Harada)* They...know?!

HARADA: *(Shakes head)* I told them that the Captain was good to my family in Japan right after war. I...want to show appreciation. The Captain's wife, she is school teacher in Tucson, Arizona. She is trying very hard to bring up children by herself. My wife and I, we go Tucson whenever we can.

OHARA: Your wife?!

HARADA: We have no children. The Tremble children, they are like our own.

OHARA: Trembel? Then, Sarah, she's...?

HARADA: Sarah is oldest of four children. Mrs. Tremble, she big trouble for not reporting income?

OHARA: No. No, she's not in any trouble. What she received wasn't income.

HARADA: *(Relieved)* Thank you. Thank you very much.

OHARA: Harada Enterprise, on the other hand, can't deduct the money given to her.

HARADA: Yes. Yes, I understand. *(As Ohara goes through tax return carefully.)* Mr. Ohara work for Internal Revenue Service many years?

OHARA: Including my service time, I've got in fifteen years.

HARADA: Oh. Very much experience. Ever think of opening tax business?

OHARA: I think about it now and then.

HARADA: If ever do, please let me know. Harada Enterprise, some day, will grow into big company in United States. We will need good tax man.

OHARA: *(Eyeing Harada)* Mr. Harada. You almost got yourself in big trouble for offering me money.

HARADA: Oh, no, no. This time, not bribery. Just in case you go into tax business.

OHARA: *(Studies tax return again.)* Mr. Harada, do you

conduct business at your home?

HARADA: Oh, yes. Lotsa times.

OHARA: I notice that Harada Enterprise didn't claim a deduction for maintaining an office at your home.

HARADA: No. We did not.

OHARA: I...also notice that Harada Enterprise didn't claim deduction for depreciation of office furniture and equipment.

HARADA: No. We not claim.

OHARA: Look, I'm going to recommend that your tax return be accepted as filed.

HARADA: Thank you. Thank you very much. About Mrs. Trembel... She find out why I give her money?

OHARA: My report will be confidential. She won't even know you were audited.

HARADA: Ah, so desuka.

OHARA: You...plan to tell her some day?

HARADA: Some day, I must. I...hope she will forgive me.

OHARA: *(Beat, then, shaking)* I'm...glad to have met you, Harada-san.

HARADA: I am very glad to meet you, too, OHara-san. Maybe, some day, when meet again, circumstance much better.

OHARA: Sayonara...

HARADA: Sayonara...

(Blackout)

TWO SHAKESPEAREAN ACTORS
by Richard Nelson

The Characters: William Charles Macready (40-50) an English actor, and Edwin Forrest (40-50) his American counterpart.

The Setting: Various locations in New York City, in May, 1849.

The Scene: When an anti-British riot puts an end to Macready's performance of *Macbeth*, the English actor seeks refuge in the dressing room of his great rival, Edwin Forrest. In the following scene, the two veteran thespians explore their jealousy, resentment and common ground.

MACREADY: *(Suddenly turns)* They were shouting your name again! *(Forrest turns to Ryder. Who nods.)* "Kill Macready! Three Cheers for Ned Forrest!"
FORREST: Why would they do that? That doesn't make sense.
MACREADY: 'Ned Forrest - an American!'
FORREST: I have made it very clear that I-.
MACREADY: I didn't want this! *(Beat)* After the other night, I...
FORREST: When you should have shouted them down. That's your mistake. You should have had the guts to shout them down! All of this could have been --
RYDER: You don't know what you're talking about. *(Pause)*
MACREADY: I was told - if I didn't perform - I'd be hurting American...American what? They made it sound like I had to...
FORREST: For 75 per cent of the house! I heard about this!
MACREADY: That had nothing to do with -. *(Beat)* Money has nothing to do with this. *(Beat. Attacking)* 'Three cheers for Ned Forrest. Hurray for Forrest!' As they try to burn down a theatre!
FORREST: Those people have nothing to do with me! *(Forrest walks away. Pause. Finally.)* You want him to stay here.
RYDER: I shouldn't be too long. We can't go back to the hotel.
MACREADY: No.
RYDER: I'll take him to Boston. We have friends. *(Beat)* He can get a boat home from there. *(Beat)* But if you don't want to...
FORREST: He can stay. *(Short pause)*
RYDER: He'll need some clothes.
FORREST: He can stay. Don't be long. *(Ryder hesitates, then*

hurries out. Pause.)
MACREADY: He didn't know where else to bring me. Could I have another? *(He holds out his glass.)*
FORREST: Listen *(Pause. From outside the noise of the mob. After a moment Forrest goes and gets the bottle and pours Macready a drink.)*
FORREST: Were they really shouting my name again? *(Macready nods.)* What the hell did they think they were doing?
MACREADY: You obviously -. For them. For some of them. Represent -. *(He shrugs.)*
FORREST: I'm an actor! *(Macready Shrugs again. Pause.)*
MACREADY: Any money I do receive I shall give away. I did not perform for... *(Beat)* I'm not a greedy man. *(Beat)* The charities I support, I should give you a list, I also give anonymously to-.
FORREST: Shut up. *(Short pause)* Please. Your generosity is well known.
MACREADY: Is it? *(Beat)* Good. *(Macready looks towards a clothes trunk, hesitates, then goes to look in it.)*
FORREST: Take whatever you need. Whatever might fit. A cape maybe... *(He shrugs. Pause. Macready begins to look through the costume trunk. From outside closer gunshots. And shouts. Suddenly turns to the noise and screams.)* Leave us alone in here!!!!!! *(Pause)*
MACREADY: *(Pulling something out of the trunk; quietly.)* Is this your Lear? *(Forrest nods.)* It's funny how we rarely get a chance to see each other's...
FORREST: I've seen your Lear. *(Beat)* I found the time to see your Lear. *(Short pause)*
MACREADY: Is that it? You've just seen it? You don't want to say -?
FORREST: *(Quickly)* I enjoyed it. *(Short pause)*
MACREADY: You've got an interesting costume.
FORREST: So did you.
MACREADY: Actually this sort of looks like mine. *(Short pause. With out looking up.)* How was your play tonight?
FORREST: Fine. *(Laughs to himself.)* There was no riot. A large section of my audience did not try to murder me. The theatre is not burning. Not a bad night. *(Beat)* They love Metamora, the noble savage. *(Beat)* Who has the decency to die. *(Smiles)* So they cheered as always. I was not very good tonight, I thought. *(He shrugs.)*
MACREADY: As we get older ... It's funny, isn't it? When we begin - when I began - I thought always about what they would think about me. *(Beat)* You want so much to please them.

(Beat) But you get older - and that's still there - but ... Well, it's us who start to judge them, isn't it?

FORREST: I'm not that old yet. *(Short pause)*

MACREADY: *(Choosing to ignore him.)* Sometimes you stand on that stage and know you are achieving a level of excellence few before you have ever achieved. And you watch an audience watching you as if on some river bank staring at the natural flow of water. *(Beat)* And then on other nights - probably like you felt tonight - you hate what you've done, perhaps even embarrassed -.

FORREST: I didn't say I was -.

MACREADY: And your audience receives you with rapturous attention and applause. *(Beat)* There seems to be no rhyme or reason. *(Beat)* The older you get, the more confusing it all becomes. The reaction. Like tonight, what you were telling me about your performance. Where's the logic. *(Forrest looks at him.)* And I'll tell you what makes it all even worse. It's going to see another performer - especially a part that you know like your own soul - and then witnessing grotesque exaggeration. Which one could forgive perhaps in a novice, but when it's an actor of some note, some ambition. And then when the crowd - the mob, one should call them in this case - greets this fraud with its misplaced adulation. I find myself in an almost state of total fevered despair. *(Short pause)*

FORREST: I enjoy watching other actors -.

MACREADY: When they are excellent! Which is so rare, as we both know so well. *(Short pause)*

FORREST: I enjoy watching other actors even when they're bad, even when they're silly.

MACREADY: But then when an audience praises -.

FORREST: I enjoyed your Hamlet a great deal. *(Beat)* When I was in London I enjoyed it. *(Short pause)* That dance you did - Hamlet's little dance before the Gertrude scene. I'd never seen anything like it. I will never forget it.

MACREADY: You're not the first to -.

FORREST: A fancy dance? I asked myself. Where does this come from in the play? I knew no reference to it. I had never before seen an actor -

MACREADY: An expression of his madness. A colour. A texture of the performance.

FORREST: And a costume for this dance which, if I remember correctly, had a dress with a waist up to about the armpits, huge overlarge black gloves -

MACREADY: True, I -

FORREST: A great big hat with a gigantic plume -

MACREADY: The character is mad!

FORREST: Is this Hamlet or Malvolio, I remember saying to myself. But still. I enjoyed it. *(Suddenly turns to Macready.)* It's true, Hamlet is mad. And in preparation for my own performance I became a student of the mind's disease. Visiting asylums and talking not only with the doctors but also with the ill. And the result of this study, Mr. Macready, was the knowledge that true madness is expressed through the ear, not the costume. Madness is not funny clothes, but a funny soul.

MACREADY: We are different actors.

FORREST: This is very true.

MACREADY: You study asylums and I study the play.

FORREST: That's not -

MACREADY: Perhaps I am old-fashioned, but I continue to believe that all one needs is to be found in the play. Mr Shakespeare knew what -

FORREST: I don't disagree. *(Beat)*

MACREADY: Then perhaps all I am saying is - from one actor to another - a little more time with the text and little less in asylums might do a world of good.

FORREST: You haven't even seen -

MACREADY: One hears, Mr. Forrest, one hears! It is a small business we're in.

FORREST: In that case, as we are talking text, perhaps - as one actor to another - I can make a suggestion as I have also seen your Othello.

MACREADY: You are a fan, I'm flattered.

FORREST: As I've said, I enjoy watching other actors whatever they do. Anyway, Othello. *(Begins to recite:)*
    'Rude am I in my speech,
    and little blessed with the soft phrase of peace;
    For since these arms of mine had seven years' pith'
(Macready joins in.)

BOTH: *'Till now some nine moons wasted,*
    they have used their dearest action in the tented field;
    And little of this great world can I speak More than
    pertains to feats of broil and battle;'
(Forrest drops out.)

MACREADY: *'And therefore little shall I grace my cause*
        *In speaking for **myself**.'*

FORREST: *'For **myself**!'* That's just how you said it when I saw you.

MACREADY: And that is the line.

FORREST: That's not the meaning though. *(Laughs)* Othello starts by saying he is rude in speech, how there is little he can speak about except battles. So what he is saying here is that he's bad at speaking, not that he doesn't want to talk or have people

194

about him. He's not being humble, for Christ's sake he's saying that he's awkward and out of place where he is! So the line should be! *"And therefore little shall I grace my cause In speaking for myself." (Beat)*
MACREADY: That's a different reading. It's interesting. But it's just a different reading.
FORREST: It's the right reading!
MACREADY: That's your opinion.
FORREST: And when I go and see your Othello again that's how you'll be saying the line, I'm sure. *(Smiles)* Here, you want another one! The same scene:
Which I observing, Took once a pliant hour, and found good means To draw from her a prayer of earnest heart That I would all my pilgrimage dilate' And so on. (Beat) 'Good means'! Not 'Good **means**'!
MACREADY: I don't hear the difference.
FORREST: He was after a good reason, a good way, a just way to get his promise. As opposed to a successful means to- *(From outside sudden gunshots which are closer. Short pause.)*
MACREADY: The other reading maybe. But not this...
FORREST: Fine. Fine. At least I got you to agree about one. *(Short pause)* I only brought it up because - What you said, about reading the ...
(Crowd noise off. Macready looks through the trunk. Long pause. Macready pulls out a costume.)
MACREADY: Richard? *(Forrest nods. Macready pulls out an identical costume.)* Why two?
FORREST: I started with the hump on my left and my left hand curled - Then I broke my right wrist, so I had to change, put the hump on the right. *(Macready nods.)* Now I keep them both. I've found that if I've got three or four Richards close together, I switch back and forth. It helps the back.
MACREADY: Kean I think did that too.
FORREST: Did he? *(Pause)*
MACREADY: Kemble too. I think. *(Beat)* Ever see Kemble's... *(Mimics Kemble's walk as Richard III. Forrest laughs.)* I don't know what it was about him. Every time he tried - Hamlet. Richard. Macbeth. *(Beat)* But did you see his Cassio?
FORREST: No, I- No.
MACREADY: Brilliant. *(Beat)* He was a first-rate actor, but only in second-rate parts.
FORREST: I've known other -
MACREADY: An incomparable Cassio. *(Beat)* You've never played -
FORREST: No.

MACREADY: Neither have I. *(Pause)* There are so many great supporting parts in Shakespeare. When I was young we'd fight for them.

FORREST: They still -

MACREADY: Not in England any more. You used to have to constantly look over your shoulder. People had ambition! Now no one wants to work. No one wants to begin. But they work in my productions. *(Laughs)* And so they hate me. *(Laughs)* You want to know what it's like in London today? I tried to correct this actor. He works for me. And he's a nothing. All I say to him is, 'Please do not speak your speech in that drawling way, sir.' I'm very polite. 'Here', I tell him, 'speak it like this: "To ransom home revolted Mortimer!" That's how you speak it!' *(Beat)* He turns to me, in front of the whole company, and says, 'I know that, sir - that is the way, but you'll please remember you get one hundred pounds a week for speaking it in your way, and I only get thirty shillings for mine! Give me one hundred pounds and I'll speak it your way; but I'm not going to do for thirty shillings what you get paid one hundred pounds for.' *(Macready laughs, Forrest smiles.)* Actors. *(He shakes his head. Short pause.)*

FORREST: What I hate is when they come late for rehearsal.

MACREADY: Which happens more and -

FORREST: Once, a rehearsal of mine was being delayed by this actor; he only had a small part, but it was quite an important part in the first scene. So we were all waiting. *(Beat)* I became visibly upset. Everyone knew enough to stay away from me. And when finally the truant - a quiet gentlemanly man, who had never before been late for one second - once he arrived I know I needed to make an example of him. *(Beat. Smiling.)* So I said, "Sir, you have kept these ladies and gentlemen waiting for a full half hour" *(Macready nods and smiles.)* 'You cannot be ignorant, sir, of the importance of a rehearsal in which every member of the company is to take part!' *(Beat)* At that moment, this actor looked at me. I could see there were tears now in his eyes. *(Macready smiles and shakes his head.)* And then he spoke. 'Mr. Forrest, sir,' he said, 'I beg your pardon. I could not come sooner.' *(Forrest looks at Macready, who snickers.)* 'My son - my only son - died last night. I hurried here as soon as I could." *(Macready suddenly stops smiling. Short pause. Forrest looks at Macready and shakes his head.)* Actors.

(Long pause. Macready goes back and looks into the costume trunk. Slow fade to blackout.)

PERMISSIONS ACKNOWLEDGMENTS

Grateful acknowledgment is made for permission to reprint excerpts from the following plays:

professional performance) may be given without obtaining in advance the written permission of the Dramatist Play Service, Inc., and paying the requisite fee. Inquiries concerning all other rights should be addressed to Lois Berman, 240 West 44th Street, New York, NY 10036.

THE DAYS OF WINE AND ROSES by J.P. Miller. © Copyright 1987 by J.P. Miller. Credit: from DAYS OF WINE AND ROSES by J.P. Miller.

DEJAVU by John Osborne. © Copyright 1992, by John Osborne. Reprinted by permission of Faber and Faber Ltd., 3 Queen Square, London WC1N 3AU.

DOWN THE FLATS by Tony Kavanagh. © Copyright 1992, by Tony Kavanagh. Reprinted by permission of the author.

EVELYN AND THE POLKA KING by John Olive. © Copyright 1991 by John Olive, Carl Finch and Bob Lucas. Reprinted by permission of author and author's agent Susan Schulman, 454 West 44th Street, New York, NY 10036.

EVIL LITTLE THOUGHTS by Mark D. Kaufman. © Copyright 1992, by Mark D. Kaufman. All rights reserved.

FOUR PLAY by Gina Barnett. © Copyright 1992, by Gina Barnett. Reprinted by permission of the author.

GERTRUDE, QUEEN OF DENMARK by Pat Kaufman. © Copyright 1991, by Pat Kaufman. A comedy about Hamlet's Mother.

GULF WAR by Joyce Carol Oates. © Copyright 1992, by Joyce Carol Oates. Reprinted by permission of the author.

HYAENA by Ross MacLean. © Copyright 1992, by Ross MacLean. Reprinted by permission of the author and the author's agent Michael Traum, 103 Eat 44th Street, New York, NY 10017.

LYNETTE AT 3 AM by Jane Anderson. © Copyright by Jane Anderson. Reprinted by permission of author; Martin Gage, 9255 Sunset Blvd., Suite 55, Los Angeles, CA 90069; and Samuel French, Inc., 45 West 25th Street, New York, NY 10010.

MAKING BOOK by Janet Reed. © Copyright 1992, by Janet Reed. Reprinted by permission of the author and the author's agent Lois Berman, The Little Theatre Building, 240 West 44th Street, New York, NY 10036.

MAN OF THE MOMENT by Alan Ayckbourn. © Copyright 1992, by Alan Ayckbourn. Reprinted by permission of Faber and Faber Ltd., 3 Queen Square, London WC1N 3AU.

199

200